EDGAR GARDNER MURPHY

Gentle Progressive

EDGAR GARDNER MURPHY
Gentle Progressive

by Hugh C. Bailey

UNIVERSITY OF MIAMI PRESS
Coral Gables, Florida

For
FRANK LAWRENCE OWSLEY
Distinguished Scholar,
Teacher, and Friend

Contents

Illustrations

Preface

EDGAR GARDNER MURPHY was a rare phenomenon for his time—a Southern social reformer who assumed a position of national leadership in the fields of education, child labor, and Negro rights. From a most plebeian background he became an articulate Episcopal priest thoroughly imbued with a sense of social consciousness and Christian activism. While he never abandoned any of his firmly held Christian beliefs, much of his success came from the realization that they required a secularized presentation in a secular age. Therefore, he was voluntarily deposed from the ministry in order to advance the Kingdom of God in this world. The positions he assumed and the success he obtained must be judged by the times in which he lived. To the liberal of today, they will often seem unsatisfactory, but in his time they were frequently advanced and gratifying.

Through a constant struggle with ill health from his early twenties until his death at forty-three, Murphy displayed an unusual sensitivity to the needs of his fellowman and a willingness to sacrifice himself for them. He was truly a gentle progressive who believed only mild reforms had any chance of success in the America of his era. He was concerned with aiding people, not in becoming a symbolic martyr, yet in his own quiet way he gave his life in behalf of the causes he felt must triumph in a Christian, democratic society.

In preparing this work I am most indebted to Samford University for a sabbatical leave and to the John Simon Guggenheim Memorial Foundation for a fellowship. Without the freedom from campus responsibilities they afforded, the research and writing could never have been completed. I cannot praise too highly the absolute independence, which permits the maximum utilization of time and resources, allowed Guggenheim Fellows.

Librarians too numerous to mention have been of incalculable aid by making manuscripts and rare books available. Particularly helpful were those at the Houghton Library, Harvard; the Howard-Tilton Library, Tulane University; the Manuscripts Division of the Library of Congress; the New York Public Library; and the Samford University Library.

In addition I am most grateful to the Murphy family, particularly Dr. Gardner Murphy, Director of Research at the Menninger Foundation, Miss Alice Gardner Murphy, and Mr. Leonard B. Murphy, all of whom furnished private correspondence, unprinted sermons, and other materials most unselfishly and at the expenditure of much of their own time. Their attitude reflects qualities reminiscent of their father and grandfather.

Most of all, I am indebted to my wife, whose patience and encouragement were supplemented by material aid in note taking, typing, and criticism of the manuscript.

EDGAR GARDNER MURPHY
MURPHY

Gentle Progressive

1.

Early Years

IN A SENSE Edgar Gardner Murphy was a man born out of time—one who believed in the need of an aristocracy to set high standards and elevate the tone of society. But he was essentially gentle and warm-hearted, with a concept of aristocracy defined less by birth than by character and education—a philosophy reminiscent of Thomas Jefferson.

It is paradoxical that Murphy had such views, since his boyhood was unusually difficult. Following his birth near Fort Smith, Arkansas on August 31, 1869, he knew the poverty of Reconstruction complicated by the fact that his father, Samuel W. Murphy, deserted the family when he was only five. At that time his sister, Ethel, was fourteen months old, and his mother, Janie Gardner Murphy, was ill with tuberculosis. Being a woman of courage, Janie refused to allow illness to ruin her life and to prevent the rearing of her children. Since a move to the West was then considered the best treatment for "consumption," she gathered all her resources for making the trek to Texas. Accompanied only by her sister, Lelia, and the children, she began the journey from Fort Smith in 1874 on a cot in a railway baggage car. When the end of the line was reached, the trip was continued to San Antonio by stage and army ambulance. Years later when he became depressed Murphy recalled his mother's stamina and took courage.[1]

Janie Murphy's spirit contributed to what seemed a miraculous recovery. Poverty forced her to forego the "rest cure" routinely prescribed by the physicians of the day for tuberculosis and to support her family by opening a boarding house at 511 St. Mary's Street. Since people then did not know the cause of tuberculosis and did not fear being near tuberculars, she and her sister had no difficulty in obtaining patrons due to her superb food and decent accommodations. Unusually thrifty, she made periodic payments on the mortgage and soon opened a small savings account for the children's education.

The Murphys' poverty forced young Edgar to seek inexpensive amusement, and as he grew older, young people often came to his home for games, food, and conversation. Among those who frequently dropped in was the personable young rector of St. Mark's Episcopal Church, the Rev. Walter Richardson, whose friendship was to be of paramount importance. Murphy's family had had no contact with the Episcopal Church, and like most rural Southerners undoubtedly regarded it as a veiled form of Roman Catholicism and a menace to American life. But knowing and admiring Richardson, Murphy was persuaded to join his church choir and easily passed to a more active role in parish life. In time he accepted the church's worship and faith and, after adequate preparation, was confirmed. While still in his teens, he resolved to become a priest, and knowing his quick mind and capacity for work, Richardson encouraged him.

At the San Antonio High School, Murphy maintained an excellent record, while at the same time working several hours each day for his mother and aunt. Both resolved that he must go to college, but this seemed impossible until Richardson persuaded the University of the South in Sewanee, Tennessee, to grant him a scholarship.

In 1885, when only sixteen, Murphy entered the freshman class at Sewanee. In some ways leaving home was both harder and easier for him than most boys. Due to his mother's illness and poverty, they were unusually close; however, for years he had assumed adult responsibilities, developing independence and resourcefulness. Despite concern for his mother, he made a quick transition to the broader, more challenging world of Sewanee. Here in "an atmosphere of plain living and high thinking," he became a member of a unique college community, including retired generals, distinguished bishops, and acknowledged classical scholars. Partially due to its relative isolation, the college, while it lacked great physical resources, formed a true community where personal attention and concern were prevalent. Murphy came to love "The Mountain," as Sewanee men referred to their school, ascribing much of his success to its training and discipline, and after graduation he came to have an almost passionate loyalty for it.[2]

Of all the forces and personalities at Sewanee, Murphy was most influenced by the Rev. William Porcher DuBose, son of a wealthy South Carolina planter. DuBose had attended the University of Virginia and studied Greek under Professor Basil L. Gildersleeve, who later distinguished himself at Johns Hopkins where he was the major professor of Walter Hines Page, who became one of the nation's leading publishers and Ambassador to Great Britain.[3] During service in the Confederate army, including three months of imprisonment, he constantly studied, and he was ordained to the priesthood before his discharge. After this, he served as rector in Winnsboro and Abbeville before coming to Sewanee in 1872. Here he became noted as a classicist in his own right but, more significantly, in 1873 he organized classes of candidates for Holy Orders—the beginning of St. Luke's School of Theology. Later, from 1893 to 1908, he served as dean.

DuBose charmed and coerced generations of students as he lectured brilliantly without notes, varying his style from austerity to humor. Always close to his students, DuBose conceded, "I was in fact more one of them, than one merely over them. . . . I claimed nothing, exacted nothing, imposed nothing of or for myself, and they both took more from me and gave me more than I ever asked or deserved." Enthralled by the man, Murphy sought him out at every opportunity, took classes with him, and came to board in his home. The two became close friends, as DuBose channeled Murphy's reading, guided his use of logic, and corrected his writing. Murphy returned many times to Sewanee to visit his mentor, and DuBose visited him in Texas and New York. He was "one of the rare personalities of the world," Murphy wrote, and "I owe to him almost all that I am in life." Naturally he could only "speak of him with reverence and gratitude."

DuBose's life and teaching made an indelible impression on Murphy, crystalizing and shaping his conceptions. A "high churchman" of an earlier mold, he was not concerned with ritualism per se, but firmly believed in the church and the sacraments as channels of God's grace. To set forth his views, DuBose wrote five major books and many articles which gained international recognition. Essentially an ethical philosopher, he contended that happiness is the main goal of life and that it "is not a state, but an activity; it is life being lived, life lived completely and fully." This was the theme of his most important work, *From Aristotle To Christ*, which stressed that a chasm does not separate God and man, that Christ's humanity is essentially the same as that of all mankind—that God and man "are for each other." In successfully basing his apologia on psychology rather than scholastic reasoning, DuBose became what W. Norman Pittinger, a leading contemporary Anglican scholar, has described as "the only important creative theologian that the Episcopal Church in the United States has produced." The impact was greatest, of course, on his own students. One of them, the poet William Alexander Percy, who later was dismissed as a Sewanee English instructor due to his Roman Catholic faith, aptly described him as "a tiny silver saint."[4]

Murphy graduated from Sewanee in 1889 imbued with DuBose's spirit and zest for learning. Despite his lack of funds, and despite his desire to repay his mother and aunt for their sacrifices, he moved to New York for a year's additional training at the General Theological Seminary. He found the work interesting and particularly enjoyed a Columbia University philosophy course taught by Nicholas Murray Butler. Life in New York also afforded cultural opportunities that Murphy had never known, and, for the first time, he was able to indulge his taste for good music and the theatre. This required a careful budgeting of time and money, since, in addition to his studies, he served as Sunday lay assistant at the Church of the Incarnation for much of the year. Its rector was Dr. Arthur Brooks, a devoted cleric and a preacher with oratorical ability. Work in his efficiently run parish was invaluable experience and gave Murphy the opportunity to know Brooks' brother, the Rev. Phillips Brooks, Rector of Boston's Trinity Church and soon-to-be Bishop of Massachusetts—a man many considered the most eloquent minister of the nineteenth century. He often conducted services for his brother, and Murphy, greatly impressed, imitated his style.[5] In addition, Murphy served for several weeks at St. Gabriel's, Hollis, Long Island, and made a sufficiently good impression that three years later its Sunday school, remembering his work, presented a brass cross to his first parish.[6]

Though a thousand miles from San Antonio, Murphy poured out his dreams and plans to Richardson in letters and wrote his mother at least weekly, a practice she came to expect whenever he was not with her. In the spring of 1890, Richardson offered him a lay assistantship in his parish; this was quickly accepted. At the end of the academic year, he returned to begin his ministry in a not unusual manner, working with a tiny mission which was struggling to survive and expand—St. Paul's located near Fort Sam Houston. Here Murphy read Morning Prayer, preached a sermon each Sunday, conducted an inquirer's class on Tuesdays, read the Litany on Wednesdays, and contacted as many parishioners and potential parishioners as possible. The small number in his congregation proved to have at least one advantage; it afforded him more time to help his family and to read and study in compensation for his limited theological training.[7]

Despite his busy schedule, Murphy made many young friends. His gentle nature, tactfulness, and infectious humor made him a joy to know, and the Murphy home was constantly filled with gay young people. A new member, Maud King, one of Mrs. Murphy's boarders, joined the group at the time of Murphy's ordination as deacon in August, 1890. The daughter of a sedate Concord, Massachusetts family, she was a Vassar graduate who had excelled in her studies and was elected to Phi Beta Kappa. A Yankee spirit of adventure led her to accept a teaching position in the San Antonio High School. Her father, George A. King, a Boston lawyer, objected to one of his four children going to "the uncivilized West," but respected her independence and made no effort to stop her.[8]

Maud was a woman of spirit and determination as well as energy and adaptability. Despite her New England background, the young set quickly accepted her, and soon she found herself strangely attracted to the young, romantic, priest-to-be. Luckily, he felt the same attraction to her. Each was conscious of the complementary nature of their personalities and, thoroughly enjoying each other, spent more and more time together. On New Year's Day, 1891, they became engaged.

The question of Maud's religion was the one issue that intruded on their happiness. She had never been baptized in any church, even though her family were members of Concord's First Parish (Unitarian). Episcopalians were a rather bizarre lot in Concord—the home town of Emerson, Thoreau, Alcott, and Hawthorne—and distinctly inferior socially to the Unitarians and Congregationalists. Maud realized that she had shocked the community by going West to teach and knew her marriage to an Episcopal priest and baptism in his church would be almost unbearable. However, loving Murphy, she did not hesitate to ask for Baptism and Confirmation, since she believed a minister's wife should be a member of his church.

Murphy was delighted by Maud's loyalty, but objected to her motives. He carefully explained that the sacraments are properly administered only to those who accept the responsibilities they entail, and for hours each week he set forth the faith as he understood it to Maud, who frequently interrupted with perceptive questions. After her return to Concord in June, 1891, Murphy wrote her once or twice daily. Later she marveled that his letters were "full of such love and such deep religion, and such searching thought—and [yet] he was only twenty-one years old." Although he frequently quoted books, poems, and sermons, Maud found nothing "so full of the religion" she longed for "as the words of his own into which he would drop unconsciously and write on and on from a full heart."[9] Following this tutelage, when he arrived in Massachusetts in August Murphy arranged for Maud's baptism by the Rev. Phillips Brooks at the Trinity

Church, Boston. She was later confirmed by the Rt. Rev. J. S. Johnston, Missionary Bishop of West Texas.

With their personal religious question settled, Maud and Edgar were married in Concord's Trinity Church on August 31, 1891, Murphy's twenty-second birthday. In keeping with the season, the church was "almost covered" with goldenrod for the 7 A.M. ceremony. Even after Edgar's death, Maud recalled the beauty of the wedding and penned the perfect tribute: "I wish I had been then as good a lover as I am now. I had to learn so much from him. I still have to."[10]

Soon after the wedding the young couple returned to San Antonio, where Murphy resumed his work with Richardson. The happy days passed swiftly and successfully until Murphy became seriously ill in January, 1893. Once before, as a child, he had suffered an attack of rheumatic fever, but the doctors failed to connect it and his new illness. In a few weeks, he apparently recovered. He had no reason to suspect that his heart was now gravely damaged and that within a decade it would take much effort simply to survive. When Bishop Johnston offered him the appointment as minister-in-charge of Christ Church, in the border town of Laredo, he eagerly accepted. He grieved at leaving his mother but knew that to fulfill his vocation he must have a church of his own. Moreover, he welcomed the challenge that the mixed nationality, great poverty, and scarcity of churchmen in Laredo afforded. He was also pleased that the offer came before his ordination as priest.

At Christ Church Murphy initiated a decade of devoted service as deacon and priest. He was an outstandingly successful pastor, winning his bishop's and people's confidence and broadening and deepening his parish's spiritual life, although his ministry added few communicants to the parish rolls. But Murphy was not content to limit his activities to routine parochial affairs. Over and over DuBose had taught and written that the Christian life is to transform men here and now, and Murphy felt his ministry of reconciliation must be as broad and comprehensive as possible without losing its effectiveness. Through speeches, articles, and books, he sought to demonstrate the vital meaning of Christianity and its practical applicability. Feeling pretense and hypocrisy to be true religion's greatest enemies, he was able to appeal to diverse groups. Yet his convictions were most orthodox.[11] As a scholar, Murphy valued freedom, but he believed the church had a mission to proclaim the full faith and held that it was dangerous to allow every man to be his own theologian. "We accede the right of the individual to go to the Bible for spiritual power, for life and the presence of God," he wrote. "We deny his right to go to the Bible as such for theology in any of its departments." Murphy, in Laredo as elsewhere, feared the image of Christ was being blurred and warned that the success of the faith did not depend upon its books, but upon the life in Christ of its adherents.[12]

In sermons written and delivered with a care that delighted Du-Bose, Murphy led his people into an understanding of the faith which revealed the comprehensiveness of his conceptions and his charity for all. He advised them, "There is no class of virtues which are the exclusive interest and property of this Church. Her message is the Christian message and no other." Parishioners need not worry about being better churchmen if they would concentrate on becoming better Christians.

At Christ Church, Murphy had his first opportunity to demonstrate that the church was truly for "all sorts and conditions of men." In many areas, particularly among the more staid groups, church budgets were met by charging pew rent, a custom repugnant to Murphy, who believed that social distinctions should end in the house of God. Here the same services and sacraments were offered to all and even in death the best taste prescribed the absence of a funeral eulogy and the use of a pall, leaving all distinctions to God. Therefore, he proclaimed that Christ Church's pews were free and, to encourage attendance, even omitted the collection of an offering at the Sunday evening service. Though the parish had few children, there were young people everywhere in the city who needed the church's ministry, and Murphy valiantly sought them out. A number were attracted to the Sunday school, and many remained for Morning Prayer. From October, 1892 to February, 1893, he administered twelve Baptisms and presented six candidates for Confirmation. His inability to effectively minister to more people and the failure of some parishioners to respond were disappointments. Although he continually stressed their responsibilities, some attended services only every third or fourth Sunday, in clear violation of their Confirmation obligations. But despite some apathy, parish life was accelerated. Throughout Holy Week, Murphy scheduled two daily services, and he persuaded the vestry to donate the Easter offering to missions even though it was struggling to meet a local budget. He declared that progress comes "by force of what men shall hope and believe can be," and that to assume larger responsibilities was the first step in stewardship.[13] As the people assumed their obligations, the church could expand its services by helping to alleviate human suffering and misery. However, Christianity must not be regarded as a magic force to free man from misfortune but as a way to free the soul from circumstances that make life meaningless and unendurable.[14]

Murphy knew that the world was full of "angers, hates, lusts" and at Christ Church sought to combat them as best he could. To aid in the effort, he encouraged the establishment of a Brotherhood of St. Andrew, which brought men and boys together for work and prayer. With delight he saw earthly distinctions crumble in their awareness of God's love, and he gloried in the fact that the brotherhood reached out to "men as men," not as producers or gentlemen, seeking to bless them and be blessed in the process.[15]

In 1893 Murphy, concerned with the spiritual estate of men everywhere, was deeply troubled by the riots at Fire Island, New Orleans, and Garland Park. As for other true reformers, these tragedies had personal meaning for him, and he assumed a share of the responsibility, stating that the riots sprang from "conditions which we are making and have made, of ideals which we make possible." He feared humanity was losing it humanity—that as man united only for revelry and murder, he was destroying the elements of strength and beauty which made him human.[16]

The situation came squarely home the same year when one of the first Negro lynchings occurred in Laredo. Murphy was horrified and demonstrated the social consciousness and moral sense that characterized his career. By offering her candy, the offender had induced a four-year-old girl to ride on his shoulders, then had abducted her, attacked her, and literally torn her body to pieces. Many people were enraged, and Murphy understood their consternation. "Yet my whole heart cried out against the form of the Negro's punishment for I then foresaw that it would be taken as a precedent for many spectacles like it."[17] In what he considered to be the "first 'public' act" of his life, he called a mass meeting to protest the lynching and induced some of Laredo's leading men to attend. Although opposed by some members of his parish, he refused to be intimidated.[18]

The meeting convened in Market Hall, where, due to the size of the crowd, officers were chosen to direct the proceedings; Mayor C. A. McLane was elected chairman and District Attorney E. M. Hicks secretary. Though the meeting had been called to object to the lynching, when Murphy introduced resolutions condemning it McLane ruled that anyone could speak, and considerable debate took place. *The Laredo News* reported an even division on the question, but the resolutions were overwhelmingly passed by voice vote. Despite this, only twenty-one men dared take a public stand by signing the document.[19] Throughout his life, Murphy remembered this episode with pride, and later he wrote Booker T. Washington, "I think if our course had been taken throughout the South there would never have been another negro 'burning' with all its imbruting consequences."[20]

Even though Murphy was outspoken in applying the Gospel to concrete circumstances, he enjoyed a great influence in his prospering parish. After a visitation in January, 1893, Bishop Johnston wrote, "The minister and people are thoroughly united in one heart and one mind, and are harmoniously and heartily working together for the good of the Church. The prospects of the parish are more encouraging than I have ever known them, for which I devoutly give thanks to Almighty God."[21]

On the Fifteenth Sunday after Trinity, in September, 1893, Murphy was ordained priest at Christ Church by Bishop Johnston at a service for which Richardson came from San Antonio to preach.[22] But within three months after his ordination, Murphy resigned to accept the rectorship of St. Paul's Church in Chillicothe, Ohio. The ministry, like other professions, is a gigantic grapevine where the successes and failures of individuals become quickly and widely known. It was not at all surprising that the brilliant, young student of DuBose, who had successfully directed a parish of his own, should be called to another one so far away. However, acceptance of the call posed a problem to Murphy, who loved his mother very deeply and enjoyed being relatively near her, his sister, and his aunt. He wrote, "All that I know of tenderness toward the Negro (and the unfortunate generally) I learned from my Arkansas mother."[23] Moreover, his work in Laredo was satisfying and afforded increasing challenges, but other factors counterbalanced these advantages. As a man of sensitivity and culture, Murphy longed to be in a cosmopolitan city where he could best perform the type of ministry he was trained to offer. But the overriding consideration was none of these. To Edgar and Maud's great joy their first child, a son named in honor of Dr. DuBose, had been born in the summer of 1893. From the first the hot, semi-desert Rio Grande Valley disagreed with him, and the opportunity to move North was welcomed.[24]

For the next three years, Murphy served as Rector of St. Paul's, Chillicothe. Few priests have worked harder or accomplished more in a relatively small parish, and few have received greater diocesan and national recognition. More socially conscious than ever after his year in Laredo, he avoided no question that he felt needed the attention of Christian people. His well-prepared sermons attracted large congregations who, due to his tact and obvious concern for all men, were not offended when he dealt with controversial subjects. Consistently, he contended that a proper study of history should convince anyone that Christianity, not its critics, had been on the side of "right thinking and noble living." When some of his parishioners were disturbed by a lecture of Robert Ingersoll, Murphy assured them they need have no fears, for Ingersoll was merely presenting a rehash of what Voltaire had said over one hundred years before. He agreed with Ingersoll that contradictions existed in the Old Testament, but the wonder lay in the fact that there were not more, considering its diversity of origin and manner of transmittal.[25]

In 1895 Murphy became involved in another controversy when he attacked the city government of Chillicothe. In a sermon entitled, "The Coming Election and Political Duty," he contended that while the law required saloons to be closed on Sundays and intoxicants could be sold only to those over twenty-one, almost anyone could buy liquor at anytime in Chillicothe. It was mockery to "teach respect of law in the schools when scorn of law is taught from the city hall." He challenged the mayor, on threat of public opposition, to "openly pledge himself" to enforce the laws. When city hall remained quiet, Murphy urged everyone to vote only for those who would uphold the law. Unfortunately, the incumbents were re-elected, but he felt he had done his duty.[26]

Murphy was successful in expanding St. Paul's ministry. When he came to Chillicothe, he was impressed by the need of an Episcopal Church in the eastern section of the city, and, with the help of his communicants and the diocese, St. Andrew's mission was organized. At first he met with the group on Sunday afternoons; after three months a Sunday school was formed, and when the mission grew to one hundred members a lay assistant was hired. By 1896, construction was begun on a frame building seating two hundred, which included three rooms for the assistant and his family, and, within a few years, St. Andrew's rose to parish status.[27]

Murphy aided a responsible Negro group to establish in a similar fashion a mission of their own. He did this when convinced that it was the only way to extend the church's ministry to the Negro community. Within a matter of months this mission, St. Mark's, paid for its furniture, including leather cushioned seats, and became self-supporting except for a contribution of $100 a year from the diocese. On February 22, 1897, Murphy conducted the first services in its new building and congratulated the people on their achievements. He told them that if their movement had been started "simply for social ambitions, or because they had quarreled with other churches or desired greater freedom to dance or attend the theatre" he would not have helped them. He knew that such indictments of the Episcopal Church were caricatures and contended that, although it was not puritanical, no segment of Christendom was stricter in its adherence to essential moral values.[28]

At St. Paul's, as in his later parishes, Murphy sponsored free dinners for poor children on important holidays, but he carefully instructed his helpers in the attitude they must maintain. As Christians they should make the children feel that they were one of the family and should feel that it was a privilege to have them in the parish hall. The opportunity to aid the needy was one of life's greatest blessings, and the Christian must fight pride as mortal sin and humbly thank God for the opportunity to cooperate with Him in doing His work in the world.[29]

To further work of this type, Murphy sponsored a men's club and nurtured it. One modern Christian custom he detested was the frequent domination of parishes by women; he felt that the church must be much more than sweet ladies meeting to do "nice things" for each other. He always reminded men that regardless of their business interests, their first duty was to truly worship God; from this flowed all the auxiliary benefits of Christianity.[30]

In Chillicothe, as elsewhere, Murphy's ministry was to the entire community as well as his parish. He gave public lectures in 1894 on the career of William Gladstone, the British prime minister noted as much for his piety as his statesmanship.[31] In January, 1895, he joined in a series of inter-denominational meetings to acquaint the public with features of the various faiths.[32] Moreover, he frequently spoke to convocations of his own and neighboring deaneries, often on matters of a housekeeping or promotional nature.[33] But it was in his writings for church publications that Murphy reached his greatest audience. In *St. Andrew's Cross*,[34] for example, he gave his view of the priesthood, stating that it called one to a unique life, always featured by a "haunting consciousness" of unworthiness. In another article, a review of DuBose's *The Ecumenical Councils*, he defended the belief that Christ is understood only through the church.[35]

Not all of Murphy's publications were so noncontroversial since he did not hesitate to attack what he found objectionable in church practices. When a Philadelphia church unveiled a life-sized portrait of "St. Charles, the Martyr," Murphy was amused and grieved. He felt that King Charles I's enrollment "in the 'noble army of martyrs' was a piece of folly traceable to a lack of reality in the ecclesiastical mind."

He attributed the rise of Puritanism to Charles' unwise policies and felt it inappropriate that "a man who found it impossible to speak the truth or to keep his promises" should be numbered with the heroes of the faith. The church had "sterner business" than "the unveiling of pictures of the enemies of religious and civil liberty."[36]

Some Episcopalians disagreed with the churchmanship reflected in "Two Aspects of Confirmation," in which Murphy held that Confirmation was more than a rite of initiation; in it action was taken by God "to enlighten and empower" man to fight the battle necessary for salvation.[37]

Murphy's perception of the faith and his desire to propagate it led him in 1897 to write and publish two books setting forth his theological views. Both grew out of sermons but were rewritten many times before publication. Neither claimed to be an original contribution, but each sought to enrich the spiritual life of the reader as well as to clarify his theology. Both were personally subsidized and, though well received and widely reviewed in the church press, did not pay for themselves commercially.

The first of these books, *The Larger Life*, dealt with specific questions continually confronting Murphy as a priest, and reflected his belief in the individuality of his presentation and the truth of his message. Much of the work was directed at those on the periphery of Christianity who needed more knowledge and insight to grow in the faith. Murphy pointed out that no man can perceive all truth, and Christianity does not explain everything. It does not banish darkness but fills it with God's presence. Some truth is not ours in order that we may battle to attain it. Certainly if one finds and uses the truths available to him, other truths come.[38] In recent centuries man had concentrated more and more on himself. Rights had superseded duties, and, with such a false center of perspective, life had lost its meaning for many. This was revealed in the Parable of the Prodigal Son where the elder brother, a typical bestower of self-approval, was surprised and irritated when confronted by a profound world.[39]

Murphy contended that no new truths are needed to live the good life; this comes from practice of old truths. Man meets inevitable failures as he attempts to follow the teachings of Christ, but tragedy lies not in battles lost but in battles never attempted. The church on earth will always remain an "Unperfected Church." It chooses man, not for what he is, but for what he may become.[40]

To Murphy, the Communion of Saints was a living reality and an important factor in the spiritual life of all Christians, who are bound to each other in a common struggle and mission. Membership, he said, requires that self-sacrifice become the habit of every heart. Satisfaction comes only to those who feel reverence for others in need and recognize that every person is a living soul and must not be regarded merely as a member of a class or group. As the cross did not witness the casting away of the body but its redemption, the advancing manifestation of God must see a purification and transfiguration of the material world. Christ calls man out of himself in order that he may know the joys of communion with Him and serving his fellow man. In later years, this philosophy served as the motivation for Murphy's actions as a reformer.[41]

The Larger Life reflected DuBose's teaching and Murphy's own Christian humanism. Not surprisingly, it received warm accolades, *St. Andrew's Cross* proclaiming it "a contribution of permanent value to sermon literature, scholarly, practical, and inspiring." *The Churchman* praised its use of language, holding that it often rose "to eloquence."[42] But undoubtedly the most pleasing review to Murphy was that of the Rev. W. A. Guerry, for many years Chaplain of the University of the South, who found in *The Larger Life* "no 'faultless fear for the faith,' no quibbling, no dodging of living issues." Instead it was "a successful attempt to show that Christianity is essentially a reasonable and rational faith," without the "fault-finding and idle abuse of the age" so common in many works. Its only weakness was the rigorous subordination of affection to reason and logic. Despite this, Guerry found the book to contain material on every page for reflection and meditation and held Murphy's style to be charming. "No one can lay this book aside," he wrote, "without feeling that the author has had something to say and said it well."[43]

A few months after the appearance of this first book, Murphy published *Words for the Church*, a brilliant rationale for the polity, dogma, and worship of the Anglican Churches. In the introduction, Bishop Thomas F. Gailor of Tennessee well described it as "the practical efforts of a priest to give his people reasonable answers to pressing questions." In the preface, Murphy expressed his conviction that the Episcopal Church could do most for God by stringently presenting her special message. When she stood for "nothing in particular," failure was imminent.

In the apostolic era, Murphy continued, although varying conceptions existed, the faith was not individualized opinion but the living heritage of the church. In modern times, however, strife, not error or heresy, had often come to be considered the ultimate evil; it was unmannerly and must be avoided at all cost. While zeal must be tempered by wisdom, charity, and patience, falsehood must not be allowed to go unrebuked. Diversities of opinion were allowable in many areas, but where the creed expressed the opinion of the Universal Church, no deviation should be tolerated.[44]

In presenting his rationale, Murphy dealt at length on the origins of Anglicanism, contending that at his ascension Henry VIII found the scandal of a foreign church and the protesting conscience of a people. By appealing for ecclesiastical freedom, the king removed the trammels which had kept him personally decent, but he took no action ending one church and beginning another. "Nowhere may be found the history of a Christian Church in which there is so little to be explained," Murphy wrote, agreeing with Gladstone that "among the English race, she speaks and moves with an Apostolic right."[45] He felt that the Reformation was perhaps inevitable but that it was unfortunate that there was no alternative to it—that the gentlest soul of the Renaissance era, Erasmus, was not "a consecrated spirit" who could bring internal reform. Since the Reformation individualism had run riot in the factionalized West. Only in recognizing "that the home of truth is not individual but social," he contended, could men do Christ's work in the world.[46]

Publication of *The Larger Life* and *Words for the Church* were a fitting climax to Murphy's years in Chillicothe, years "rich with friend-

Maud King
before her marriage

Edgar Gardner Murphy
at age eleven

Edgar Gardner Murphy
at Sewanee

Edgar Gardner Murphy
and the Rev. Matthew Brewster

Edgar Gardner Murphy and two Montgomery friends

ships [and] full of successful service." The family had been happy
there and blessed with the birth of a second son, Gardner, in 1895.
Few parishes could offer a greater challenge than St. Paul's, but the
Scioto River Valley was noted for its malaria, and the entire family
was sick much of the time. Murphy blamed the climate for his recur-
ring attacks of fever and weakness. These factors and an urgent request from a parish in distress led him to accept the call in October,
1897, to St. John's, Kingston, New York, a Hudson River town of
22,000 located at the foot of the Catskills and two and one-half hours
traveling time from New York City. The parish and community alike
received his resignation "with surprise and regret." Bishop Boyd Vincent expressed the sentiments of many when he wrote, "It is a very
sincere sorrow to find that you are really going away. You have done
a devoted, noble and most efficient work at Chillicothe, and I shall
never cease to be grateful to you for it."[47]

Murphy's call to St. John's, a fine old parish of 425 communicants,
was instigated by the Bishop of New York, who had been impressed
with Murphy's publications and felt he was the man to heal the severe
internal difficulties between the Catholic and Evangelical factions in
the parish.[48] In the late nineteenth century the Oxford Movement's
effects began to be felt in America and were eventually to transform
the Episcopal Church. The movement, emphasizing apostolic succes-
sion and the sacraments, was increasingly concerned with ritual. Ultimately its leaven resulted in the reinstitution of at least one celebra-
tion of Holy Communion each Sunday, the return of the altar as the
center of worship, the use of candles and vestments, and in the scheduling of weekday services. But the High Church or Anglo-Catholic
victory was never complete, and the struggle, in greatly abated form,
even now continues. Bitterness was intense at St. John's in 1897, and
there was danger that the parish would destroy itself. Low Church
forces, those that opposed the High Church restorations, were offended by the recently established advanced ritual and other practices.
Murphy knew that most of the parishioners were loyal churchmen
who, though upset, were united by many factors. He realized that in-
novations themselves often cause disputes and that externals could

pendent upon it. Christ speaking through the church provided a resolution of all questions. At first there could be no appeal to "a completed and authoritative Scripture," since it did not exist. "The New Testament itself took form and outline only under the test and authority of the Christ-Spirit in the Christian Church." The church as a body determined that Christ was indeed God as well as man. Murphy agreed with Edward Pusey, the Oxford Movement leader, "that the personal truth—if truth at all—will be confirmed by the response of the collective heart." He had no doubt that God had additional truths to reveal to man and that these were delayed, not by the teacher, but by want of a "unified and spiritually responsive Church."[57]

Kingston was proud of the distinctions Murphy attained, and after a year at St. John's he could state, with gratitude, "The spirit which prevails among the people is one of comity and good will." Despite this, in November, 1898, he resigned to become Rector of St. John's Parish in Montgomery, Alabama. As Murphy continued his sacerdotal work he became more and more conscious of the unity of man's life— that it is literally impossible to segregate the spiritual and the non-spiritual. He was a devoted Southerner who loved the region of his native birth while understanding many of its weaknesses and shortcomings. He was keenly aware of its social problems and felt that his training and background fitted him to work best in this region. Upon the recommendation of Bishop Johnston of West Texas, the vestry of St. John's issued the call, which he quickly accepted. In assuming his new position, he devoted himself not only to his new parish but to the imminent problems of the South, a task that came to dominate his life.[58]

2.

Montgomery Priest
and Racial Reformer

WHEN MURPHY CAME to St. John's, Montgomery, he assumed the spiritual leadership of one of the oldest and most influential Alabama parishes. It had six hundred and twenty-five communicants, and many others regarded it as their church home. Its members included state leaders through whom Murphy came to have an influence greater than he had ever known. The churchmanship of the parish and the entire Alabama diocese was much lower than Murphy's, but this posed no problem. He soon began to devote so much effort to Christian social relations that there was little time for theological controversy. No internal disputes existed at St. John's when he arrived in Montgomery shortly before Christmas, 1898. He was distressed, however, to find that only ninety-three persons paid a stated sum to the parish, and of these only twenty-nine gave as much as three dollars a month. This lethargy in fund-raising was a characteristic of the Episcopal Church in the South and did much to stunt its development. Many of St. John's expenses were met by voluntary guilds staging a perennial round of money-raising activities. Deploring the situation, Murphy promptly began to rectify it. He believed that man had a need to give to the church and, equally important, needed time free from money-raising to worship God. By March 30, 1899, $2,700 in additional funds was obtained, and all money-raising guilds were abolished.[1]

Although St. John's income doubled in six months, it was still not great enough to support a curate, an assistant that Murphy felt he must have. Bishop Richard Wilmer of Alabama wrote him, "Tell your people that, from my Heart, I beg them to follow your lead. . . ." Knowing the need of the entire church and continuing a practice begun in his first parish, Murphy led his vestry to pledge the 1899 Easter and Christmas offerings for missionary use, despite local needs.[2] Constantly stressing the responsibilities of Christians to support the church, he obtained sufficient funds to employ the Rev. Edward E. Cobbs as an assistant in the summer of 1899. Cobbs, a grandson of the venerable first Bishop of Alabama, was an unusually able and dedicated young deacon. From the first, he and Murphy were one in spirit and action, and his presence freed Murphy to undertake many non-parochial activities.[3]

Always first in Murphy's heart was a desire, as Rector of St. John's, to meet the spiritual needs of his people, but illnesses made this difficult during his first six months in Montgomery. He arrived with the flu and later relapsed. In January, 1899, Gardner had scarlet fever, and, two days after the quarantine was removed, DuBose contracted the disease and almost died.[4] Murphy was not sufficiently recovered from another illness to conduct Ash Wednesday services, but, true to his responsibilities, he counseled his parishioners to make their communions as "a true beginning to a devoted and fruitful Lent."[5] He urged them to abstain from "the lighter interests of the world" during the penitential season. The noblest persons saw no evil in dancing, theatre-going, and card games during the rest of the year, but during Lent they refrained from all of these and other gala activities as in bereavement. "The Church is in watching with her Lord," and her sons must behave accordingly.[6]

One of Murphy's greatest joys at St. John's was the faithfulness of its people and the "gratifying degree" to which the parish was made up of men. Capitalizing on this, he organized a vigorous men's club whose charter provided that no dues or fixed obligations would be levied. Monthly meetings were held in the homes of members, where refreshments were limited to coffee and sandwiches in order that sessions could be held with the "only moderately well-to-do."[7]

The cooperation of the men's club aided the parish in undertaking an ever-expanding program. When Murphy visited the mill workers in Montgomery's West End, he was appalled at their poverty, poor housing, and grueling working hours, and he began a program to help them. A mission, served by Murphy and Cobbs, was opened in their region, and a corps of teachers came from St. John's to maintain a Sunday school. "Neighborhood House," consciously modeled after Northern settlement houses, was established as a social center for the people of the area and a means to give simple instructions in hygiene and self-help; also, a library was opened for the children. For the first time, Murphy became familiar with the particular problems of the mill workers, and his warm, sympathetic nature led him to resolve that a Christian society must do something to improve their intolerable conditions. Experiences here furnished him with the moral indignation necessary to initiate the crusade against child labor a few months later.[8]

The Negroes were another segment of the city's unfortunate people that soon attracted his concern. When he found that the Episcopal Church made no attempt to reach this half of the city's people, he was shocked and undertook a ministry to them wholly as "a labor of love."[9] In June, 1899, he invited all interested Negroes to meet at St. John's in the belief that the Episcopal Church could provide a ministry "peculiarly adapted to their needs and aspirations." He quickly warned them, however, that they should turn to the church purely for spiritual reasons. "I do not want any distinction in this church between the rich and the poor, or between the fashionable and unfashionable."[10]

To further the plan, Murphy appealed to a select white group, confident that their assistance would bring spiritual growth to them as well as to the Negroes. Many persons felt that Negroes "should be left wholly to those forces of a crude and emotional Protestantism that are already so largely at work among them." Strongly contesting this view, Murphy declared that the Episcopal Church could "give them the Christian faith without dependence on those degrading influences of frenzy and hysteria that have so often made religion a fetish to the ignorant and a stumbling block to the intelligent." The church, he said, stands for qualities of character "that are developed not merely by preaching, but by training and education" and imparts a "wholesome conception of religion through the attractive and ennobling forms of a conservative ceremonial." When correctly presented, its "ministry of symbolism" appealed particularly to Southern Negroes. It must minister to Negroes in the Alabama capital, where "thinking men" came from all sections of the state and which was a city adjacent to a county where Negroes outnumbered whites six to one.[11]

With the aid of the Bishop of Alabama, St. John's, and the Negroes themselves, the new Church of the Good Shepherd was given a well-located lot and a comfortable frame building with adjoining rooms for a Sunday school, a day nursery, and a kindergarten. One of the church's first bulletins explained, "Mr. Murphy has told us that the best way to give money is just to give it, that the way to contribute is to contribute; that the community will appreciate an attitude on our part which exalts the dignity of Christian benevolence by its simple dependence on the powers of courage and faith and love."[12]

St. John's heeded Murphy's counsel on giving in 1900 when, with one-twelfth of the communicants of the diocese, it provided one-tenth of the total income and furnished one-half of the contributions to domestic and foreign missions. When a church journal asked how this was accomplished, Murphy's aversion "to any unbecoming advertisement of a parish" made him reluctant to reply, but he did so in hopes his experience would be useful to others. The church had wise governing agencies to oversee the use of funds, and he advised that they be trusted and sustained. He knew that Alabama Episcopalians were generally no wealthier than the average members of their communities. "With the exception of some six or eight families, the members of St. John's are people of only average means," he wrote. The parish's success stemmed from the sacrifices of men and women of moderate income, and he urged that the opportunity to give sacrificially be extended to churchmen everywhere.[13]

One problem on which the faithful parish could give little help was the lack of appropriate teaching materials for the Sunday school. After studying the situation, Murphy developed his own curriculum based on the reproduction of great works of art. Knowing that a child forms mental pictures, he concluded that any successful teaching system must present an appealing projection of Christ's personality. Accordingly, he selected fifty-two famous paintings, including five works of Raphael and three of Millet, and placed a text on the back of each for instructional and devotional use. The Perry Picture Company of Boston issued the collection (and a smaller set of twelve) packed in small portfolios. Dr. Lyman Abbott, among others, praised the system as "a fresh and original kind of lesson-help," warmly commending it to "progressive Sunday School workers" of all faiths. Its use was a blessing to St. John's and many other parishes and was a great satisfaction to Murphy.[14]

Even greater freedom to work beyond the parish came to Murphy when Cobbs was raised to the priesthood on October 28, 1900. In the ordination service, which he preached, Murphy attributed much of the parish's success to Cobbs' work. "Believing in each other, sustaining each other, with the same plans at heart, with the same prayers for the guidance of a common people," they had worked as "brothers in a common household."[15] He realized that at times as a priest Cobbs would be distressed when confronted by "the unintelligent misjudgment of petty minds" and when men would leave him "alone to perform the tasks that their God had given alike to them." Yet he could look for human rewards also. Murphy had found, "No man is condemned so lightly as the Christian minister, but no man is really believed in so deeply."[16]

Sensing his religious duty, in late 1898 Murphy called for the practice of the Golden Rule to lessen the tension on the churchmanship issue. The vast majority of Episcopalians, while they might label themselves as "high" or "low" churchmen, were united by a strong bond of common belief and practice and were "neither disguised Romanists nor ill-concealed Non-conformists." Many failed to realize that the church was both Protestant and Catholic—Protestant in rejecting provincial additions to the faith and believing in "direct access to the Father of spirits" and Catholic in recognizing that superior to the individual was the "religious conscience of Christendom."[17]

Addressing the Churchman's Club of Providence, he extended his plea for cooperation to include a call for the reunion of all Christendom, a goal in keeping with the resolutions adopted by the 1886 General Convention of the Episcopal Church. While much of the world was on the side of simplicity, he warned, a unity of value must be based on the historic faith. In a striking analysis, he contended that Christ's influence came largely from "the social vitality of the idea he presented to man." The implementation of the Parable of the Good Samaritan seemed a logical approach to unity. Murphy ascribed much of modern Christianity's difficulty to the clergy's failure to speak their minds on vital issues. They had become "too much occupied with the generalities of the Christian religion." Fearful of being accused of interference in state affairs, they allowed moral problems to be resolved without exerting their God-bestowed responsibility of speaking for the right and against the wrong. In a democracy, Murphy said, it is vital that all men think through major issues, and if the clergy were to be other than paper men, back slappers, and semi-comic actors, they too must be free to think and speak. "There may be worship, preaching [and] deeds of love without freedom, but there can be no thinking without freedom." With a free and responsible clergy, Murphy hoped that there would "come into the national life a new influence and a vitality of conscience."[18]

Murphy's utterances were warmly received, and he spent an increasing portion of his time dealing with social and civic questions. More and more, he perceived that the great issue was the implementation of the faith, and to attain priestly ends he was forced to delve into the secular arena.

No person as sensitive as Murphy could have lived and worked in the South at the turn of the century and failed to be concerned with the injustice and misery of the Negro. One of the most enlightened Southerners, Walter Hines Page, wrote that the problem had not left his mind for twenty years and that he found the pathos of it eternal. In both North and South since the 1880's there had been a constant abandonment of the Negro's rights as an American citizen until by the turn of the century it seemed that the nadir was reached. Joel Chandler Harris found the situation "worse than it ever has been—far worse than I ever expected it to be." In 1903, the editor of *The South Atlantic Quarterly* declared that a crest in Negrophobia had arisen in the last five years as evidenced by "restrictions of the negro vote, in the passage of 'Jim Crow' cars, in an increasing resort to lynching, and in a general augmentation of that sensitive disposition on the part of Southerners to take fire at the hint of a 'Negro outrage.' "

Paradoxically, this trend came while white society was being democratized, while the Negro was decreasing his illiteracy from 79.9 per cent (1870) to 44.5 per cent (1900) and was creating his own middle class. Undoubtedly much of the difficulty both directly and indirectly arose from the Populist revolt. Not only, after initially attempting an alliance with the Negro, did the Populists turn upon him, but too often the conservatives, alarmed by the white's assertion of power, raised the Negro issue and rended him also. Perhaps John E. White, the pastor of Atlanta's Second Baptist Church, was correct when he said, "The least responsible elements of our population lack the restraint and guidance of the more responsible elements to which they have the right to look for statesmanship. . . .The state of anti-negro sentiment, which we know exists in the lower sections of Southern society, is in a great degree due to a hopelessness and inaction they see in the ranks above them."[19]

Murphy agreed with the Alabamian, William Garrot Brown, who was teaching at Harvard, that "men of the better sort," the Southern upper classes, must lead the masses to a peaceful, moderate, and just solution of the race question. At the turn of the century, Murphy had not arrived at his own definition of what that solution should be, but he knew it would include an absolute end to lynching. This stain on civilization reached an all-time high in the decade of the 1890's, when an average of 187.5 persons were lynched each year (1889–1899); of these, 138.4 were in fourteen Southern states and over 67 per cent were Negro. The number of lynchings was cut in half from 1900 to 1909, but Negroes constituted almost 90 per cent of the victims and most of the lynchings took place in the lower South. Tragically, in the years between 1885 and 1907 "more persons were lynched in the United States than were legally executed." As late as 1919, Robert R. Moton, Booker T. Washington's successor at Tuskegee Institute, believed that lynching caused more unrest among Negroes than anything else and found it the most frequently given cause for the Negro migration that began in large volume from the deep South at the time of the First World War.[20]

George Washington Cable, the New Orleans local colorist, was unique among prominent white Southerners in demanding not only an end to lynching but absolute civil equality for the Negro. The unpopularity of his stand was a factor in his self-imposed Northern exile in 1884, but his indictment of lynching bore fruit. "Words like yours," wrote the Rev. Quincy Ewing, "waken in me an awareness of spiritual companionship," and he proceeded to preach and write effectively against the evil, strongly motivated by a lynching near the Episcopal Church he served in Greenville, Mississippi. "My soul is sick within me today!" he confided to Cable. "Not content with battering in the jail-door in broad daylight, while the sheriff sat in the court-house, near by,—not content to lynch the Negro prisoner in the jail-yard— a mob of our best citizens led him up Washington Ave., the leading thoroughfare of the town, and hanged him at the two main business streets. My baby in his carriage and Enid [his seven year old daughter] were just ahead of the mob down the street, and Enid—whose little heart and soul we have tried to fill with only fair and beautiful things—saw the Negro hanging! She explained to me—'I couldn't help but see it, Daddy,'—and of course she couldn't." When Ewing heard that two of the city's Presbyterian ministers sympathized with the lynchers, he wrote, "Alas!! Has 'the Galilean conquered?'" and resolved to move to some more appropriate area to rear his children.[21]

With the exception of Atlanta's John Temple Graves, editor of *The Atlanta Times*, who in 1906 offered a prize of $1,000 for a successful lynching, the Southern press generally condemned this form of outlawry, a much more liberal stand than it assumed on any other aspect of the race question. Murphy believed the press reaction was indicative of Southern opinion and felt the most certain way to end the terror was for constructive Southern forces to assert themselves. When the influential *New York Evening Post,* a militantly anti-Southern newspaper edited by William Lloyd Garrison's grandson, Oswald Garrison Villard, indicted the South as a section for Georgia lynchings in 1899, Murphy wrote a letter to the editor. He sincerely feared the intemperate attack would inflame Southern opinion and induce conservatives to withhold their influence. In this case and afterwards, Murphy was extremely conscious—perhaps overly so—of Southern sensitivity to outside interference. His reply to Villard reminds one of recent contentions that Southerners alone understand the Negro and that outside intervention is unwarranted. There was no doubt, however, that Villard had overstated his case and that he had failed to realize that Southern society, "as elsewhere, is a fabric woven of coarser and finer elements." Moreover, Murphy was correct in thinking that responsible Southern groups were refusing to join lynching parties and that with the loss of "any semblance of decency and order" mobs would eventually cease to be. If he could have foreseen the time and horrors involved before lynchings would end, however, he probably would have sought additional correctives.[22]

As time passed, the question of race relations bore increasingly on Murphy's mind. He realized the problems involved were intricate and that much of the South's and the nation's future depended on their proper resolution. He knew that the older conservatives had lost power or had compromised on the race issue, that by 1898 when South Carolina joined the Jim Crow car movement a pattern of segregation had been settled on the entire South, and that beginning with Mississippi in 1890 and South Carolina in 1895 disfranchisement of Negroes regardless of ability had been initiated and was continuing. He believed even the poorest Southern white man was potentially a fine human being, and his greatest fear was that hysteria and inertia would prevent the natural leaders of the South from leading their people in the right direction. To avert this he concluded that the forces of intelligence and decency must be brought together, confront the issues, and have a forum to propagate their concepts.[23] Since there was no agency to fill these needs, he resolved that one must be established. He induced twenty-four prominent Montgomery men, including the Mayor, Dr. J. B. Gaston, a Methodist minister, and a Presbyterian minister, to join with him in forming the Southern Society. Its constitution stated that the society was "to furnish, by means of correspondence, publication, and particularly through public conferences, an organ for the expression of the varied and even antagonistic convictions of representative Southern men" on the race problem. With great confidence it proposed, by educating the public mind, to bring about an "understanding of the remedies for existing evils."[24]

The society's first action, in January, 1900, was to call a Conference on Race Relations to meet in Montgomery in May. Murphy as Secretary of the Executive Committee assumed the responsibility for developing plans and promoting the conference, and with his accustomed zeal he quickly began to advertise the event and formulate a program. Within a matter of days, he and other members of the committee were invited to Tuskegee for the dedication of the Slater-Armstrong Memorial Center, the new trades building on the Institute campus. This was certainly the most important trip of Murphy's career, and he always considered the spontaneous sequence of its occurrences as near miraculous.

By 1900 Tuskegee Institute already enjoyed an international reputation and commanded the respect of much of the nation. Primarily, it was the embodiment of the ideals of Booker T. Washington, its founder and principal. Washington was a graduate of Virginia's pioneer industrial school, Hampton Institute, which was developed by Samuel C. Armstrong, a former Union general and son of missionary parents, after he realized the great need and potential of the Negro people while serving as a Freedman's Bureau agent. Washington's humility and efficiency, his school's industrial training which produced such effective farmers and craftsmen, and his insistence on his students' personal cleanliness, courtesy, and high morals endeared him to the white community while earning Tuskegee national stature. Northern philanthropists first began substantial aid to Tuskegee Institute when William H. Baldwin, Jr., then Vice-President of the

Southern Railway System, after weeks of entreaty, was persuaded to visit the school in 1894. Not only did he and his friends prove generous benefactors, but they led Congress and the Alabama legislature to grant 50,000 acres of land to Tuskegee and the Alabama Industrial School. By 1900 the reputation of Washington's school had come to equal or excel that of Hampton Institute.

Much of Tuskegee's fame rested on Washington's personal acceptance as a herald and prophet in the field of race relations. In his most famous address given in 1895 at Atlanta's Cotton States and International Exposition, and known afterwards as the "Atlanta Compromise," he clearly set forth the doctrine that segregation should be accepted, at least temporarily, in return for economic aid. "The central theme in Washington's philosophy was that through thrift, industry and Christian character Negroes would eventually attain their constitutional rights." Due to his success and the hope he offered in an era of savage repression, he became the leader most Negroes accepted following Frederick Douglass, the ardent contender for full civil rights who died the year of the Atlanta address. Washington was never fully accepted by many intellectuals, but the most important of them did not break openly with him; W. E. B. DuBois, professor of sociology at Atlanta University and later a leader of the N.A.A.C.P., delayed doing so until 1903. In 1900 Washington stood on the brink of his greatest power, a period in which Presidents Roosevelt and Taft used him as their principal patronage adviser for the South and during which he exercised a virtual veto over Negro affairs in many areas.[25]

Washington's quiet dignity and cordial hospitality were an ideal introduction of Murphy to Tuskegee Institute. The Slater-Armstrong building, constructed of 800,000 bricks made by the students, was a living memorial to the indomitable spirit of man, and the surprising number of Northern philanthropists present gave new hope that man's humanity to man was still alive. But most inspiring were the students themselves—many from miserably humble backgrounds— who were overcoming apparently insuperable obstacles to obtain educations and to prepare themselves for useful lives.

As these impressions revolved in his mind, Murphy, to his complete surprise, was introduced by Washington and asked to give an account of the coming Montgomery Conference on Race Relations. Aroused emotionally, he responded with the finest speech of the day and one which was most significant for his career. He explained that the conference by its nature would not be handicapped by Southern prejudice against solutions proposed from the North. He hoped by establishing "in our own Southern country an annual Conference representative of Southern opinion on this subject—a Conference working along broad, liberal, and inclusive lines, we can move toward a solution which shall be honorable and just for all." The race question was sectional in the sense that the majority of Negroes were in the South, and the South must come to grips with the problem. "We believe, therefore, that we shall preserve the South just in so far as we fail not to preserve the manhood and the womanhood of this Negro race." Further, he said that these conditions were not static, and they were not gifts bestowed but rights earned.

Murphy told the eager students that they had a responsibility to carry forward an enlargement of liberty. He reminded them that the Declaration of Independence was at first a prophecy and the Emancipation Proclamation "represented but a liberty in the document." They must attain and utilize a "freedom of accomplishment" and advance the "whole conception of emancipation until it shall mean not merely the right to vote, but that faculty and fitness for efficient life which is everywhere the crowning authority of the citizen." Emancipation must be obtained not merely from political dependence but from ignorance, uncleanness, idleness, and wrong. The only free man is the one "who lives worthily, who works faithfully and well, and who carries within his own person the availing and qualifying arguments of merit and fitness. When we have all reached that conception of the emancipation of the Negro of the South, we have brought to him enfranchisement indeed." This was precisely Washington's philosophy, and it was logical that Murphy concluded his address by telling the students that Tuskegee was "the Temple of your liberties."[26]

The speech was repeatedly interrupted by applause, and, at its conclusion, the audience rose as a body in an ovation, waving handkerchiefs and cheering. Spontaneously the two-hundred-voice choir began the joyous spiritual, "Lay On Your Harps, Hallelu," in which the audience joined. When order was restored, Washington stated, "It is worth every dollar that was ever expended on this institution to have heard such an address as that to which we have just listened." The press was equally laudatory. *The Montgomery Advertiser* reported that Murphy's address "won all hearts" and that it "seemed to mark the beginning of a new day." Even *The New York Evening Post* declared it the highlight of the convocation, quite a compliment since the venerable J. L. M. Curry, head of the Peabody and Slater funds, had also spoken. If the speech were representative of any considerable segment of white, Southern thought, the *Evening Post* conceded it would be "difficult to see what they could learn from any outside source."[27]

In the evening following the address, Murphy and the Rev. George B. Eager of Montgomery met with the Tuskegee Board of Trustees, a group largely composed of outstanding Northern philanthropists. The impressions Murphy created opened avenues of advancement he had not known existed. His conservatism, respect for the successful businessman, and belief in self-help, as well as his sincerity, warm humor, genuine good will, and distinctive Southernism made him exceedingly attractive to the group.

Among the trustees was the man who had spoken immediately prior to Murphy, William H. Baldwin, Jr., Chairman of the Tuskegee Board of Trustees and President of the Long Island Railroad. Born in Boston in 1863 and a Harvard graduate, he early became identified with many social reforms in his home town, ranging from evening school classes to open air farms for children. A veritable dynamo, the Episcopal Bishop of Massachusetts later said of him that his greatness came less from being "so *good* a man, [as that] he was a man rich in suggestive power." He began work as a railway clerk and advanced to Assistant Vice-President of the Union Pacific Railroad. While serving as Vice-President of the Southern Railway System, he became vitally interested in the welfare of the Negro and accepted a position as a trustee of Tuskegee Institute in 1897. He persuaded Andrew Carnegie to give the school $600,000, and after 1902 he was influential in obtaining some of the first grants from the General Education Board. As a liberal on the race question, he believed that there was no "place" of inferiority for the Negro and that the Tuskegee method was the best means for him to advance toward full equality. In addition to concern with the Negro, he was beginning a brief but intensive period as Chairman of New York's "Committee of Fifteen," which investigated and sought remedies for prostitution and other social abuses in the nation's largest city.[28]

A second trustee at the meeting was Hollis Burke Frissell, a New York native and graduate of Phillips Andover, Yale, and the Union Theological Seminary. As a young minister, he served as an assistant in New York's Madison Avenue Presbyterian Church, but when he visited Hampton Institute in 1880, Dr. Armstrong induced him to accept the chaplaincy. A short while later he assumed the duties of principal, and upon Armstrong's death in 1893 succeeded him. A man of determination and ability, Frissell was associated with many reform movements throughout the South and nation.[29]

The trustee most strongly attracted to Murphy and who became one of his closest friends and co-workers was the sixty-four year old Robert C. Ogden. A native of Philadelphia, he began work in a dry goods store at the age of fourteen and first traveled through the South as a clothing agent in early 1861. The same year he was introduced to the twenty-two year old Samuel C. Armstrong, who throughout his years at Williams College spent part of his vacations with him. Together they discussed Armstrong's theories of Negro education and formulated the plans for Hampton Institute in Ogden's parlor. The saintly but dynamic Armstrong frequently said he had to choose between being a pirate or a missionary, and the tactful, business-like Ogden served as a beneficial influence on him personally and was one of the school's major benefactors. He had unlimited respect for Armstrong and declared him to be "the greatest man it was ever my privilege to know." He became a Hampton trustee in 1874 and served as board president from 1894 to 1913. He often took guests to the graduation exercises, which he missed only once in his lifetime—a fact he deplored since it was the year, 1875, of Washington's graduation. The Institute's publication, *The Southern Workman*, correctly declared, "No man except General Armstrong himself has had more to do with the upbuilding of the Hampton School. . . ." A recent convert to Tuskegee's support, Baldwin induced Ogden to come to the school whose work and Washington's personality captivated him; however, even though later serving briefly as chairman of the Tuskegee board, Ogden always felt that Hampton did superior work.

Ogden's business success and personal frugality made possible his charity. He was a partner with his father and Daniel Devlin in a New York clothing firm until 1879, held various positions with John Wanamaker in Philadelphia until 1896, and when the latter took over the A. T. Stewart Co. in New York Ogden became its manager. One of the first to use extensive advertising, he was most successful in his new business. His deep religious faith and practical bent of mind were factors in his work in the South. Though a devout Republican, who had attended the Lincoln inaugural ball in 1861 and voted for every Republican presidential candidate since 1860, he was completely committed to the Washington philosophy of racial compromise. "Perhaps, it may truly be said that slavery has harmed the poor white more than the Negro," he wrote. "They should have sympathy, pity and patience, not resentment and bitterness, even though they are very provoking and trying. They are a dead weight upon the whole body politic. They must be educated. The joint intelligence of black and white created by painful steps and slow, is the only basis of hope."[30] Holding these views, Ogden in 1900 was on the threshold of transforming the Conference for Southern Education into one of the most important educational movements in American history.

Meeting with men such as Baldwin, Frissell, and Ogden was an exciting experience for Murphy. All the trustees had been impressed by his address, Baldwin to such an extent that he was almost speechless afterwards.[31] In the ensuing conference, which lasted until midnight, they had a better opportunity to explore Murphy's ideas and to appraise his personality. The more they talked with the bril-

liant, earnest young man the higher he rose in their estimation. Before
the session ended, they gave a hearty, unanimous endorsement to the
impending Montgomery race conference, and Murphy was invited
to make a major Philadelphia address.[32]

Murphy's meeting with Washington was equally important. They
became fast friends and from this time often consulted and aided each
other. Washington's influence proved as appealing to Murphy as to
most Americans, and he accepted his philosophy on many major questions. Murphy was even more concerned than Washington in not
offending Southern white sensibilities, and there was a sincere doubt
in his mind as to how far the Negro could advance. While it is true
that Washington "so thoroughly subscribed to the 'White Man's
Burden' of leadership and authority that, in seeming forgetfulness that
he was a Negro, he actually took up the burden himself," there seems
no doubt he felt his people could and must attain the standard of
white America. This is most clearly apparent in Washington's post-
humous article, "My View of Segregation Laws," but much of his correspondence also reveals the same attitude. For example, in 1904 he
wrote Oswald G. Villard, "The fact is, all of us are aiming at the same
thing; we may be pursuing different methods, trying to reach the
same goal by different roads, and there is no necessity for quarrelling."
Washington pointed out that the Negro had lost most of his Southern political power before Frederick Douglass' death, that in every
case where racial disfranchisement had been proposed he had spoken
against it, and that he had raised a cry opposing lynching as often as
he dared do so without losing press coverage. He stated also that his
stand on industrial education was misunderstood. "In all my writings
I have emphasized the necessity for college and professionally trained
men and women as well as those with industrial education." How
could he do otherwise when Tuskegee employed more graduates of
liberal arts colleges than "any other similar institution in the world."
Washington knew that many of his critics attacked him because of
frustration. "I become just as impatient as they do, and wish just
as much as they do that I could change conditions," but he felt
this could only come slowly as Negroes acquired "property, edu-

cation and character." Others judged the ability of a Negro leader "in proportion as he cursed the Southern white man regardless of the effect of such cursing." Washington felt that cooperation with the Southern whites was the route to success. There is a serious question as to whether he contributed to the degree of Negro repression by providing in his Atlanta address and elsewhere a rationale for segregation and second-class citizenship, but at least his intention was not to do this. Being a pragmatist, he was pursuing the one road he felt would lead to success. Significantly, he opposed repeal of the Reconstruction amendments even though the federal government made no effort to enforce them.[33]

Murphy and Washington, sharing many ideals and beliefs in the same methods, worked closely in planning the Montgomery Conference on Race Relations. Washington visited the rectory to give his advice, and during the rush of Holy Week Murphy met him at Montgomery's Union Station for a between-trains conference. Proofs of the Southern Society's promotional literature were sent to him and changes were made based on his recommendations. In an action indicating his own true opinion, Washington suggested as speakers two advocates of full civil rights, Senator Chauncey Depew and ex-Governor William A. MacCorkle of West Virginia. Murphy accepted MacCorkle but vetoed Depew because he was "known through the rural districts of the South chiefly as a Republican." He believed that a non-politician or a Northern Democrat would carry greater influence.

Murphy's own timidity was reflected in the decision not to invite Negroes to participate in the public sessions. In committee meetings he argued for the inclusion of two Negro speakers but was overruled. He acceded to the majority and came to feel his action was wise; to have Negroes on the regular program would have aroused prejudice and defeated the purpose of the conference. Certainly Washington did not like this stand. In 1890, when the Mohawk Conference in upstate New York failed to invite Negroes while considering the Negro question, George W. Cable protested and Washington congratulated him. "Were it possible for any action of yours to increase my respect and love for you, your position in this matter would certainly do so many fold," he wrote. He did not consider himself a sensitive man, but he found "the disposition on the part of many of our friends to consult *about* the Negro instead of *with*—to work *for* him instead of *with* him—is rather trying and perplexing at times." Despite reservations, he did suggest appropriate Negro leaders who were invited for private discussions at the time of the Montgomery conference.[34]

Murphy's racial views were first presented in detail in Philadelphia on March 8 when, through Ogden's, Frissell's, and Baldwin's influence, he spoke on "The White Man and the Negro at the South" at a meeting sponsored by the American Academy of Political and Social Science, the American Society for the Extension of University Teaching, and the Civic Club of Philadelphia. His one-and-one-half hour address and its publication as a 55-page pamphlet received widespread recognition.

He directed his remarks to "The Northern man who, by unsympathetic legislation would oppress the White Man of the South, and to the White Man, North or South, who would oppress the American Negro." Indicting both Northern and Southern radicals, Murphy contended that no one had the right to speak "as a representative authority" on the serious race problem. All anyone could do was give conclusions based on his own experience and judgment. The South was a diverse land and conditions varied; it was quite incorrect to speak of the problem as being the same everywhere. The race question was greater than the Negro issue, however, because within it was entangled "the whole bewildering problem of a civilization";[35] all Southern issues were related to it. Murphy's sense of Christian ethics led him to believe that man must learn to live with his fellow man in a spirit of love which law could not decree, an opinion shared by an increasing number of Northerners. One of them, Dr. Lyman Abbott, editor of *The Outlook*, expressed it in this way: "I have more faith in the power of an awakened public opinion than I have in any form of legislative action."[36] Yet Murphy realized there was a national responsibility in race relations since all America was involved. Unfortunately, Reconstruction converted a national issue into a sectional one and blinded Southerners to the realization that they needed Northern wealth and interest to grapple with the issues.

Influenced by Washington's philosophy, Murphy commended those who were attempting to improve the Negro's "industrial and personal efficiency" before seeking political and social rights and who were supporting "those forms of education which open to him the actual opportunities of his life." In taking first things first, Murphy felt that these reformers were being realistic and were not abandoning a desire for civil rights. The Southern white man constituted the average Negro's world, and the Negro would not be helped if his world were turned against him.[37] In taking even this moderate stand, Murphy was bucking a rising trend which saw Negro education as ruining good field hands.

As the agitation of social equality "befogged the problem" of Negro rights, so, Murphy believed, obsession with lynching resulted in a lack of adequate concern with the more important question of Negro rights before juries, a view reflected a few years later by the historian James W. Garner who wrote that lynching "is the natural result of the failure of courts to discharge their natural functions." But Murphy was not attempting to excuse lynching and wrote, "It is hard for the Negro to get justice" anywhere. "Justice at the South is secure, everywhere, just in so far as the surface frictions of class and caste and race are met by the sweetening and healing forces of experience, education and religion."

Murphy knew that such Southern political leaders as Senators Benjamin R. Tillman and James K. Vardaman wished to restrict the Negro's educational and economic opportunities, but he believed the Montgomery conference would demonstrate that the majority of Southerners disagreed. The power of those opposed to Negro education was declining. Most agitation was against teaching a classical curriculum to the masses before they were taught to make a living. Murphy's aristocratic bias emerged when he stated that no trouble existed between trained, efficient Negroes and upper class whites; the major opposition always came from the poorer Southern whites. But his sense of *noblesse oblige* was apparent when, unlike so many others, he did not castigate these whites. Instead, he found them the most helpless of Southern people, and like Washington he felt that industrial training was needed for them also. He could understand how a poor white mother on visiting Tuskegee would wonder why her sons could not have similar advantages, and he cautioned Northern philanthropy not to neglect the underprivileged Southern whites and expect all to go well with the Negro. "There is not an evil at the South for which education—thorough education, more education—and education of the right kind, will not bring availing and abiding remedies," he wrote.[38]

Murphy next turned to the question which most deeply divided Southern men in 1900, that of the franchise. At the time, the South was in the midst of disfranchising the Negro while leaving loopholes for poor, ignorant whites to vote. Even progressive leaders like governors Charles B. Aycock of North Carolina and Andrew J. Montague of Virginia supported the movement. Walter Hines Page, in the midst of a Southern tour in 1899, wrote that the people would not tolerate disfranchisement of Confederate veterans but "*the nigger cannot & shall not rule. This is the central doctrine everywhere.*" George W. Cable was in a tiny minority when he wrote of the Negro, "We have no warrant for the assumption that we dare not accord him full political fellowship—We have never fully tried it—so far as it has been tried he has always met conciliation & forbearance half way."[39]

Murphy's position was the same as that of Ogden, Page, Dr. Albert Shaw, editor of *The Review of Reviews*, and other moderates, North and South. He held that any civilized person would oppose wholesale Negro enfranchisement in areas where Negroes predominated until they were literate and had acquired higher moral and cultural standards. To insist "upon the supremacy of the forces of intelligence and property" was not prejudice but realism. Personally he wished an honest treatment of the situation—the reduction of Southern representation in the House of Representatives, under terms of the Fourteenth Amendment, and the withdrawal of all attempts at national coercion of the South. He advocated equal property and literacy tests for both races, but unlike most liberals he believed that a modification of the Fifteenth Amendment to make the franchise a local issue was the best means to attain this. He felt the amendment served only to arouse local passions against the Negro and was a political football for aspiring politicians. It did not give the vote to a single Negro since many of the new state constitutions contained "grandfather clauses," "understanding clauses," and other subterfuges. If the Fifteenth Amendment were rescinded and the threat of Negro power were removed, he was sure that qualified Negroes would be given the vote. Southerners as Americans would recognize that no people would accept "as a working principle of life the theory of taxation without representation," and even the most prejudiced would see that the enfranchisement of the whites as a race and the disfranchisement of the Negroes gave only the blacks "an incentive to the acquisition of an education and a home."

Murphy's plan overvalued the Southern white man's sense of justice and reflected his tendency, most becoming in a cleric, to always see the best in others. He was not the only one deluded, however. D. H. Chamberlain, South Carolina's last Reconstruction governor, held as late as 1904 that the "educated and capable negro" would "be freely admitted to vote" in his state, and Washington himself was victimized by the white South's failure to keep its "gentleman's agreement," which promised equality in applying voting standards in return for Negro and national acquiescence in the new policies of the states. But Washington disagreed with Murphy's attempt to have the amendment formally modified, and Walter Hines Page felt it was foolish to raise the question. He believed its original passage was a mistake, but Northerners would regard a repeal movement as one for Negro disfranchisement. Unhappily, Murphy's position placed him in company with the most noisy advocate of repeal, the racist James K. Vardaman, who made it an issue in his 1903 campaign for the governorship of Mississippi.

Murphy knew his appeal would be opposed by men in both sections who could "neither forget nor forgive." Many Northern men mistakenly believed that by coercing the Southern whites they could force them to cease punishing the Negro. Murphy assumed there was a rational basis for disfranchisement and explained it as a reflection of the fear of ignorance. Unfortunately, too many Southern whites felt it was easier to coerce the Negro than to educate him.[40] However, the

Negro's economic progress indicated he could raise himself to be a suitable voter. As Washington pointed out, the South had opened labor, industry, and business to him and had afforded him "something more merciful than sentiment and something more necessary than social assimilation." Therefore, increasing numbers of Southerners should realize that in dealing with the Negro they "have faulted him for ignorance and then left him ignorant . . . have called him brutal and then have treated him with violence . . . have blamed him for indolence and then have denied him the great civic inspirations of labor —the inspirations of political responsibility, the quickening and steadying powers of a vote freely cast and freely counted." To be just to himself, the Southern white man would be forced to be fair to the Negro.[41]

While naïve in some respects, Murphy's advice portrayed his own fine, ethical sense, his opposition to the militant racism gaining control in the South, and his belief in a true spirit of community. His strong religious convictions were often apparent, and his belief that society is one—that no segment can suffer without all being injured— is related to his faith in the Communion of Saints—a consciousness that all Christians are members of one body and that they have a responsibility to each other.

Throughout his Philadelphia address, Murphy's select audience of almost one thousand remained attentive.[42] The Philadelphia press gave it favorable coverage, and he was most pleased by approval of his appeal for the poorer Southern whites.[43] *The Churchman*[44] proclaimed the speech "an auspicious event in our social history" and predicted it would influence Northern philanthropists to modify their programs and work with the liberal Southern forces. Trends in this direction were emerging, and Murphy's articulate voice and pleasing personality became a powerful force accelerating and channeling the development.

From Philadelphia, Murphy went to New York City, where he preached at Grace Church and visited for several days with the men he had met at Tuskegee. He and Robert C. Ogden spent hours in serious discussion and, finding they shared many deep convictions, they resolved to work together for their implementation. At the time, no opportunities were open, and no specific plans could be formulated.[45]

Returning to Montgomery, Murphy continued preparations for the Conference on Race Relations. His Eastern contacts proved valuable, and he used Ogden's and Baldwin's names in seeking support. While in New York, he talked with W. Bourke Cockran, the Irish-born, Democratic congressman, whom he persuaded to become the concluding speaker and the principal Northern one on the program. Before inviting him, however, Murphy carefully outlined his views on the Fifteenth Amendment and became convinced that Cockran would take a similar position.[46] When Washington learned of Murphy's attitude, his support of the movement began to waver and was sustained only by tactful explanations. Murphy assured him that the Southern Society had no policy on the amendment. Personally he did not advocate its repeal but its modification, and he had said that he "would not have the *potential* citizenship of the Negro destroyed." He only wished to make the franchise a local issue since he believed that this was the one means of expanding the suffrage to qualified Negroes. He suspected the average Southern white man would oppose his solution because under the present state he could "count the Negro out in the election, and can count him in for representation."

After being attacked by the Philadelphia Negro press, Murphy realized that Washington could not afford to be identified with his proposal. "They are not ready for what I am trying to do," he wrote, advising Washington to say he disagreed on the Fifteenth Amendment but accepted the remainder of Murphy's philosophy. He assured Washington that this issue would not cause the slightest break in their relationship. "I have absolute faith in ideas," he wrote, and a dispute as to method would never create dissention. "I admire you and I believe in you absolutely, and I trust that in the future, whether we agree or not, we shall be united in sympathetic co-operation for the welfare of the poor and dependent of both races."[47]

Washington was not the only conference supporter who was troubled by Murphy's attitude. Ogden had advised him not to introduce the subject in his Philadelphia address or at Montgomery, and Walter Hines Page withdrew as a speaker when he learned that it would be. Though he and Murphy were later to work closely together on the Southern Education Board, he now wrote strongly to him. He declared that the consideration of repeal "shows such a hopelessly impractical and theoretical state of mind" that any conference proposing it would be considered an impractical body. Having made magazine programs for years, he assured Murphy that a mistake in judging public opinion "outweighs all good intentions." Confident in his views, Murphy stood his ground even when Page challenged Cockran's character and his status as a "representative Northern man."[48]

As the day of the conference approached, Murphy assumed responsibility for many of the details for the gathering. One of the most onerous was obtaining invitations to private homes for the many visitors, a necessity since the city's few hotels were poor in quality. Newspapers throughout the country were contacted, and leaders of public opinion were invited to attend. The group that assembled in Montgomery on May 8, 9, and 10 was a distinguished one, and Murphy was pleased to find among them Hollis Frissell and Hampton Institute's recently chosen treasurer, Alexander Purvis, Ogden's son-in-law.[49]

The largest audience ever assembled in Montgomery gathered for the conference. The presiding officer was Hilary A. Herbert, eight-term Montgomery district congressman and Cleveland's Secretary of the Navy.[50] In his opening address, Herbert deplored the use politics had made of the Negro and contended that the carpetbagger was the first to draw the color line. In a note reflected throughout Southern politics, he defended the disfranchisement features of the new constitutions of Mississippi and Louisiana as a means to purer elections.[51]

Alfred Moore Waddell, the mayor of Wilmington, whose racial violence had spurred North Carolina disfranchisement, assumed the negative position taken by Prudential Life Insurance Company statistician, Frederick L. Hoffman, in his book, *Race, Traits and Tendencies of the American Negro*, and held that the Negro had become less fitted for civilization each year since Reconstruction. He urged repeal of the Fifteenth Amendment, defended the North Carolina constitution, and disagreed with Murphy as to the desirability of equal voting qualifications. He challenged Murphy's belief that applying literacy and property tests to Negroes only placed the whites at a disadvantage, holding that fallacies lay in assuming that the white exemption would be permanent and in identifying education with thrift.

Waddell was mild in his rejection of Murphy's proposals compared to the rabid Atlanta editor, John Temple Graves, who challenged all of them. "Separation is the logical, the inevitable, the only way," he declared. "Every year of enlightenment increases the Negro's apprehension of his position, of his merit and attainment, and of the inconsistency between his real and his constitutional status in the republic." Negro education, he said, would only complicate the problem.[52]

In a position similar to Cable's, ex-Governor MacCorkle disagreed with Graves, advocating the immediate granting of all constitutional rights to the Negro. "The question of Negro franchise has never yet been fairly tried," and the South has most to gain from it, he declared. The system of repression required all the South's attention, precluding progress in many fields. MacCorkle was certain that an attempt to modify the Fifteenth Amendment could "again rend in twain this great nation." In effect it meant "the practical turning over to the South of the Negro Question as a local question," and he left his audience with the haunting query, "Are we able to bear it?"[53]

In his address, Hollis Frissell, assuming the positive public attitude taken by Hampton and Tuskegee spokesmen, turned from the franchise issue to education. He advocated an expansion of industrial training, holding it was "capable of producing a class of hard-working, docile Negroes, which will place the South in the foreground among the industrial countries of the world." At least one good school for each race should be maintained in each of the South's 1,300 counties, he urged.[54]

The educational theme was continued in the presentation of the dean of Southern educators, J. L. M. Curry. As head of the Peabody Fund from 1881 and the Slater Fund after 1891, two major efforts of Northern philanthropy to aid Southern education, he had not insisted that Negroes obtain a fair distribution of grants, but he belonged philosophically to the older school of Southern aristocrats who did not understand the new cult of repression. Pronouncing the conference a success on the basis of Herbert's and Frissell's addresses, Curry, overemphasizing the meager Southern contribution, praised "the liberality of the Southern people in providing the means of education for those who were recently their slaves." But he knew that much remained to be done, particularly through a combination of the industrial education and academic training which seemed most appropriate for the Negro in his present state of development. Society could not afford to let one-half of its people retrogress from lack of adequate instruction. He could not see how "to unfetter the faculties, giving wider intellectual horizon, developing the true manhood and womanhood should have a different ethical effect upon a man with a black skin than upon one with a white." He reminded those who advocated that the Negro should provide for his own education that no one had ever been educated by his own resources.[55]

Next on the program were two pessimistic addresses given by the Chief Statistician of the United States, W. F. Willcox, and by the chairman of the faculty of the University of Virginia, Paul B. Barringer. These men, like the Dean of Harvard's Lawrence Scientific School, Nathaniel S. Shaler, who wrote an essentially racist article for *The Atlantic Monthly* in 1884, brought the prestige of science to bolster their preconceptions. Willcox described the Caucasian as being a superior, Aryan race and held that when "higher and lower races meet and interpenetrate, only two permanent solutions have thus far been recorded in history. Either the lower race has disappeared, or the two have fused." Since emancipation, the Negro population had first slackened in growth, secondly, became stationary, and, finally, was declining. Therefore, he predicted its eventual extinction. He had not seen the census returns for 1900 or he could not have made this evaluation; it revealed an increase in Negro population in the 1890's.

Barringer, agreeing with Willcox, held that the Negro when "subjected to natural law" would "go like snow before the sun." He believed that since the war the Negro had lived "on the stamina and morality of slavery days," but that these were running out. Money was squandered even on the type of Negro education associated with Hampton and Tuskegee institutes. "The wealth of the Indies could not give this entire race technical training any more than it could satiate the appetite of those thriving on the brokerage of philanthropy. Industrial training should be reserved for a more industrious people."[56]

Murphy was shocked by Willcox's and Barringer's speeches, but pleased that their opinions were aired. His own optimism and faith in the soundness of the masses when given the right leadership prevented despondency, and he was delighted with W. Bourke Cockran's address, which largely reflected his own views. Cockran proclaimed that the Negro's progress and that of the South generally refuted the belief that the Negro had deteriorated. If freedom were destined to destroy the Negro, this would have occurred when he was freed. Instead, he had not reverted to savagery but had learned to labor for himself.

Cockran felt the real problem came from the Constitution, which gave the Negro theoretical rights denied him by public opinion. Reflecting Murphy's views, he held that removal of the threats of outside coercion and potential Negro domination would result in literate, responsible Negroes receiving their civil rights. If accompanied by widespread industrial education the Negro would also gain economic security. With "a Tuskegee in every community," he predicted "that the next generation, instead of troubling about the Negroes will be celebrating a glorious success in settling a question graver than any presented to a nation in the history of the human race."[57]

Cockran's address set a tone of confidence on which the conference ended. Herbert, in a conciliatory manner, concluded the sessions by firmly, but politely, challenging Barringer's reasoning and use of statistics. He reminded him that tabulating the Negro's savings gave no accurate barometer of his economic worth, which lay mainly in his labor for others. Herbert's pride in Negro achievements and hope for his future were evident to all.[58]

The conference's success "exceeded the most sanguine expectations" of Murphy and his friends. All shades of opinion were expressed, and "the net result of the Conference" appeared to be "hopefulness, courage," and a desire for justice. It placed particular emphasis on education; Frissell's paper was tactful and forceful, and Washington and many of his friends declared Curry's address to be the greatest of his career. The audience for the last session was composed of "the best thought and life of the state and the South." Although Murphy felt Barringer's address was "odious in spirit," his voice "was too ineffective to give his words any extended influence." Most thoughtful people, "including even the representatives of the press, regarded the speech with distinct disfavor," and the paper "wrought its own cure," evoking successful rebuttals. "No man was ever more thoroughly smashed," Murphy wrote, rejoicing that this occurred at a conference in Montgomery sponsored by the Southern Society. Cockran's two-hour address of "surpassing power and beauty" was an effective corrective. "In point of intellectual sincerity, of moral enthusiasm, of philosophic weight, as well as in diction, it is the greatest speech I have ever heard," Murphy said. The intelligent Negroes of Montgomery almost unanimously regarded it as a fine plea for their cause.[59]

The Negroes, of course, disagreed with the racist speakers, but they were not alone as critics. None of the people with whom Murphy talked agreed with Graves' proposal for separation of the races; many sympathized with Waddell, but local criticism of Barringer was severe. Murphy was encouraged by these opinions and the more enlightened white attitude that emerged while the conference was being planned. In its infancy, Murphy could not obtain approval for admission of Negroes to the conference audience, yet when the plans were concluded there was no opposition. At the final evening session, three- to four-hundred Negroes occupied seats "that were wanted by some of the best *white* people of Montgomery," and there were no complaints.

Murphy hoped the conference demonstrated that thinking men

could deal with major issues "without going into hysterics." He trusted others would come to share the opinion of William W. Screws, editor of *The Montgomery Advertiser*, who declared, "the welfare of each race is involved in the welfare of the other; and whatever is a difficulty for one, is a difficulty for both, and that the true removal of difficulties must open the way of development for all classes of our population."[60]

The conference received not only local but national coverage, the most interesting account being by Washington in *The Century Magazine*.[61] He stated that its sessions and those of the Confederate Congress were the most important gatherings in Montgomery's history. That such a conference could be held only thirty-nine years after secession in itself afforded cause for encouragement. Few movements had created so much interest and discussion. "I have known the promoters and officials of it for years, and believe that they have in view but the permanent elevation and highest good of both races in the South," Washington wrote. He applauded the diversity of thought represented, declaring, "Any movement that brought merely the friends of the negro together would mean little in the way of distinct gain." Though leaving something to be desired in freedom of speech, the conference did represent the "Silent South." "For years we have heard the voice of the North, the voice of the negro, the voice of the politician, and the voice of the mob; but the voice of the educated, cultivated white South has been largely silent." Only four of the conference's nineteen speeches were antagonistic to the Negro, but Washington felt it well they were given. "The man who speaks out truly and frankly is not a person to be feared." Barringer's address contained "the most discouraging views" Washington had ever heard, and, as he listened, he kept wondering what their effects would be on a Southern audience. Fortunately his views were challenged, and the audience agreed with the challengers. Washington concluded that Barringer's extravagances, by motivating whites to come to his defense, would aid the Negro. Men would be stimulated to make first-hand investigations of Negro life, and many would, for the first time, see its "higher" side. Only then when the American people came "to

judge the negro much as they do other races—by the best types and
not by the worst"—could he expect justice.

Only the press of New England proved to be critical, but it was
aroused, as Ogden and Page had foreseen, by the suggestion of a
modification of the civil rights amendments. Murphy rationalized
this valid objection, though it severely troubled him. Maud was from
Concord, and he had a host of friends in New England, but, he
explained to Cockran, the New England mind worked on a priori
knowledge. As the original seat of abolitionism, it had not yet admitted "either the patriotism or the sincerity of the South." *The
Boston Transcript* and *The Springfield Republican* were in character
when they issued the "most ignorant and wanton misstatements."
Murphy interpreted their editorials to mean "that any word said in
behalf of the white population of the South or in sympathetic interpretation of the actual conditions of Southern life is necessarily unreasonable and unjust."

Despite the attitude of the New England press, Murphy was hopeful. Even *The Boston Transcript* recognized that the Fourteenth and
Fifteenth amendments would amount to nothing unless the masses
of Southern whites had the proper attitude toward the Negro.[62] An
overnight change could not be expected, and Murphy counseled patience when Cockran was perturbed at those opposed to his viewpoint, including Washington. "Washington himself is not a mer-
curial man," he wrote. "He is one of the best men I know. At the
same time, he cannot help feeling the pressure of New England
philanthropists, and his conversion to your wise proposal will naturally be a slow one."[63]

To further disseminate the work of the conference, Murphy edited
its proceedings and persuaded the B. F. Johnson Company of Richmond to publish a 220-page, 5,000 copy edition. It took much of the
summer to complete the project since Cockran, who had spoken from
notes, was extremely slow in writing a paper. But at last this was
received, and the volume appeared in the fall.[64]

Its success led Murphy to plan a magazine, similar to *Everybody's*,
that would investigate the serious aspects of the race question. The
Montgomery Conference on Race Relations had received much at-

tention, but newspapers everywhere had ignored many of its most valuable aspects. Murphy felt modern journalism to be concerned primarily with the sensational and wished a journal which would deal with race relations "in so broad a light and so interesting a manner, that we can educate without the general public finding out that they are being educated." He believed three policies reflecting Washington's philosophy should dominate the publication: belief in the broadest nationalism, achievement of universal education, and the attainment of "industrial and economic efficiency" as a prelude to suffrage. He had "never seen any racial friction between two representatives of different races when *both* the individuals considered were really educated." Moreover, he disagreed with James Russell Lowell's contention that the ballot itself was an education, holding that the recent political history of New York and Pennsylvania demonstrated its invalidity.

To promote his magazine, tentatively entitled *Race Problems—A Journal of Information and Discussion,* Murphy asked Walter Hines Page if Doubleday, Page and Co. would be the publishers, and he offered to assume the editorship for two years for $1,500. He believed publication should be in New York, "our one cosmopolitan city" and "one of the most incurably democratic communities in the country," a location that would not arouse Southern prejudice. He also suggested that Frissell, Curry, and Washington be appointed as an advisory board to deal with Negro-white relations in America, but, realizing the magnitude of the issue, Murphy wished the magazine to consider the world racial problem as well.

Page, while sympathetic, felt Murphy's recommendations were infeasible at the time. Unlike Murphy, he knew the cost and labor involved in such an undertaking and advised him to use the publications of Hampton and Tuskegee institutes to enlighten national opinion. Murphy was forced to acquiesce, but he knew the alternative Page suggested was inadequate. By their nature, the industrial schools' publications were forced to concentrate on a narrow aspect of the race question, and, among other issues, could never carefully consider the overseas problem.[65]

While planning his journal, Murphy dreamed of other conferences that would continue the process of informing the American people, particularly the masses of Southern whites. He and Washington had a number of meetings to formulate plans for a 1901 conference. An agenda was prepared, and President McKinley and J. G. Carlisle, Cleveland's Secretary of the Treasury, were invited to speak. Despite this, the meeting did not occur. No city offered to serve as host, and the very success of the Montgomery meeting made the Southern Society fearful of holding subsequent sessions that might be more explosive. Since practically every segment of racial opinion had been presented and was available in permanent book form, Murphy and his associates decided to allow constructive Southern forces to operate a few years before calling for a reappraisal. In the interim, Murphy's time was absorbed in other aspects of the racial question, which he now realized affected every facet of Southern life. Education, in particular, seemed the hope of the South, and henceforth he concentrated much of his energy on its relationship to the race question.[66]

Even while social questions dominated his time, Murphy was still Rector of St. John's and conscientiously sought to minister to his people. As always, his strength was severely sapped by prolonged hard work; he was exhausted for weeks following the Conference, but his parish continued to flourish. In the summer of 1900 the church was redecorated, and a fine new organ was installed by late January, 1901.

During this period, Murphy visited his ever-widening circle of New York friends, who accepted him both as a genial companion and something of a seer on Southern problems. It was probably at about this time that he approached the recently retired steel millionaire, Andrew Carnegie, for a contribution to the Montgomery Public Library. Early in 1901 Carnegie offered a gift of $50,000 if Montgomery would provide a site and an allocation of $5,000 for maintenance. *The Montgomery Advertiser* praised Murphy for his "representations" to Carnegie, and the city council appropriated the $5,000. To comply with Carnegie's conditions, Murphy became a leader of the library trustees and raised $14,000 from private sources to purchase the library site. Murphy and the shrewd Scotsman got on well together, and Carnegie agreed to come for the dedication ceremonies, but a sudden illness forced a last minute cancellation.[67]

Another friendship cemented during Murphy's New York visit was with George Foster Peabody. A distant cousin of the Peabody Fund founder, he was born in Columbus, Georgia of New England parents, who, impoverished by the Civil War, moved to Brooklyn when he was fourteen. He was forced to educate himself by reading nightly in the Y.M.C.A. library, which he termed his "alma mater." At the Brooklyn Heights Reformed Church, he became the friend of a young investment banker, Spencer Trask, and they formed a partnership that prospered greatly through investment in beet sugar, electrical utilities, and Western railroads. Despite his acquired wealth, Peabody kept the "common touch" and was always interested in philanthropy and reform. He became a devotee of the single tax after reading Henry George's *Progress and Poverty* and was an ardent Democrat, taking vigorous parts in national campaigns and serving as Treasurer of the Democratic National Committee in 1904. After his conversion to the church in 1880, he was an equally ardent Episcopalian and served as a delegate to a number of General Conventions. Peabody's religious and political views and a mutual interest in Southern progress explain the very close relationship which developed with Murphy.[68]

While with Peabody in 1900, Murphy told him of the recreational needs of Montgomery's young men. Impressed by Murphy's interest, in 1901 Peabody contributed $14,000 to purchase a lot for the Y.M.C.A., $2,000 for its furniture, and $5,000 of the $30,000 needed to erect the building. Murphy and his friends assumed the leadership of a local campaign which successfully raised the remainder.[69] Services such as these led *The Alabama Journal*[70] to praise Murphy as "a cultured scholar and a working man of deeds." It believed him to be "the most valuable acquisition in the way of a citizen that Alabama has had for years. No man ever came to us and made so profound an impression in twice the time. He does things, a man of actual deeds—a most rare man."

Murphy did not confine himself to work for Montgomery, and, in

1900, accepted a second invitation to address the annual Church Congress. On this occasion, he dealt with the nature of the church and its relation to the search for truth in an address entitled "Analysis and Synthesis in Religion," which was more appropriately renamed, "Reconstructive Forces in Religious Progress," when reprinted in *The Outlook*.[71]

In his speech Murphy challenged the intellectually shallow forces all too present in the churches of his day that sought to stifle scholarship and inquiry. Only two years before, the President of the Southern Baptist Theological Seminary, William Heth Whitsitt, had been fired when the contents of one of his books published in 1880 became known. In *A Question in Baptist History*, he had contended that before 1641 the English predecessors of American Baptists had not been immersionists and that even Roger Williams had been only sprinkled. Three years later, North Carolina Methodists unsuccessfully attempted to have John Spencer Bassett fired from Trinity College for lauding Booker T. Washington, and only by determined efforts were North Carolina state colleges saved from economic strangulation by denominational forces which felt freedom of inquiry was a menace to the faith.[72]

Murphy denounced such efforts as thought control and contended that the raising of religious questions was a constructive force since every sincere question springs from a genuine need. Questions had produced the Reformation, which, although it had its negative side, was a constructive movement. It even forced the Roman Catholic Church to undertake a revival of her own, "a movement of piety" which preserved her as a leading segment of Christendom. Murphy told those who feared "modern criticism" that with it had come the greatest expansion in Christian history. Genuine scholarship could never discredit the faith because it could reveal only truth. Instead, it had "accredited anew" the concept of Christ "which the historic creeds enshrine"; similar results could always be expected.

Murphy's brief address portrayed his intellectual liberalism—a belief that in a free market of ideas the truth would ultimately be discovered and accepted—and it was well received by his 1,400 member audience. *The Living Church*, an influential Episcopal publication, characterized it as "one of the best addresses of the Congress" although the topic was an intellectual one requiring close reasoning.[73]

Returning to Alabama, Murphy joined the Rev. Neal L. Anderson at Camp Hill where, in December, they spoke at Southern Union College in support of industrial education for white boys. In early 1901, he staged a large reception for the Bishop of Alabama, and led the Montgomery Ministerial Association in opposing the "questionable sideshows" and "rowdyism" associated with the city's street fairs.[74]

During the year, Murphy found himself increasingly concerned with racial affairs. He was distressed by a book, *The American Race Problem*, written, ironically, by a Negro, William Hannibal Thomas. Ostentatious and sensuous, it contained absurd generalizations such as that 90 per cent of Negro women were immoral and that J. L. M. Curry had mismanaged the Slater Fund. *The Southern Workman* reported that it "is neither accurate nor reliable, and the book is written by a Negro who is filled with hatred for his race." Unfortunately, Thomas Nelson Page accepted it as authoritative and quoted freely from it in his articles, not a surprising fact following the favorable reviews that greeted its publication. Murphy considered popular acceptance of Thomas' views to be "a calamity" and sought to prevent this by writing a review published by *The New York Times*.[75] He questioned Thomas' contention that the Negro was deteriorating. Knowing nothing of the South before he came to South Carolina in 1871, how could his comparisons be valid? Freedom was producing a new class of Negro leaders, and Thomas was most unjust in contrasting their simplicity with that of slaves. Murphy's one consolation was "the thought that the first conspicuous repudiation of the book may come from a Southern white man."[76]

Alabama events kept Murphy from concentrating on racial developments elsewhere. In March, 1901, he became engrossed in the question of the proposed Alabama constitutional convention. The Negro had been disfranchised by constitutional conventions in Mississippi in 1890, South Carolina in 1895, Louisiana in 1898, and by an amendment in North Carolina in 1900. Georgia became the seventh Southern state (1908) and Oklahoma the eighth (1910) to adopt constitutional changes excluding the Negro vote, while elsewhere in the South the same ends were accomplished by the levying of poll taxes and other subterfuges.

Frightened by manipulation of the Negro vote, and knowing that political suicide would be involved in any appreciable white disfranchisement that literacy and property tests imposed, Mississippi invented the "understanding clause." This permitted registrars to use their discretion in registering whom they pleased. South Carolina adopted the clause, but placed a two-year limit on its use. Louisiana's contribution was the attempt to bring some semblance of regularity through the "grandfather clause" providing for registration of those entitled to vote on January 1, 1867, and their descendants. This proved so popular that with modification as to the time for qualification it was used elsewhere. In Mississippi an amazing spectacle occurred when the one Negro delegate supported the changes which not only disfranchised the Negro but froze the Black Belt's hold on legislative power.[77] The six Negroes in the South Carolina convention did not acquiesce, and in the opinion of the contemporary historian, David D. Wallace, "made good the claim of their race to being natural orators." But they were abused, two being "exposed" on the convention floor "as illustrations of the venality of Negro politicans."[78] Booker T. Washington fought the constitutional changes everywhere, seeking not to prevent levying of literacy and property tests but their arbitrary usage against the Negro. "Let the law be so clear that no one clothed with state authority will be tempted to perjure and degrade himself by putting one interpretation upon it for the white man and another for the black man," he wrote Louisiana voters in 1898. "I beg you, further, that in the degree that you close the ballot box against the ignorant that you open the school house." Failing to influence the Louisiana decision, Washington began a campaign to prevent similar tragedy in Georgia, but success was not to be attained. "I have been corresponding with leading people in the state but cannot stir up a single colored man to take the lead in trying to head off this movement," he wrote in 1899.[79]

Some opposition did develop, particularly in Louisiana where New Orleans politicians and *The Times-Democrat* opposed the "grandfather clause." In South Carolina *The Columbia Daily Register* feared the "understanding clause" would be invalidated by the courts with many whites disfranchised and, on a higher plain, *The Charleston News and Courier* believed the entire program could result in only discredit and moral injury. John Mitchell, Jr., the editor of *The Richmond Planet*, Virginia's leading Negro newspaper, attempted to defeat the movement by flattering the conservative whites. He felt that much of the motivation for disfranchisement came from those jealous of the tiny, affluent segment of Negro society, and he tried to demonstrate the impossibility of Negro domination.[80]

Although some protested, Negro disfranchisement became a holy crusade for much of the South, where the initiative was often taken by the emerging progressive leaders. These men, like their Northern counterparts, were usually middle class businessmen seeking to perfect the capitalist system and democracy "for whites only." Their racism was more a reflection of their times than an original contribution and was adopted both as a means to gain popular favor and a phase of their reform programs. They truly believed that the removal of the Negro was necessary for the emergence of a two-party South and purity in Southern politics.

North Carolina was one of the first states to attain disfranchisement under progressive auspices. Here the movement was held so sacred that it was initiated on Memorial Day, 1898, with Senator Furnifold M. Simmons and Josephus Daniels, editor of *The Raleigh News and Observer*, leading the fight. A white supremacy convention at Goldsboro attracted eight thousand, and Simmons and Governor Thomas G. Jarvis, to insure Baptist support, pledged that there would be no additional appropriations for state colleges and the University of North Carolina. Success depended on Democratic victory in the 1900 gubernatorial race. This was insured when the popular progressive, Charles B. Aycock, was chosen as the candidate, and when the whites resorted to the most diverse forms of threats and intimidation. As Daniels wrote, "The bulk of the white people of the State made up their minds to win at any hazard."[81]

Virginia's Governor Andrew J. Montague told Walter Hines Page[82] that he knew of only two pieces of "large constructive statesmanship that Southern men had done since the civil war"—Alabama Senator John Tyler Morgan's work for an isthmian canal and Mississippi Senator James Z. George's development of his state's disfranchisement program. When men like Aycock and Montague who were liberal on many questions zealously promoted disfranchisement, Murphy must have realized its inevitability. The issue had been prominent in Alabama politics since 1890, and the convention was probably postponed due to fear of the Farmers' Alliance strength. Apparently Alliancemen and their allies elected Reuben Kolb governor in 1892 and 1894, but an unfair count prevented his assuming office. With this challenge over but still frightened by the Negro vote, the Democratic party endorsed the plan to call a convention and voted to make it a party issue. There was much opposition, however, from North Alabama, where white counties feared white disfranchisement. In an attempt to overcome disapproval, the party specifically pledged that no white man would be denied the vote unless convicted of infamous crime. To gain the necessary public support in a state-wide referendum, John V. Smith, President of the Alabama Railroad Commission, was chosen Chairman of the Democratic Campaign Committee, and he called on the clergy to bring pressure on the electorate and party delegates to vote for the convention.

Murphy believed that racial disfranchisement was unjust, undemocratic, and immoral. Angered by the attempt to use the pulpit for partisan purposes, he replied to Smith in a series of letters defending the disfranchisement of "ignorant and vicious" Negroes and whites alike and opposing the calling of a convention under the terms of the party pledge. These letters were published in several pamphlet editions and formed one of the most potent arguments ever presented for an equal franchise. When the calling of a convention was approved, April 23, 1901, by a 70,305 to 45,505 vote, he converted the letters into an argument for a just franchise clause in the new document, and copies were sent to each convention delegate, the newspapers, and leaders throughout the state.[83]

Murphy reminded the delegates to the convention, which assembled in Montgomery on May 21, 1901, that they had no mandate to enfranchise all whites and exclude most Negroes. Of the state's sixty-seven counties, twenty-five, all in North Alabama, had voted against holding the convention, and such "progressive communities" as Birmingham and Mobile were carried only by narrow majorities. Less than one-third of the state's Democrats voted for it, although the official organization applied strong pressure to gain support. In fact, the issue had been decided by those counties where Negro votes were manipulated by the whites. Under such conditions, Murphy felt that to modify or reject demands of the platform was not to betray the people since it was "unauthorized, impossible and inexpedient." There were some promises no one had a right to make, and the members of the constitutional convention were "not the servants of the literal demagoguery of a partisan instrument, but were servants of the broad and permanent welfare" of the state.

Before the Democratic Party made its immoral pledge, Murphy had supported a revision of the constitution hoping to eliminate the subterfuge in Alabama politics, but when the party usurped the power of the convention he went over to the opposition. The contents of the projected constitution had not been an issue in the primaries, and for the party delegates to determine the constitution's contents was completely undemocratic. Murphy believed that the party wished the convention to meet "not to propose, but to ratify" its decisions.[84]

Moreover, Murphy felt the platform demanded the impossible. It promised to deprive no white man of the ballot except for infamous crime, implied that Negroes would be excluded, and pledged to achieve this constitutionally. Although he hoped the Fifteenth Amendment would be modified, Murphy pointed out that it was still the law of the land, and the party's pledge could not be carried out legally.

Furthermore, the platform demanded the unnecessary. Murphy did not favor Negro domination in any county, regardless of their numbers, since in general Negro literacy and culture were inferior. "White supremacy in the present stage of the development of the South" meant "the supremacy of intelligence, administrative capacity and public order." It afforded "those economic and civic conditions upon which the progress of the Negro is itself dependent." But white rule was securely established throughout Alabama, and the idea of Negro domination was "the merest 'bogie,'" which was employed by scheming politicians to advance themselves. Its use made "cowards of those who should be men" and had resulted in a pledge guaranteeing the ballot to white men who, among others, were chronic vagrants, illiterates, and even those found guilty of election bribes.

Murphy's views were similar to those of Albert Shaw, who wrote Governor Montague that an educational test for voting was perfectly justified and had been accepted for years in Rhode Island.[85] Certainly, "Illiteracy is not a crime, but literacy is a duty," Murphy wrote. "No man should vote who cannot read the ballot which he casts." Special consideration could well be given to veterans who had fought for the state, but this should be limited to a two or four year respite in which the veteran could prepare himself for the literacy test. Murphy wholeheartedly rejected the conferral of civic virtue by inheritance through the "grandfather clause." The white people needed the incentive "a slight educational test" would give. "The South must, of course, secure the supremacy of intelligence and property," but this could not be obtained by disfranchising intelligent and wealthy Negroes. An effort to do so would only depress Negro development and retard the state.[86]

Murphy knew many anti-Negro leaders were demagogues who would be surprised if their program was incorporated in the constitution. A suffrage test exclusively for the Negro might even be considered the best possible means to promote Negro supremacy. While driving Negroes "into restlessness and discontent," it would provide a stimulus to them alone. Could this be why "the South-haters at the North" accepted it with such composure? It would result in persistent agitation which would unsettle Negro farm and industrial labor. Always recognizing the unity of Southern life, Murphy declared, "Whatever strikes at the industrial contentment and the productive power of the Negro, strikes at the wealth of the South," and the income of every investor and wage earner would be affected. Moreover, unlike some political leaders of the 1960's, he realized the capital necessary for Southern development would be "frightened away by the 'scare head' articles on 'Negro Persecution' or the 'Race Riot' in the sensational newspapers of the land."

Suspicious of Northern tolerance of Southern injustice, Murphy predicted that court decisions and a new force bill, like that of 1890 which would have provided federal regulation of congressional elections, would right injustices if Southern economic pressure became evident or Republican control was endangered. It seemed foolish "to put into the law itself the injustice that is done outside the law." The only satisfactory permanent solution was to place suffrage restrictions "without consideration of race," and then "the Federal Constitution will never be invoked against us."[87]

Despite his clear thinking on this portion of the question, Murphy believed white supremacy had to be maintained until the Negro had acquired sufficient education and property to vote constructively. He advocated that this be done through the temporary levying of a $2.50 per year poll tax.[88] He failed to consider that regardless of his training and wealth the Negro had needs and wants which deserved governmental representation. In addition, Murphy still cherished the hope that the upper class' sense of *noblesse oblige* would see that the Negro in tutelage obtained justice. This viewpoint is surprising in the light of the selfishness and corruption Murphy had witnessed in the last few years, but his own distinctive romanticism led him to nurture his delusion.

Many of Murphy's friends and parishioners disagreed with his views. Conceding he could be incorrect at some points, he stated, "I am not such a bigot as to assume that a monopoly of all the infallibilities finds its center in myself." However, when a correspondent challenged his knowledge of the means used to debar Negro voters, he replied that, though he was familiar with the techniques, he did not dwell on them since his writings would be quoted in the North, and he did not "wish to advertise the misdeeds of Alabama."[89]

During the convention the Montgomery press printed everything Murphy wrote, *The Advertiser* not infrequently using it as editorial matter. Its editor, William W. Screws, was a vestryman of St. John's and one of Murphy's closest friends.[90] Another friend, former Governor Thomas G. Jones, concurred in Murphy's opinions and was largely responsible for his writing an open letter opposing the convention's majority report.[91] Under it the governor would appoint three registrars in each county who would pass on the qualifications of all voters. Murphy contended the only person satisfied with the proposal was the man who would cast his own vote and "the votes of all his negroes (living and dead)," and he distrusted the arbitrary authority given the registrars. There was nothing to prevent them registering every Negro in sight and from discriminating against anyone they wished. "I can see nothing in the scheme but the formalizing of our perennial fraud," Murphy wrote. In fact, the present conditions were better than those being invited. The "grandfather clause" and exemptions for veterans were simply outrageous, even implying whites could not meet the standards of Negroes. This would drive many intelligent Negroes from Alabama and place the state at the mercy of the United States Supreme Court.[92]

In spite of Murphy's outspoken objections, he was asked to compose the convention's opening prayers for the week of June 17 to 22. Undoubtedly he felt his petitions on June 18 were unanswered. In them he prayed: "Defend us from the perils of the ignorant, and from the pitfalls of the proud. Keep us from the spirit of the oppressor, and the touch of the unholy; that the glory of our hearts may be found in the welfare of the people, and the fruitage of our labors may be garnered in the lasting harvests of their security and dignity and peace."[93]

The constitution in its completed form contained many features Murphy opposed, but it was an improvement on the majority report, due partially to the influence he had exerted. Modifications included the disfranchisement of vagrants and those guilty of buying and selling votes, and the levying of a $1.50 poll tax, which Murphy hoped would be a temporary measure. However, he felt the success of the entire document would depend on the fairness with which the boards of registrars conducted their business. He distrusted the delegation of such great powers to men who would earn only $2.50 a day for weeks at a time, another betrayal of his aristocratic bias. But, ever the optimist, he hoped that the new document, which was approved by the voters on November 11, would lessen tensions and that fair-minded registrars would behave justly. Some weeks later, he hoped he detected "a growing disposition to exclude the unqualified white man and to include the qualified Negro." If this trend existed and continued, he felt even yet it would be possible for Alabama to avert the potential disaster in its new framework of government. Unfortunately, his hopes were unfounded.[94]

Murphy's sense of the historical saved him from extreme pessimism over the grave injustice done the Negro not only in Alabama but throughout the South. "There are always men in every epoch and in every State who devote all their energies to resisting changes in public sentiment," he wrote. "They are sometimes unable to perceive a revolution even when it has occurred. Their whole force is devoted to reiterating ancient prejudices in new forms, and to hopeless endeavors to turn back the shadow of the sun-dial." He could not say that the majority of Southerners agreed with John B. Knox, president of the Alabama constitutional convention, in his wish that qualified Negroes not be disfranchised. He stated with confidence, however, that Knox's attitude was that "of the thoughtful men in the South, of an increasing number of men in the South, of the certain majority in the South of the future." He urged Northern patriots to ally themselves with these men and aid in the attaining of "justice and equal rights" throughout the land.[95]

Murphy was most pleased that Thomas G. Jones, a close friend, a progressive, and a thoughtful man—one to whom the future belonged —was appointed to a federal judgeship and delighted that he played a role in the choice. He wrote to President Roosevelt in his behalf and induced Washington to use his potent influence at the White House, all of which was sufficient to obtain the appointment for the distinguished Alabama Democrat.[96]

The increasing national recognition that came to Murphy was indicative of the contact between Northern men and Southern liberals, a mutual relationship that led Northern progressives to compromise

on the race question. His election in the spring of 1901 to membership in the American Academy of Political and Social Science was a
well-earned honor, and one that encouraged him to pursue his writing
and speaking on the national level.[97] The increasing Southern repression of the Negro spurred him to maintain his study of race relations,
hopeful that he would be heard. But when the child labor question
arose, its urgency demanded his equal attention. He sincerely believed
that he could not refuse any ministry which would aid in the process
of bringing the entire world to Christ and achieving His will among
men.

3.

Child Labor Reform

WHILE MURPHY WAS deeply engrossed with the franchise issue, a political and social question of the first magnitude arose which he could not neglect. Alabama had pioneered in establishing a law to protect its children from the dangers of early and excessive labor. In 1887, when the industrialization of the state was in its infancy, a law was enacted prohibiting the employment of children under fourteen and limiting those under sixteen to an eight hour work day.[1] However, with rapid industrial growth in the next few years, the pressure to use child labor—particularly in the cotton mills—became intense, and the law was repealed in 1894. Without a law, in the period from 1890 to 1900 there was a 386 per cent increase in children under sixteen in the Alabama mills; by 1900 they constituted one-fourth of the textile laborers. Their exploitation posed a major threat to the health and well-being of the state, although a comparatively small portion of the people knew about the existing conditions.

Alabama's situation was not unique; similar conditions existed in the other Southern textile states—the Carolinas and Georgia. The census of 1900 showed that 25 per cent of all Southern mill operatives were between ten and sixteen. In North Carolina, the only Southern state with a statistical breakdown of age groups under sixteen, 18 per cent of the workers were under fourteen and had an average wage of twenty-nine cents a day, a decline from thirty-two cents in 1880. If

North Carolina percentages held true for the other states, in 1900 there were at least 32,000 children under fourteen and 10,000 to 12,000 under twelve in Southern mills. Illiteracy of factory village children was three times as great as that of children throughout the state in North Carolina, more than three times in South Carolina, and four times in Georgia. In one North Carolina factory village only 8 per cent of the children were in school, 50 per cent were at work, and the rest were "waiting in ignorance till they were old enough for work in the mill."[2]

The employment of children not only harmed them personally but was a drag on the entire Southern economy. Originally mills were devoted to spinning, a simpler operation than weaving, and to production of cheaper grade materials in order to exploit child labor. Even when Southern mills began to produce goods comparable to those of the East, they could not be sold at equal prices due to "the bad reputation that southern mills have won for the indifferent products of unskilled, that is child labor."[3]

Child labor was a national evil in 1900, and in terms of absolute numbers there were more children under sixteen working in Northern states than in the South. The difference lay in the fact that the problem had been recognized and was being attacked in the North while the opposite was true in the South. In 1881 at the first meeting of the Federation of Trades, Samuel Gompers attacked child labor, reviving a previously defeated resolution condemning it. Henceforth the American Federation of Labor sponsored much of the agitation for better laws and their enforcement. In 1894 Gompers submitted four proposals on the subject to the New York constitutional convention and, the same year, began publication of *The American Federationist*, which fully exposed the horrors of the system. Due to this and the work of such reformers as Florence Kelley, laws were enacted in all the Northern states, most of which forbade child labor under fourteen. As a result, the number of employed children under sixteen was reduced from 15.6 to 7.7 per cent of the work force between 1880 and 1900.[4]

Conditions in the South made the adoption of Northern-type leg-

islation very difficult. Manufacturing was a relatively new development, one that was welcomed with open arms and presented by the
advocates of the "New South" as the solution to all Southern problems. Moreover, the mill workers themselves were ardent individual-
ists who lacked the class consciousness and sense of injury that would
lead them to seek redress through labor unions and state aid. Even
the progressive Riverside Cotton Mills, later the Dan River Mills,
employed 700 children and young people in 1896, and only in January, 1901, was its work day reduced to eleven hours from April to
September and ten hours from October to March. A contemporary
critic correctly stated, "There is not now a manufacturing country in
the civilized world, except a few States in the South, where children
without age limit are allowed to work in factories." He was amazed
that the Southern press and pulpit remained "largely deaf and dumb"
on the question of legislation when such countries as Russia and Japan
took action.[5]

Murphy did not remain in the "dumb" category once he became
aware of conditions in 1898–1899. When he extended St. John's ministry to the mill workers of Montgomery's West End, he was shocked
by the squalor and misery, and grieved by the extent of child labor
and absence of educational facilities. He found these people to be
among the most helpless he had ever known. Most of them had abandoned tenant farms within twenty or thirty miles of the city, which
ostracized most of them; yet they were proud to have any jobs at all.
He quickly sensed that the mill offered the only opportunity for many,
yet his whole spirit rebelled against its abuses.

In 1898–1899 a very weak bill imposing some limitation on child
labor was introduced in the Alabama legislature, but did not receive
serious consideration. This upset Murphy; he was not surprised, however, knowing the decades of agitation required in Great Britain following the initial protests from Manchester physicians in the late
eighteenth century.[6] Murphy hoped that the democratic process would
supply the corrective for political callousness, and this seemed likely
when the civic clubs of Birmingham and the Women's Christian
Temperance Union took up the issue. Their growing awareness of

the problem was to have great political significance, but equally important was the intervention of the American Federation of Labor. In 1900 it sent to Alabama Irene Ashby, a graduate of Westfield College, London, where she had performed the seemingly impossible— the organization of the working girls in Sir Thomas Lipton's tea packing factories. By January, 1901, she completed the first thorough investigation of child labor in any Southern state and prepared a report revealing that in twenty-five Alabama mills 430 children under twelve were working twelve or more hours a day.[7]

Shortly before Miss Ashby's report was completed, a new legislator from the Birmingham area introduced a child labor bill in the Alabama House. The bill was killed by the Committee on Mining and Manufacturing. Afterwards, another measure, introduced by Representative A. J. Reilly of Ensley and Senator Hugh Morrow of Birmingham, provided a twelve-year age limit except for children of widowed mothers or disabled fathers, in which case the age limit was ten. It also forbade night work for those under sixteen, required all employed children to be able to read and write, and authorized the state employment of a factory inspector at an annual salary of $1,500.

Realizing that labor unions had little political strength in Alabama, Miss Ashby began a search for some interested person who could use her study to advance the bill before the legislature. Various people in Alabama told her that Murphy was the active, influential leader who could best help her, and she took her completed study to him and asked his aid. He was horrified by the statistics and immediately began to devote much of his energy to obtain the Reilly-Morrow Bill's passage. He obtained the Montgomery Ministerial Association's support, and in February, 1901, when the bill was considered by a joint session of the House and Senate committees on Mining and Manufacturing, he was the chief spokesman for its supporters. Although the session was an executive one, the Alabama Federation of Women's Clubs sent delegations to Montgomery (including one headed by Julia Tutwiler, a well-known reformer), which were present when spokesmen announced that the House committee had rejected the bill by a nine to four, and the Senate by a five to two vote.

Refusing to give up, the bill's supporters reintroduced the measure in the House. This time it was referred to the Committee on Immigration and Labor. Murphy again was its chief advocate and, in a brief but lucid address, outlined the ideas he was to develop in the next few years. Carefully arraigning the child labor system rather than the employers involved, he contended that the system was undemocratic since it always resulted in "compulsory ignorance." Its presence lowered wages for everyone, kept skilled labor out of the South, and threatened eventual disaster for the entire region. It was a menace to peaceful race relations since the Negro depended for his advancement on white leadership, which could emerge only when the masses of whites were educated. Murphy warned that if state regulation of child labor was not instituted, federal controls were inevitable, a development that could mean "the entire overturning and readjustment" of Southern conditions at a "frightful cost" few were willing to pay.[8]

But many Southerners, including most of the mill owners and managers, did not agree with Murphy. Unlike industrial leaders in Great Britain and elsewhere, Southern mill men generally did not reply to the advocates of reform with a straightforward laissez faire rationale. Instead they cloaked their selfish motives by paternalistic arguments, by invocation of the sacred state's rights dogma, and by personal attacks on the reform advocates. The nature of their opposition is best seen in the attitudes of one of their most admirable representatives, Daniel Augustus Tompkins. A prime builder of the "New South," Tompkins was born in 1851 on an Edgefield County, South Carolina plantation. After graduation from Rensselaer Polytechnic Institute, he worked for Bethlehem Iron Works and as a machinist in Germany before returning to Charlotte, where he began a crusade that did much to convince Southerners that the coming of the cotton mill offered economic and social salvation. He became the major owner and president of three large mills, a director of eight, and a stockholder in many others. In his own and other mills he sought to obtain humane working conditions and the establishment of mill-village schools for primary education. Despite his great service in promoting industrialization and education, Tompkins had a negative influence on the development of Southern society. Personally and through *The Charlotte News and Observer, The Charlotte Evening Chronicle* and *The Greenville News*, newspapers which he owned totally or in part, he fought the advocates of child labor reform, contending that they were impractical, uninformed, notoriety seekers who would spoil children by depriving them of the discipline of hard work. The mills were doing all they could for the children, he held, but his definition of the desirable was questionable. When a nineteen-year old applied for employment as a machine shop apprentice, he refused, stating he needed him when he was twelve, and he placed his own nephew as an apprentice in a mill when he was only a lad. While advocating compulsory education laws as a substitute for child labor legislation, his proposals were of a nature to keep the children in the mills. He wished eleven to twelve-year olds to be given six months in school and three in the mills, but fourteen to fifteen-year olds would be in school only three months and in the factories seven, while fifteen to sixteen-year olds would attend classes only two months and work ten. Naturally, Tompkins opposed labor organization as an unjust interference with the rights of capital, which could be depended upon to make the best possible provision for its workers. Considering his opinion and others, Broadus Mitchell, a leading historian of Southern industrialization, concluded "southern capitalism did not know that the world had moved in a hundred years." But many of the leaders of Southern society agreed with Tompkins. After observing some of the more progressive mills, William P. Few, President of Trinity College, wrote, "if legislation and public opinion shall continue to safeguard the interest of the stockholder as well as the interests of labor, I believe there is before the State a great future of industrial prosperity and industrial peace."[9]

Backed by a sizeable segment of Southern society, the mills' representative at the Montgomery hearings replied to Murphy's arguments for a child labor law with a degree of vituperation which amazed him and which implied that the advocates of the bill were being paid by Eastern mills. Murphy was outraged and refused to accept his private apology after the committee killed the measure, in a polite way, by voting to report it without recommendation. With tact but candor, he told him that a public attack required a public apology, which was not given.[10]

The lack of newspaper coverage and public interest in the bill convinced Murphy that a campaign to inform and arouse the people was essential if child labor was to be regulated. In seeking to fill this need he gave great impetus to the modern child labor movement in America. It was natural that he turn for aid to the men with whom he had worked on the Conference on Race Relations. After consultation, this group decided a propaganda and political pressure organization was needed, and in 1901 they formed the Alabama Child Labor Committee. Murphy assumed the leadership of the group and became its secretary. Members of the initial Executive Committee were former Governor Thomas G. Jones; Lucien V. LaTaste, Montgomery; Dr. J. H. Phillips, Superintendent of Birmingham Schools; two legislators, John Craft, Mobile, and A. J. Reilly, Ensley; and Murphy. The Rev. Neal Anderson and the Rev. George B. Eager of Montgomery were other members of the organization who played important roles.[11]

In the summer of 1901 Miss Ashby presented a report to the Committee entitled, "The History of the Child Labor Bill in Alabama." It catalogued the bitter opposition to the measure by Northern owners of Alabama mills and surveyed the activities of their lobbyists in the legislature.[12] The report confirmed Murphy's belief that Northern owners were primarily responsible for the killing of the bill as they had been for the repeal of the 1887 law. Therefore, on October 1, he wrote "An Appeal to the People and Press of New England"; this was signed by the Executive Committee and published in *The Boston Evening Transcript*. By this action the Alabama Child Labor Committee began a program of education and propaganda which was to have national significance. This and the committee's later publications written by Murphy were published in pamphlet form and distributed free, or for the cost of mailing. They became a major force in every state where the battle against child labor was waged. As one of his contemporary reformers later wrote, his arguments "will suffice for our time."

Murphy's keen reasoning powers and knowledge of psychology and of the people whom he addressed were apparent in "An Appeal to ... New England" and all the committee's publications. He did not discount the apathy of a great many Southerners who, "fearful of losing capital investments, shied away from reform." However, he appealed to New England since twice as many children under twelve were working in Northern-owned Alabama mills as in Southern-owned ones and since "the most aggressive and effective opposition" to a child labor bill "came from the salaried representative of Massachusetts investments." Although a few mills had exemplary working conditions, most did not, and New England investors needed to know that they were "supporting a system under which hundreds of our little children are denied the most elementary opportunities for health and happiness."

The committee asked the press to carry Murphy's appeal and any replies made to it, in the hope that free discussion could result in informed action. It felt "that Massachusetts, having defended her own children from a cruel and unnecessary industrial system, will question the heartless policy with which her capital is using and is striving to perpetuate the defenselessness of the children of the South."[13]

Murphy's "Appeal" was answered[14] by J. Howard Nichols of Boston, treasurer of the Alabama City Mill, who conceded that the employment of children under twelve was a mistake both from an economic and humanitarian standpoint. He had never gone South without protesting against it to plant management, but he contended the mills could not apply age restrictions since parents would seek employment at mills that would also employ their children. Nichols traced the origin of the Reilly-Morrow Bill to organized labor and attacked it with great vehemence. "The labor organizations at the North imported from England a very bright and skillful female labor agitator and sent her to Alabama," he wrote. "The manufacturers and other business men of Alabama resented this outside interference" and also believed Northern manufacturers were contributing funds to "incite labor troubles in the South." They felt the bill "was only the entering wedge" and "determined any action must come from within the

State." At the same time, they resolved that Georgia—with twice as many spindles—must act before Alabama. In conclusion, Nichols declared there was nothing within or without his company's mill "of which any citizen of Massachusetts need be ashamed." He challenged the Alabama Child Labor Committee to name any other installation that could compare in the quality of housing, religious facilities, schools, and working conditions it provided for its workers.

Murphy was disgusted with Nichols' arguments, feeling them to be deceitful and full of distortions and half truths. He met them with a prompt rejoinder, noting that his "Appeal" had been signed by "six representative citizens of Alabama," while Nichols was anything but a "disinterested" resident of Massachusetts. The most amazing portion of Nichol's retort was its admission of "the social wrong and the economic error of child labor under twelve"; yet his company had been largely instrumental in killing the Reilly-Morrow Bill. Nichols held that parents placed such pressure on the mills they could not refuse jobs to children, a condition the bill was designed to alleviate by removing from the mills all children under ten.

Murphy felt Nichols' indictment of organized labor and New England manufacturers was a smokescreen. It seemed that "evils may be supported from the East, but the remedies must be indigenous!" Murphy realized the danger of this appeal to class and sectional prejudices, however, and hastened to assert that the efforts to pass a child labor bill were indigenous in origin and directed by local forces. Miss Ashby, "earnest and devoted woman that she was, had worked under the absolute command of the local forces of the State." To deny the children the limited protection that they needed to grow in stature and intelligence on the grounds that this constituted the "entering wedge" for other reforms was an absurdity. It was equivalent to saying that "we must not do a compassionate and reasonable thing, because, forsooth, somebody might then demand an inconsiderate and unreasonable thing!" The same lack of logic was displayed in the demand that Georgia must act before Alabama since she had twice as many spindles. Logically it would be twice as hard for Georgia to protect her children as for Alabama, and therefore Alabama should seize the opportunity to pass a law before conditions became as bad as they were in Georgia.

Murphy believed that for the owners and management the "course of humanity is always the course of wisdom," and he sought their support. Barbarous conditions "must gradually invite the hatred of the people, must inevitably goad the great masses of our population into the fixed belief that the corporation desires to live, not by production but through destruction; that it is a force to be feared and bound rather than a force to be trusted and liberated." The exceptional facilities of Nichols' mill merely furnished additional proof of the need for a law. "If the Alabama City Mill is so unique, then it is not representative or typical." Its owners and management should not oppose efforts to establish a minimum standard in more ordinary establishments.[15]

Nichols did not attempt a reply to Murphy's devastating arguments, but passed the responsibility to another Bostonian, Horace S. Sears, treasurer of the West Point Manufacturing Company of Langsdale, Alabama.[16] The less moderate Sears contended that appeals such as Murphy's subverted the children's welfare, "which many manufacturers have more truly at heart than have the professional labor agitator and the well-meaning but ill-advised humanitarian." He was sure that if any Alabama Child Labor Committee member had attended the Montgomery hearings on the child labor bill, he would have recognized that a compulsory education law was the remedy for the problem. This would give unemployed children something to do and would remove parental pressure to give them work. To avoid jeopardizing Alabama mills, Sears felt any compulsory education law must not precede similar legislation in Georgia, South Carolina, and North Carolina.[17]

Murphy insisted that Sears' arguments were ruses; he was saying, "We are not to attempt a possible reform until we have first secured another reform which every practical man in Alabama knows is just now impossible." But Sears made his own remedy dependent on its acceptance by other states, a strategy "very familiar to the students of economic progress." "Over in Georgia and the Carolinas, some of the

mill men are claiming that they 'are only waiting upon Alabama,'"
Murphy wrote. Amazingly enough, the compulsory education law
Sears supported originated with Miss Ashby, whom Nichols heartily
condemned. It failed despite untiring support from members of the
Alabama Child Labor Committee. The result would have been different, Murphy believed, if the mill forces had exerted one-fifth the support in its favor which they used in opposing the child labor bill.

It was absurd that forces which opposed laws prohibiting six-year
olds from working twelve hours a day could truthfully support a compulsory education act. Child labor was "a system of compulsory ignorance." The Massachusetts capitalists had shown their real beliefs
when they helped defeat the Reilly-Morrow Bill, which contained an
admirable education law. Murphy found it difficult to understand
New England's lack of interest in mill children, and, knowing the
region's concern with racial affairs, partially attributed it to the fact
that the workers were white. "Suppose the conditions were reversed,
and the mills of Southern men were full of Negro children under
twelve—how quickly and how justly New England would ring with
denunciation!"

Sears used the "idle hands" theory to justify his position, contending that without a compulsory education law unemployed children
would not go to school and would get into trouble. To challenge this
opinion, Murphy told of a mill within twenty miles of his office which
employed seventy-five children from 6 A.M. to 6:30 P.M. When a
night school was opened by Sears' "well meaning but ill-advised humanitarians," fifty children enrolled, who, even after a twelve hour
day, clamored for instruction. This convinced Murphy that the first
step in the education of mill children was to get them out of the mills.
In foreseeing doom in idle hands, Sears forgot that the proposed legislation would remove only those under twelve from the mills. What
possible trouble could a child twelve or younger find in the rural South
or model mill villages that Sears described?[18]

The Murphy-Nichols-Sears correspondence attracted wide attention. The Alabama Child Labor Committee, realizing that the January,
1903 legislature would be the last regular session for four years,

sought to pressure the lawmakers by issuing a 40-page pamphlet entitled *Child Labor in Alabama, An Appeal to the People and Press of New England, With a Resulting Correspondence.* Published in December, 1901, the pamphlet filled the need for a convenient, convincing argument for effective legislation, and its success was greater than anticipated; demands for it came from the entire nation.

In November, 1901, Murphy, after much soul-searching, resigned as Rector of St. John's to become Executive Secretary of the newly organized Southern Education Board. This decision reflected his growing awareness of the Christian's responsibility to see that God's will is done in society. Though frequently away from Montgomery after this, he did not slacken his efforts to obtain a suitable Alabama child labor law, and the success of his first pamphlet led him to write nine others in the next few months. Often he had to underwrite the cost himself, although all were published under the auspices of the Alabama Child Labor Committee.

One of the most useful pamphlets was based on material gathered in the spring of 1902 for use in preparing a paper for *The Annals of the American Academy of Political and Social Science.* A renewed attack of rheumatic fever delayed writing beyond the publication deadline, but Murphy incorporated his findings in *The Case Against Child Labor: An Argument.*[19] Not only did he present a complete indictment of child labor, but he sought to answer every counterargument that had been presented to his previous charges. He held that a state had as much right to protect a child from unnatural labor as from parental cruelty, and he commended the Democratic party of South Carolina, the second largest cotton manufacturing state in 1900, for endorsing a law prohibiting child labor under twelve. Without legislation, the Southern situation was not improving. The mill owners conceded this when they, in contradictive fashion, stated the number of mill operatives under twelve was insignificant but their removal would destroy the Southern textile industry.[20]

From his study of children and the mills, Murphy concluded "that among the most distinctive of the rights of the little child is the divine right to do nothing." Even the horse breeder recognized that the "abnormal straining of muscles and nerves, in the period of immaturity, is an injury to all life." The most vocal opponents of child labor laws charged that state intervention was "paternalism," but they did not admit that their alternative, compulsory education was paternalistic also. Murphy suspected the pleas for school laws were fraudulent means to defeat legislation for protecting the children. On one occasion, Daniel A. Tompkins, the principal spokesman for the North Carolina mill owners, said, "The South is too poor to attempt to have public schools more than three months" in the year. In Murphy's opinion this was a key to the mill men's program, which could be put in one sentence: "For the little children of the poor— three months in the school, nine months in the mill!"

Mill owners and management were not greatly disturbed by the lack of formal education for children, since they seemed to feel that "labor in the average cotton mill" offered "children of the poor the progressive advantages of the kindergarten, the grammar school, the high school, the great university—and a trip to Europe—all in one!" In addition to its other advantages, the factory gave each child ten to thirty cents pay for twelve hours of work.

While presenting an effective emotional appeal, Murphy was careful to refrain from indicting mill men as a class or of impugning their motives. He knew that men like Tompkins were benefactors and hoped that their myopic vision would be cleared. He noted that recently many were shocked when an eight-year old had "the two larger fingers of her right hand torn from their sockets at the greater knuckles," while working "in one of the largest and most pretentious of the Boston factories in Alabama." This was one of hundreds of similar accidents which should demonstrate to reasonable mill men that under prevailing conditions the child was bearing "in its tender strength the greatest burdens and the heaviest curse of the new 'prosperity'. . . instead of receiving as childhood should the maximum of immunity from distress, and the largest freedom which the new environment affords." "Let us not be guilty of mental confusion," Murphy wrote in a phrase he often reused. "Let us not credit the good fortune of the family to the misfortune of the child."[21]

Next, Murphy revealed the sense of history which so often characterized his work. Southerners, he said, must realize they could not "war against the practice of the whole world," and industry must recognize that a moderate compliance with public opinion offered the optimum condition for its development. In every civilized country, child labor was under attack, and eventually it would be destroyed. Since mill profits were high, Murphy concluded that a tight budget could not explain mill owners' opposition. He suspected the real motive was "the dread that any sort of restrictive or protective laws will further, in some way, the cause of the labor union." While approving the labor movement, he wisely avoided the issue of unionization and, for argumentative purposes, assumed "for the moment, that the essential interests of the factory are in conflict with the interests of the labor union." In such a case, management could only injure itself by opposing "the collective experience and the established judgment of society itself." "If the struggle between capitalism and trade unionism" was to be joined on the question of child labor, there could be no doubt the unionists would win. In a paragraph pregnant with insight, he warned the mill owners not to underrate the sentiments of Southern society. "Of all the sections of this world the South—the land of chivalry, of tenderness, of homes—the land where, if we have learned anything, we have learned to suffer for our ideals—the South is the very last place in which to laugh at sentiment, least of all at the sentiment which touches the promise and freedom of our children."[22]

As long as child labor continued, Murphy knew there would be a "sacrifice of the childhood of our poorer people, the repression of their best skills and their fullest intelligence and efficiency." Though originally from this class, he had risen to the heights of intellectual and social acceptability. Yet one of his most admirable qualities was a sincere respect for the potential of the Southern masses from whom he differed so greatly. He detested child labor mostly because it closed the opportunity for development to the average Southerner. Should it prevail, he would be forever consigned to poverty, and the entire South would be "condemned to the production of the coarser grades of goods." The intelligent, trained worker was the key to personal, regional, and national prosperity. Murphy found great significance in the fact that a bale of Southern cotton worth $50 could be converted into finished Paris products valued at over $100,000. "The magic touch of intelligent and skillful labor" made the difference. When it was recognized that "the function of the child is not productive, but receptive," the South would be on its way to prosperity. Four decades before automation, Murphy realized that the exploitation of workers before they received a basic education was "condemning them to the lot of the underprivileged . . . thus creating a backward industrial class." Enlightened self-interest demanded the outlawing of labor for children under twelve. "The families of workers elsewhere lived without the tiny wages of their younger children," and so could Alabamians. Formal education should replace the monotonous grind of factory labor, and Murphy urged the mills to "yield a small portion of their large profits" to aid in financing day nurseries, kindergartens, and public schools. Only in advancing society through its children could the textile industry hope to reap its greatest reward.[23]

Murphy's strong advocacy of child labor laws was most detestable to many textile leaders and their journals, the most able and militant of which was *The Manufacturers' Record* of Baltimore, a magazine characterized by a reformer as "the most conspicuous opponent of child labor legislation in this country." Edited by the gifted, rugged individualist Richard H. Edmonds, it was one of the most ardent champions of the "New South" and attacked any proposals for regulation or taxation that it believed would interfere with industrial progress. *The Case Against Child Labor* provoked Edmonds to devote a six-column editorial to a thorough refutation, which gave Murphy's pamphlet unpurchasable publicity.[24] Edmonds was disturbed by the work's favorable Northern reviews and in an emotional vein sought to correct those "individuals who think from the midriff" and who had been taken in by the "inflammatory, . . . impractical, . . . bryanesque, . . . wandering, . . . and radical" pamphlet. He praised the factory owners who, he contended, by employing children at a financial loss demonstrated a "practical philanthropy—a philanthropy that does more good in one day than may be accomplished in a century by the theoretical philanthropy of overheated faddists who wish to do something, but who don't know exactly what it is they wish to do or how to start doing it." He held that Southern child labor was a necessity due to the poor educational system and the inadaptability of Negroes to mill work. He warned that child labor would be cast off "only by the unimpeded and unantagonized efforts of the representative Southern men, who have already accomplished so much of their own initiative for the improvement of a long neglected folk." The mill men "in resisting the demagogue and hysterian, especially the hysterian of the masculine gender, are conferring a distinct benefit not only upon the South, but upon the whole country."[25]

Murphy charged that *The Manufacturers' Record* had quoted him out of context and in *The South and Her Children: A Rejoinder in the Child Labor Discussion* set the record straight and exposed Edmonds' fallacies. Most galling to Murphy was the contention that those opposing the child labor law were "representative Southern men," while those favoring it were not. "The most aggressive opposition to the proposed measure came from the representative of New England investments." He knew of no "outside" influence responsible for agitation in behalf of the law. Southern mill men were no more representative of the South than any other segment of the population. Since they had made no progress against child labor in twenty years, they could not be relied upon to divest themselves of it. Though rather comprehensive, Murphy said, the report of *The Manufacturers' Record* failed to favor or oppose "the one essential point of the whole discussion," a law limiting mill labor to children over twelve. If it would support such a bill, Murphy gave it permission to call him any names it liked.[26]

Threats to a workable bill came not only from journals outside the state but even from local allies of the Alabama Child Labor Committee. In the summer of 1902, Mrs. Lillian Milner Orr, president-elect of the powerful Alabama Federation of Women's Clubs, announced her support of a voluntary agreement among mill owners instead of a law prohibiting child labor. Realizing the ineffectiveness of such an agreement, Murphy immediately set forth his opposition in *A Child*

Labor Law. There was no assurance that the mills were generally ready to enter such understandings, and agreement by the best mills would do no good whatsoever since the mills with poorest conditions were the ones that needed to be regulated. Voluntary agreements of the type proposed placed the honest mills at a disadvantage and had always failed. The North Carolina agreement was proving inadequate according to the state commissioner charged with its supervision, and in South Carolina the failure was so great the Democratic Party had committed itself to pass a law. Some Alabama manufacturers favored the voluntary "Georgia" agreement used in the neighboring state. Yet even if enforced it was little better than no limitation since children over ten could be worked as much as ten hours a day if they could read and write, and those over twelve could work nights. Murphy insisted that an effective measure must have a minimum age of twelve and provide for inspection. Mill men who were honestly attempting to comply with the law should not object to an impartial check.[27]

Believing that the support of humane and intelligent business leaders was essential for success, Murphy appealed specifically to them in *Child Labor and Business*, which he introduced with a review of the deplorable conditions prevailing under a laissez faire policy. Since the movement for a law had begun, a number of children under twelve had been withdrawn from the mills; however, many were still at work, and if fear of a law were removed conditions would revert to what they had been, he predicted. "If there are but few children under 12 in the factories of the state, and if there is no deliberate intention to employ more of them, why should the mills expend so much money, energy and time in opposition to a law which would keep them from the factories?"

In a positive vein, Murphy counseled the business leaders to support a child labor law for industry's sake. Other states excluded children; why must Alabama mills have them when cotton was locally produced, power was abundant, and a fine climate was present? Ten investors were detracted to every one attracted by the use of child labor, and Alabama mills should prosper as never before under a sound, workable child labor law.[28]

Turning from the mill men to the masses of people, Murphy wrote *Child Labor and the Public.* He urged them to organize local committees, circulate the state committee's literature, write their legislators, and give information and advice to the state committee. The question must be discussed "without acrimony," the featuring of personalities, or the impugning of bad motives. Cautioning against the faulty reasoning that the child was better off in the mill than outside, he compared this to arguments used by Eastern sweatshop owners. He quoted *The Chattanooga News'*[29] contention that New England manufacturers had killed child labor bills for twenty-five years by using a compulsory education bill as a diversion.

The South was proud of her industry, yet her main interest was "not in her factories, but in her children." The Southern press reflected this and "with marked unanimity" supported child labor laws. The conversion of Southern newspapers to the reform cause was so notable that Murphy used fifty-two excerpts from thirty-nine newspapers to write *Child Labor in the Southern Press, Bulletin A.*[30] In it he demonstrated that criticism of child labor was indigenous to the South and that demands for a law were "not confined to 'agitators' and 'reformers,'" but were "coming from the representative and conservative opinion of the South."

Child Labor and "Politics," a reprint of an editorial published in *The Montgomery Advertiser,*[31] ridiculed the Republican party for attempting to exploit child labor as a partisan issue. It pointed out that the 1898 bill had first been introduced by a Populist, and the later ones were first espoused by Democrats.[32]

To demonstrate the South's backwardness, Murphy condensed the child labor legislation of each of the states, after tedious research, in *Child Labor Legislation, A Review of Laws in the United States.* He hoped the readers would not conclude that the issue was a sectional one, but that they would see the positive result of Northern legislation. By comparison, the review revealed the conservative nature of the proposed Alabama law and the mildness of its effective features.[33]

For emotional effect and to reach those who threw the average pamphlet away, Murphy prepared one of the most effective publica

DuBose and Gardner Murphy in 1898

Maud and Gardner Murphy in 1907

DuBose and Gardner Murphy in 1905

tions in the child labor dispute, a twelve-page leaflet containing ten personally taken photographs and entitled *Pictures from Life. Mill Children in Alabama.* It presented as words could not the true plight of Alabama's working children. Included was a photograph of a six-year-old boy at the machine where he worked twelve hours a day for fifteen cents. Three barefoot boys—nine, eight, and seven—were next shown with the information that, although their parents were living, they worked from 5:20 A.M. to 6:30 P.M. six days a week. In rush periods their hours were longer—until 9:30 or 10:00 P.M. each day. Among other "heart-rending" photographs, Murphy presented that of an eight-year-old girl whose father had not worked for two years. He queried, "Is this the sort of 'parental right' that the State must guard and respect?" With the portrait of a little eight-year old at lunch, Murphy noted that it would be incorrect to say she was "on her noon hour," since she was allowed only forty minutes, and many received only twenty.[34]

In contrast with these gruesome sights, *Pictures from Life* concluded with an inviting pastoral scene taken one-hundred yards from a mill. This view illustrated "where the children *might* have been." Murphy noted, "We are told that we must work our little children 12, 13, and 14 hours a day in order to save them from 'the gutter.' The above is the 'gutter.' The animals and the birds are there, but the children are in the mills."[35]

Murphy's pamphlets were "the first body of printed material of any considerable extent or value" in favor of child labor legislation in the South.[36] Moderate in tone and written by a Southerner, they did a work that would have been impossible coming from another source. Twenty-eight thousand copies were mailed throughout the nation, and their data and arguments were extensively quoted.[37] Wherever the battle continued, Murphy's reasoning was used. He was recognized as a prominent child labor reformer in every section and was asked to speak and write on the question for national meetings and journals.

But in 1902 and 1903 Murphy's chief interest continued to be in Alabama. For weeks before the legislature convened in January, 1903, he worked on the strategy to obtain the passage of an adequate law. Personally he welcomed support from all sources, but knew that success demanded prevention of the movement being labeled as Northern or labor union; this proved difficult and embarrassing. He was genuinely fond of Miss Ashby, now Mrs. Macfadyen, but he was fearful that she and the A. F. of L. were injuring the cause. In the state campaigns Mrs. Macfadyen spoke in behalf of labor oriented candidates. Samuel Gompers encouraged her and ordered union leaders to support publicly those pledged to the labor program. This was precisely the policy Murphy most feared, and he clashed head-on with Gompers. Previously he had accepted $100 from Gompers to distribute *The Case Against Child Labor*, but he now returned the money. "The committee are well-meaning men, but have left the work almost entirely to myself," he wrote Gompers. "Under these circumstances, I have had to thoroughly canvass the situation and to take my course accordingly." Murphy believed the defeat of a child labor bill in Georgia was due to organized labor's promotion of it, and he was determined the same mistake would not be made in Alabama. A few weeks later the two men met in New York, and Murphy convinced Gompers of his policy's wisdom.[38]

The opposition was "making the most effective possible use of whatever seems to be sectionalistic criticism from the North," and Murphy warned Oswald G. Villard to consider this in writing his editorials for *The New York Evening Post*. While the sensitivity of many Alabamians to Northern criticism was absurd, allowance must be made for it. Murphy told Villard his "most effective line" would be "criticism of the Northern men who have stock in the mills and who are quietly doing all they can to oppose us." Also, "Some strong words should be said about the responsibility of the New England pulpit." Not one New England clergyman of prominence had spoken on the question, although the American Unitarian Association passed a resolution condemning child labor.[39]

When the new legislature convened, essentially the same bill was introduced as in 1900, but Murphy immediately realized that its chances for passage were dim. The legislature would not reconvene for four years, and the average lawmaker was under little pressure to comply with popular wishes. Even the zealousness of some leaders in the fight was questionable. For example, though Mrs. Orr had announced her support, Murphy questioned it. Her father had been a major opponent of child labor legislation, and she and her family were stockholders of Birmingham's Avondale Mills, which employed fifty-six children.[40]

Under the circumstances, Murphy reluctantly agreed to a compromise. After formal sessions with leaders of the mills, he, J. B. Gaston, and Alexander T. London signed an agreement with the manufacturers' representatives, the future Governor Braxton Bragg Comer, John W. Tullis, and D. T. Goodwin. While setting an age limit of twelve for child laborers, it allowed children of ten to work up to sixty-six hours a week if they had widowed mothers or dependent fathers. Tragically, no provision was made for inspectors to enforce the law. While the original measure prohibited night labor of those under sixteen, the compromise permitted those thirteen or above to work at night up to forty-eight hours a week. Affidavits giving children's ages were required of all parents; misstatements were made subject to fines of $5 to $100. Manufacturers who violated the law were to be fined only $200.

The Federation of Women's Clubs and Mrs. Orr received almost exclusive credit for the compromise, perhaps because they alone were satisfied with it.[41] Murphy was displeased with its essential features and was distressed at the thought of ten-year olds continuing in the mills regardless of the cause. There was no place for a child under twelve in any factory "even though that factory were equipped with the elegance of a Pullman car, were provided with nothing but ball-bearing machinery, and were conducted by a board of nursery governesses." His place was in "God's outdoors, in the home, or in the schoolroom."[42]

Even after the compromise was reached, there was difficulty in getting the bill through the Senate. A motion to table the measure was defeated by only two votes, following presentation of Nichols' and Sears' arguments and the indictment of Mrs. Macfadyen as a labor agitator. Only Murphy's courting of the "most progressive" mill men saved the measure. He was the first to acknowledge this and henceforth used it as evidence of the mistake in condemning all manufacturers.[43] The struggle had been long and hard, and Murphy realized the victory was limited. Yet the enactment of the law of 1903 was a solid achievement, an acceptance of the principle of public regulation that opened the way for more adequate laws. This convinced Murphy that state laws could deal with the problem and that any movement for federal control would only alienate needed support. Of course, he resolved to continue the fight until all of Alabama's children were liberated.

While working for reform in Alabama, Murphy's pamphlets played an important role in a score of states which either passed their first child labor laws or improved their legislation between 1901 and 1903. As early as 1899, Andrew J. McKelway, a Charlotte minister who edited his church's North Carolina newspaper, *The Presbyterian Standard*, became interested in the question. After 1901, "when Edgar Gardner Murphy . . . had pointed the way to reform for all the editors of the South," McKelway became the champion of a North Carolina state law. He wrote an excellent series of editorials, utilizing Murphy's arguments, and won the unqualified support of Governor Charles B. Aycock. As a result, North Carolina passed a law similar to that of Alabama. McKelway looked forward to meeting Murphy and eulogized him as the leader of the Southern reform movement.[44]

National demands came increasingly to Murphy from those who wished to regulate child labor. He eagerly accepted an invitation to address the National Conference of Charities and Corrections, which met in Atlanta in May, 1903, and chose as his topic, "Child Labor as A National Problem." He contended society was one, and its maximum prosperity depended on the optimum development of all its people—a condition which could not occur when children were deprived of their freedom and education. The prosperity of business and the welfare of the child were nowhere in conflict; the enactment of just laws everywhere would liberate the child and be equally advantageous to industry. The mission of the humanitarian and the reformer was to implant this message in the minds of men and to arouse a nationwide movement against child labor.[45]

Murphy made a very favorable impression. *The Boston Evening Transcript*[46] wrote, "For oratorical effect the palm must be given to Mr. Edgar Gardner Murphy, who has won his fight in Alabama and done more than any other man perhaps to awaken the South to the wrongs inflicted on child laborers." Following the address, Jane Addams, who had appeared on the same program, came to Murphy offering her congratulations and friendship. Afterwards he felt meeting her had been worth the effort of the speech. McKelway, also in the audience, was delighted to find Murphy could speak as well as he could write. Years afterward he recalled the address vividly and still considered it "the greatest speech against child labor ever delivered in America."[47] Murphy's warm personality attracted other serious-minded people of similar convictions. As in the case of Baldwin and Ogden at Tuskegee, he and McKelway became close friends at the Atlanta meeting, and they too resolved to work together.[48]

In effect Murphy's Atlanta address was a call for the formation of a national anti-child labor organization, although it did not explicitly spell out the request. In 1903 a committee similar to the Alabama one was formed in New York, and four Northern governors called for improvements in their laws. While in New York, Murphy and Dr. Felix Adler, Professor of Political and Social Ethics at Columbia University and head of the Society for Ethical Culture, discussed the formation of a national organization. In the fall of 1903, as they surveyed the wave of interest and the need for stronger laws, they considered the time opportune. In October, Adler, after consulting Murphy, led the New York Child Labor Committee to appoint Baldwin, Mrs. Florence Kelley, secretary of the National Consumers' League, and himself as a committee to develop a national organization.[49]

As part of the organization strategy, in March, 1904, Murphy delivered a major address on "Child Labor in the United States" before the Society for Ethical Culture.[50] In it he combined solid facts and keen analysis with a non-sentimental yet emotional appeal. Child labor presented both economic and sociological questions, and, being an expert in neither field, he chose to speak only as a concerned citizen. Among the important changes convulsing the United States was a concurrent movement of men to the city and into industry. These resulted from the need to "more cheaply and more effectively perform the labors" and "secure the advantages of life." With them had come child labor, which was tolerated to gain a short-term productive goal and was partially due to parents not recognizing the difference between children working at home, as they always had, and working in a factory. They did not comprehend the depersonalization of factory labor where the system subordinated the child "to the interest of the work."

While proportionately the South had more child laborers, the actual number was greater in the North, Murphy reiterated. Everywhere child labor was defended on the basis that the work was "light," yet the question was not the momentary physical exertion but the prolonged "nervous tension required by the work." Twelve hours with twenty minutes for lunch was a killing grind, particularly for immature bodies and minds. Furthermore, greater productivity was often required of the child than was just. "The factory works as one machine," and the child was asked to produce at an adult level.[51]

Murphy believed all America should know the scandalous conditions of child labor. He knew that very few foremen or superintendents were cruel men, but he felt they were victims of an evil system. On one occasion, as Murphy examined a seven-year old's hand that had three fingers torn from it, the owner of the mill explained that the child had been careless. Murphy could only reply, "My God! Hasn't a child seven years of age got a right to be careless?" He wondered what the world would be "if its little children were all careful, were all solid philosophers of probabilities!" Child labor should be careless "in the sense that the child is as yet care-free, not wrought upon by those burdens of apprehensions, and by those agencies of solicitude which haunt and steady the mind of man." A child's "elementary prerogative is growth, its secondary prerogative is labor," but man's is the reverse since labor enables him to grow.[52]

Legislation furnished the only remedy, he continued, but it was difficult to obtain. As in personal morals, the most dangerous man is the good man who supports conditions which make bad ones, so the greatest difficulty lay with the progressive industrialist who protested that regulatory laws reflected on all industry. While he impeded action, "the bad man stays off in the shadow and smiles and works his devilish work upon his children." Every American's cooperation must be enlisted through the enactment of state laws. Their help would come only when they realized that ethics in production were as important as price.[53]

Murphy's address gave the New York committee a needed stimulus to complete its plans, and on April 15, 1904, a nationwide organizational committee of twenty-five members was formed. Adler became temporary President, Murphy temporary Secretary, and both became members of the Executive Committee.[54] The committee called itself the National Child Labor Committee and, as its first action, published a leaflet stating its purpose: "To promote the welfare of society with respect to the employment of children in gainful occupations." It proposed, through investigations and reports on working children, to raise standards of opinion and "parental responsibility." It pledged an effort to obtain suitable state child labor laws and aid in their enforcement. The method of operation was to be primarily through the coordination and support of local committees.[55]

Knowing the strong laissez faire sentiment in America, Murphy and his colleagues sought to present a rational, appealing image to the public. In late April, announcement of committee plans was made in *Charities*, and a few weeks later, in the same magazine, Murphy described the program of the organization. As the factory system came South, he noted, Southern states saw the need for child labor laws, and by 1904 eight states had the beginning of legislation. "The factory evils at the South were much censured by the Northern press. But the deepening of interest in the general subject brought the question, 'How are matters at home?'" The reforms of Florence Kelley, Jane Addams, and others had resulted in Northern gains, but the need to sustain and expand them everywhere led to the formation of the national committee. It was founded on the belief that sentiment had to be educated as well as aroused in order to see not only that good laws were on the books but that they were enforced. The National Child Labor Committee hoped to aid local committees by "(1) offering sympathetic counsel, by (2) acting as a clearing house for information and methods, by (3) making specific independent investigations, and by (4) extending through its agents—whenever requested—supplementary aid and influence."[56]

Murphy played a critical role in founding the committee and directing its early policy. As Homer Folks, a member of the Executive Committee, wrote, Murphy made "the primary suggestion for the organization," and over a period of months he, Florence Kelley, Adler, and Baldwin "secured a membership . . . of commanding influence" which obtained for the committee "a respectful hearing in every state in the Union."[57] Adler was more precise and characterized Murphy as "the father and founder of the National Child Labor Committee."[58]

Once the committee was launched, Murphy's other obligations and ill health forced him to turn the secretaryship over to someone else, but he continued as a most active committee leader. He and the chairman of the Finance Committee engaged Samuel M. Lindsay, a Professor of Sociology at the University of Pennsylvania and, temporarily, Commissioner of Education in Puerto Rico, as Secretary of the National Child Labor Committee.[59] When the time came to choose an Assistant Secretary, Lindsay, Folks, and Murphy were empowered to make the choice, and all felt that the appointee should come from the South. Murphy immediately suggested A. J. McKelway, who accepted when the proposed salary was increased from $2,500 to $3,000 a year.[60] This choice gave the committee an untiring, able Assistant Secretary who soon assumed direction of the committee's Southern work when an assistant for the North was appointed. Although later he and Murphy were to break over the question of federal controls, and while some moderates were alienated by McKelway's zealousness, Murphy never regretted the selection. Murphy also recommended the committee rent rooms in the United Charities Building, a most advantageous location for its work, and, as a member of a three-man committee, he aided in framing a constitution which was the basis for the National Child Labor Committee's incorporation by Congress in 1907.

It was in determining the nature and scope of the committee's operations, however, that Murphy wielded his greatest influence. As a public leader and scholar, he was convinced that success depended on arousing public opinion, but he knew before this could be done that investigations must be made and accurate statistics compiled. He urged the committee to devote itself to these fields at first, and his views prevailed. Initially, in 1904, welfare and labor officials throughout the nation were asked to supply information, and investigators were dispatched to the Pennsylvania coal mines, the cotton mills of Georgia, and the glass factories of New Jersey, Pennsylvania, and Ohio. Although limited funds prevented other investigations immediately, reports from these fields gave the committee ample ammunition.

As one of four members of the Publications Committee, Murphy, drawing on his experiences, persuaded this committee to issue a series of pamphlets based on its findings. He also obtained acceptance of an offer from *The Annals of the American Academy of Political and Social Science* for publication of materials. Thus the committee became not only a clearinghouse for information but the prime molder of opinion on the child labor question. In less than a decade it issued hundreds of copies of pamphlets, and *The Annals* devoted one volume each year to papers presented at the committee's annual conventions.[61]

In its first year the National Child Labor Committee extended its operations into many areas, in most of which it worked with local forces. As a result, of the thirty-nine state legislatures which met that year, twelve passed some form of child labor legislation—Delaware for the first time. In seventeen states and the District of Columbia, state and local committees were organized which cooperated with the national committee. Lindsay held meetings in twenty states, traveling 50,000 miles. The committee developed a select mailing list of 2,500 names, distributing 48,500 pamphlets and thousands of shorter releases. The actual expenses for the fifteen months from July, 1904, to October, 1905, were $18,000, much of which was contributed by thirty-four individuals, including Henry C. Frick, Daniel Guggenheim, Andrew Carnegie, Robert C. Ogden, and John D. Rockefeller, Jr. After the fall of 1905, however, most operating capital came from annual dues, which gave the committee a degree of freedom enjoyed by few such organizations.[62]

The first annual meeting of the National Child Labor Committee was held in New York City, February 14–16, 1905. Addresses were given by committee officers, Chancellor James H. Kirkland of Vanderbilt University, Jane Addams, and others. Interest proved to be surprisingly keen, and attendance was greater than had been expected. Three topics were considered: "The Forces Arrayed Against Child Labor and Their Better Utilization," "Review of Legislation on Child Labor, Methods of Enforcement, and Present Problems in the Several States and Territories," and "The Need of Protective Legislation for Working Children." In December, a second meeting was held in Washington with a White House reception given by President Roosevelt, and there were supplementary sessions in Chicago and Philadelphia.[63]

Despite Northern needs, Murphy's most intense concern continued to be with the South, and on his recommendation McKelway's office was moved from Charlotte to Atlanta in November, 1905, even though an additional $1,300 yearly was needed to maintain it there. In his opinion, this was necessary since Georgia was holding the South back, and the South the nation.[64]

Murphy felt the "increasing confidence" expressed in McKelway's efforts was a Southern counterpart to national progress. Murphy continued to furnish materials and advised him to vigorously counterattack when the enemies of reform opposed his work. He knew that Daniel Tompkins, *The Manufacturers' Record*, and others were charging that the committee was financed by New England to prevent the development of Southern industry. He urged McKelway to refer to his long standing personal interest in child labor reform and demonstrate that the national committee was not a Northern one. How could it be when among its members were Senator Ben Tillman, Clark Howell, Hoke Smith, and many other Southerners? When sectionalism was used to attack him, Murphy advised McKelway to defend his membership and leadership in a national organization. His action and that of others was slowly establishing the contention "that the Southern man has a right to make a national alliance and to associate himself with great national forces." Although the road might be hard, it led "toward the freedom of the Southern publicist to be a citizen of the whole country." Southerners must realize that they could best serve the South by cooperating with national movements—that provincialism was the route backward, not forward.

Murphy recommended that in local affairs McKelway must have a spirit of magnanimity and kindliness whenever he could. Remembering his experiences in Alabama, Murphy suggested that if any mill men showed a desire to cooperate he should display "hearty appreciation." By this means his labor would seem "less like class legislation and will have a good effect generally."[65]

During their first three years of effort, despite sound advice and intense labor, McKelway and the committee made little progress in the South. A bitter setback came in North Carolina in 1905 when the legislature defeated a bill based on the model child labor law submitted by Florence Kelley's National Consumers' League. Among other features, it established fourteen as a minimum age for working girls and sixty hours per week as maximum employment for all children under sixteen. McKelway intensely angered some mill men by photographing children in their plants and using these pictures to illustrate the dramatic article, "Do Not Grind the Seed Corn." This was first published by Josephus Daniels in *The Raleigh News and Observer* and then became a very useful committee pamphlet. Joseph P. Caldwell, editor of Tompkins' *Charlotte News and Observer*, became so angry that he referred to McKelway as a "preacher, reformer, editor of a so-called religious paper and common liar." Perhaps through fear, he resolved to have "no debate with the dog" and wrote, "You have the kick which you have so long begged for and so richly earned."

In the hearing before a legislative committee, McKelway was the sole advocate of the North Carolina bill. He gave a splendid defense of the measure and tried to present his relationship to the National

Child Labor Committee as well as justify its work. In his rebuttal, however, he failed to answer the charge that the committee was a tool of New England. This may have been responsible for the bill's defeat. Tompkins and his associates agreed to the passage of a law in 1907 but only when changes were made in accordance with their suggestions—the minimum age was placed at thirteen, but exceptions were allowed for apprentices.[66]

Some Southern success came in 1906 when Georgia passed an act similar to the 1903 Alabama law. But South Carolina failed to act, and especially discouraging was the fact that few Southerners affiliated with the National Committee.[67] However, Murphy believed the work of state and local committees in the South was having its results and in time action would be taken. This optimistic view was not shared by a majority of the National Committee's trustees—a new title for the Executive Committee. Therefore when Senator Albert Beveridge introduced a bill excluding from interstate commerce the products from all plants which employed children under fourteen, many on the committee felt this was the one means to deal with the situation in the foreseeable future.

Murphy was shocked that the committee would even discuss the Beveridge Bill. He was not opposed to all federal activity in the child labor field, however, and had joined in the committee's endorsement of a federal Children's Bureau to investigate and publicize conditions. He believed this was within the scope of the powers granted the central government and that the agency would not arouse Southern opposition.[68] Opposing federal regulation of child labor from the earliest days of the committee, he had assumed leadership only when it pledged "not to advance the interests of federal legislation."[69]

To advance his bill, Beveridge first appeared before the National Child Labor Committee's trustees on November 23, 1906. "Considerable difference of opinion as to the wisdom of federal regulation was expressed," and the opposition, particularly of Southern members, was so intense that a decision on committee support was postponed for two weeks. On December 6, a second meeting was held with Beveridge. Murphy was absent from both sessions, but he presented his views by letter. The distinguished Alabama attorney Francis G. Caffey, who had recently moved to New York, and Robert W. deForest vigorously argued against endorsement, but a majority of the committee voted to endorse the bill.[70]

When Murphy learned of the approval of the Beveridge Bill, he promptly resigned both from the Board of Trustees and the committee. For different reasons he had attempted to do this in 1905, stating that his poor health and concern with educational matters limited the time he could give the committee and that he feared his name was his only contribution. The Secretary denied this, writing, "there is no other member of the National Committee who has given me as much help since I have been connected with it as you have done."[71] This time his letter of resignation, presented through Adler, left no doubts as to the finality of his action and the reasoning behind it. He felt the Board of Trustees had violated a compact since at the first some members argued for federal regulation, yet all had signed an agreement not to accept it. But this was "the least of the issues involved"; his opposition arose from the belief that the Beveridge Bill was "contrary to sound public policy"; if enacted it was "sure to work the gravest injury to the cause of the children," North and South. He did not doubt that as a law the Beveridge Bill might "be temporarily successful," but he questioned its ultimate effect on public opinion, which in the long run would determine both legislation and administration. Murphy disavowed any questioning of his fellow trustee's motives, but due to his convictions he felt he would best serve the cause of the children by resigning. With profound regret, the trustees accepted his resignation on January 29, 1907 and instructed Lindsay to prepare a resolution of appreciation for his services.[72]

Some trustees wrote Murphy asking that he reconsider. Most perceptive was Lindsay, who declared there were certain to be differences of opinion in a widely representative group and that Murphy should abide by the majority decision. The National Committee had aroused more interest than anticipated and needed unity to attain victories. Even before his resignation could be formally presented Lindsay could feel the loss of his support and wrote, "I feel that more than ever this cause needs you."[73]

In January, 1907, the National Child Labor Committee began a campaign to obtain passage of the Beveridge Bill. Lindsay, McKelway, and others with whom Murphy had worked for years believed it offered the one effective means of dealing with business organizations that had become national in scope. As Lindsay expressed it, the measure was endorsed by the trustees only because the states were proving "impotent" in the enforcement of child labor legislation and because manufacturers were able, with some justice, to defeat laws on the grounds that other states without them could destroy their business. The committee sent letters to 10,000 clergymen asking that they preach sermons in the bill's behalf, and McKelway took personal charge of Washington lobbying, spending most of his time working with Southern congressmen. On January 23, 1907, Senator Beveridge began a three day speech in which he attempted to overwhelm the opposition by presenting an impressive array of facts and statistics showing the need for the law.[74]

At the same time, Murphy effectively launched a campaign against the measure by publishing a well conceived attack, which soon afterwards became a widely distributed pamphlet, in *The Montgomery Advertiser*. Murphy also contacted a number of influential men, receiving aid and assurance of their support. Charles W. Eliot, Harvard's president, telegraphed, "Use my name against the Beveridge bill at your discretion." George Foster Peabody and Oswald G. Villard, both of whom were outspoken liberals on many questions, refused to renew their contributions to the National Committee after corresponding with Murphy. Villard succinctly summarized much of Murphy's reasoning when he wrote, "this running to Washington for aid will do the cause a great deal of harm and set back its local state progress immeasureably." Most significantly, Murphy wrote President Roosevelt, suggesting a delay of six months or a year for closer study of the measure and to enable the country to be adequately informed. The departure was so radical, he declared, that if the idea was sound nothing would be lost by delay.[75] In return he received two "confidential" letters from the White House from which he inferred that if he published a complete exposé of the bill "the President may wholly withdraw his support from Beveridge's measure."[76] "Your letter came just at the right time," Roosevelt wrote. "There is no one whose judgment on such a matter would more affect me than yours, and it definitely decided me not to send in any message on the subject of the Beveridge bill at present nor until I have gone more carefully over it. I have a very profound regard for your knowledge of what is the best means to do in cases of this kind."[77]

When Villard offered to publish a rebuttal by Murphy to arguments for the bill in *The New York Evening Post*, Murphy consented, partially through fear that Senate attacks on the bill would be from a corporation standpoint, which would aid passage. He also hoped to correct McKelway's statement that the committee's endorsement had not hurt the child labor movement in the South. Consequently, he revised and expanded the article which had appeared in *The Montgomery Advertiser*. "I think I have accomplished my purpose," he wrote upon its completion. "I think that if I can get my argument before the country the Beveridge bill will be dead." Even more importantly, he hoped to "check and turn one of the most dangerous tendencies in our country in reference to social reform," the tendency of "the best people" to look to Washington for direction of all changes.[78]

Murphy's article, which in its reissued pamphlet form was entitled *The Federal Regulation of Child Labor, A Criticism of the Policy Represented in the Beveridge-Parsons Bill*, contended that the child labor question was national but not one for the national government. It revealed his sincerity and tremendous power of analysis, but demonstrated that he was a keener student of logic and psychology than of America's economy and politics. He was so immersed in the state's rights concept that he believed any attempt at national control would defeat the goal being sought. Once the federal government assumed local police jurisdiction "the sense of local responsibility is lowered and confused, the local processes of social education are arrested, the cause of the children is set backward and the interests of the Nation are defeated rather than advanced," he wrote. If the states allowed the federal government to acquire more and more of their powers and responsibilities, would the people be able to maintain the standards they had been too weak to establish? He wondered if the bringing of debility to the states would not also bring it to the nation.[79]

Federal interest had been aroused in child labor through the activities of the states, and McKelway himself had written that the campaign in Alabama was "the beginning of the present fight for the children that has extended over the Nation." The problem still remained everywhere, but, in the aggregate, it was mainly a Northern one. The relatively small number of Southern child laborers was responsible for much of the difficulty in obtaining action from rurally dominated legislatures, but they were being persuaded to act by the slow, inevitable forces of local agitation. Much remained to be done, particularly in the enforcement of legislation, yet one could scarcely read a newspaper without seeing that "the people have been reached and have been aroused."

Murphy thought that there was insufficient state negligence to warrant federal intervention. While he did not question Senator Beveridge's sincerity, he traced the origin of the bill to "a political opportunism which is not necessarily either illegitimate or insincere." Only methods, not goals, divided most supporters and opponents of the bill, and this division was based on "varying conceptions as to the very nature of our government."[80]

Senator Beveridge largely ignored the question of governmental powers in his Senate speech but assumed that the continued presence of evils proved the futility of state regulation. Murphy felt that the same conclusion could be made about control of vagrancy, arson, etc., and this only proved that "the powers of the local police are derived from the local will and are answerable to it." Federal control in any of these areas would destroy the nature of the American government, while there was no reason to believe it would be any more effective. Federal laws were "repeatedly outraged," especially those dealing with counterfeiting, bootlegging, and customs inspections, which were "the occasion of endless scandal and irritation." Could anyone retain confidence in federal regulation who had studied the control of Indian affairs? It seemed only logical that the more complex the administration, the greater the chance for "cupidity, or discrimination, or plain bungling." Until the Beveridge Bill was introduced, the last session of Congress seemed ready to approve a local child labor bill for the District of Columbia. It was appalling that the federal government failed to act in an area where it had exclusive jurisdiction yet wished to intervene in the states.[81]

Moreover, Murphy challenged the effectiveness of the Beveridge Bill. Of necessity, federal control would be indirect and would not be as efficient as that of the states. Large numbers of child laborers, particularly those in agriculture, would not be covered. (*The New York Times* estimated the bill would effect only 300,000 children, a figure Murphy believed to be excessive.) Also, the bill provided such high penalties that juries would hesitate to convict anyone. Its greatest weakness lay in the assumption that an age limit would eradicate the evil of child labor. To be effective, the law must provide for inspection and enforcement, have provisions for compulsory education, "and —more important still—must place a humane limitation upon the periods and hours of labor." A system of controls was needed that Murphy thought could not be constitutionally supplied by the central government but was being slowly created by the states. Many state laws were "full of tragic weaknesses and humiliating stupidities," but these defects, unlike those of a federal law, were curable.

To the argument that one federal law could be more easily passed than forty state laws, Murphy asserted that selfish corporate interests would also find one legislature easier to manage. Even though a federal law were obtainable, campaigns for state laws were essential to awaken the people to their responsibilities. "Local agitation" furnished the means of "slow and inevitable education of individuals and communities," for which there was no substitute. A national law could not create uniform conditions. If passed in such a diverse country, the struggle would simply be transferred "from the field of law enactment to the field of law enforcement." True competition between the states was raising standards, and the reputations of mills employing younger children were becoming odious. A national law would kill state initiative as it had in the regulation of obscene literature and counterfeit money. The great tragedy lay in the fact that the Beveridge

Bill, with only an age limit provision, was no substitute for adequate state control.[82]

The Beveridge Bill divided the forces of reform as well. Everywhere federal intervention was welcomed as a "short cut from local responsibilities," but it aroused a resentment at national intrusion, perhaps founded in stupidity. In the Southern states and Pennsylvania, the opponents of reform had regained sympathy that they had almost completely lost.

Since to him the state seemed to offer the ultimate solution, Murphy felt any diversion in the development of its control system was a mistake. Too many assumed "that anything which the States fail to do, the federal power can necessarily do better." The system of public schools, "by far the best as well as the most distinctive of our contributions to modern society," was a state creation. It rested upon the "same solicitude for the children" on which child labor legislation must rest.[83]

As a final argument, Murphy turned to the constitutional issue, holding that Beveridge failed to prove that the federal government could legally exclude from transportation articles which in themselves were "devoid of evil or injurious qualities." This was quite different from excluding impure food and drugs on the grounds that their transportation would result in injury to people of a state by those of another state. Furthermore, the bill prohibited distribution of goods of factories employing young children even though child labor might be used in only one small department. Murphy stressed that this was not regulation; it was punishment! United States law did not prevent the employment of children under fourteen; how could the government punish what it did not prohibit?

Murphy knew some would think his concern for the rights of employers strange, but felt he must be just. Any injustice would not aid the children but only "harden" the "moral sensitiveness of the people." He concluded:

> There is little help to moral clearness or humane distinctions in a bill which reaches first to the regulation of commerce . . .

to the regulation of the age of producing labor . . . to an arbitrary classification of the product (not according to the more predominate but according to the less predominant element engaged upon it), and from an unjust classification of products upon which the prejudicial labor has been slight, to the unjust *exclusion* of products upon which it has been wholly absent! But what, indeed, is the Constitution of the United States "between friends"?[84]

"No more able statement of the objections to federal child labor legislation" was ever made.[85] It was especially effective in pointing out the limited nature of the Beveridge Bill and the need for an aroused public opinion. However, Murphy failed to realize the inadequacy of state controls in an age when interstate corporations and trusts were coming to dominate American business. Neither did he realize that public opinion could be aroused on this issue nationally as well as on state bases. While always most conscious of the need to handle Southern sensibilities tenderly, on few other issues did he so completely accept the state's rights rationale. He often urged Southerners to think nationally, and he previously had endorsed federal aid to education.[86] Apparently he was so encouraged by the Alabama campaign of 1903 and the limited success of the National Child Labor Committee at the state level that he assumed this was the one road to success.

Murphy did not confine his activities to use of the pen, and, although no longer associated with the National Child Labor Committee, he sought to have it reverse its endorsement of the Beveridge Bill. He retained a close relationship with several members of the committee, to whom he presented his views. Ironically, McKelway, who owed his position to Murphy, was not among them, and this was not due to a disagreement on policy but to what Murphy believed was a definite insult which came in a letter of McKelway's to the editor of *The New York Evening Post*.[87] In it he impugned Murphy's knowledge of Southern conditions. He acknowledged Murphy's "zeal in behalf of the toiling children," stating that he was "entitled to the credit of inaugurating the agitation in their behalf that has resulted in the passage of State child labor laws for the first time in many States, and the amendment of former ineffective laws." But he added:

> . . . it is also fair to say that the pressure of other important work in his present state of health has not allowed Mr. Murphy to keep as fully abreast of the developments of this movement as some of his colleagues, and that perhaps his prolonged absence from the South has prevented him from recognizing the most significant sign of the times in the South, the growth of the national spirit in the best sense of that term.

Murphy was stung by McKelway's attitude, feeling that he and some others were "incurably personal in controversy." However, this was not true of his good friend, Adler, and in May, 1907, Murphy met with him for a discussion of the trustees' policy. Specifically, he asked why they had not been told Senator Ben Tillman was against the bill before they voted to endorse it. He inquired if they were being kept fully informed of the bill's effects in the South, if they knew the attitude of the Maryland Child Labor Committee, and that the Alabama committee would cooperate only if all references to the bill were suppressed.[88] Murphy told Adler that he was unwise to defend coercion as a policy when the minds of the people were unprepared for it.[89]

In the midst of the 1907 campaign against the Beveridge Bill, Murphy, working with a rejuvenated Alabama Child Labor Committee, assumed much of the leadership for a more effective Alabama law. The new Governor, the railway and educational reformer, Braxton Bragg Comer, was also president of Avondale Mills, one of whose plants McKelway characterized as next to the worst factory he had ever seen. During the gubernatorial contest of 1906, *The Montgomery Advertiser*[90] carried a letter of Murphy's stating that Comer had opposed all legislation in the 1903 conference. "Mr. Comer has seemed to me the most bitter opponent of child labor legislation I have ever known."[91]

Because of his personal position, Comer could not afford to oppose this legislation, and the State Democratic convention of 1906, controlled by his forces, pledged additional reform. Yet Murphy knew that Comer opposed the bill privately and that its supporters would need all the help they could get if they were to succeed. One of the best child labor bills ever proposed in the South was introduced in the new legislature, but Murphy and his associates decided not to press for its immediate passage, feeling that they could muster more votes after the spring recess. Before adjourning in the spring of 1907, the legislature enacted a law providing that the State Inspector of Jails should inspect factories four times a year.[92] This was a distinct advance, but it gave Murphy the opportunity to make another popular appeal through a poem entitled, "With the Jails." Its concluding stanza read:

> There are men of lawless passion
>   In our prisons bound secure;
> But what are the crimes of the children
>   Who are bound though their hands are pure?
> For Eleven hours—a strong man's day—
>   They toil till Spirits fail.
> And thread by thread they spin the cords
>   That bind up your mills with the jails.[93]

In another poem, "Beneath the Shield," Murphy advised:

> Have done with the senseless slaughter
>   of the strength our children yield;
> That the child of the land may also stand
>   secure beneath the shield
> Of a State grown sick of a traffic
>   from city and village and plain,
> That would barter the treasure of ages
>   for a moment of brutal gain.[94]

Before the legislature reconvened, Murphy became ill and found the strain so great that he had to leave Montgomery. However, he had hopes for a better law and cautioned Villard not to be misled by the pessimism of *The Montgomery Advertiser.* Although its editors were his friends, they were bitterly opposed to the Comer administration, and their accounts spoke as if the legislature "had adjourned *sine die*(!)"[95]

Immediately before the legislature reassembled, Murphy sent an article entitled "A Plea for Immediate Action" to each of the members; to avoid further antagonizing the Comer forces, it was not published in *The Montgomery Advertiser.*[96] In it he urged the legislature to face its responsibility without attempting to place blame for child labor conditions on earlier legislatures or leave their mitigation to later ones. At the first session, laws had been passed to safeguard the fish, game, and wild birds of the state; certainly no less could be done for the children. Murphy recalled that he had agreed to the 1903 compromise with intense reluctance, and its weaknesses must be remedied to give Alabama an adequate law. The first reform should be the end of exceptions to the twelve-year age limit, an opening "to numberless excuses and evasions" that put additional hardships on "those whose fate is already hard," i.e., orphaned ten-year olds who were forced to do eleven hours or more work each day. In cases of real need, "the burden of the emergency should fall . . . on the mills (which make enormous profits from the cheap labor of their operatives) and upon the community—rather than upon the child of ten—the one least able to bear it." At one time "Alabama led in the fight," but other states had moved so fast they had passed her. Now in effect she had a ten-year age limit. Subterfuge must be eliminated; at "whatever point or age, the limit should be clear, unequivocal, decisive." In the most severe statement he ever made against the mills, Murphy declared that the man who defended child labor as a necessary corollary to prosperity traduced the South and its industry.[97]

In addition to establishing a fourteen-year age limit, Murphy hoped that "the horror and scandal of *night* work" (from 7 P.M. to 6 A.M.) would be eliminated for all those under sixteen. He demanded that provisions be made for inspection and enforcement and that a compulsory school term be established. He earnestly advised a shortening of the work day, since mills worked children eleven hours or even twelve if they granted a half day of freedom on Saturday. To those who said the children were given light factory work, Murphy replied, "Why, gentlemen, children cannot continuously *play* that many hours per day without exhaustion—much less work." It was impossible to pick up toothpicks, one by one, and transfer them from one pile to another, for twelve hours "without tasting something of the numbing, maddening monotony" enshrouding the working children; action must be taken![98]

Some of Murphy's friends cautioned him to be moderate, but he replied, "I have *seen* these children. I have photographed them, not as an intruder but with the consent of superintendents who themselves detested this evil and desired its mitigation." The "cruel absurdity— to all our normal human thinking and feeling" demanded action.

Murphy held personal animus toward no one but felt that the Comer forces must be challenged to provide an effective child labor law. They had won the governorship by promising to bring the railways under public control and reduce their influence in government. By the same token, they must see that public control prevailed over factory conditions. "We are told that the people do not wish the railroads of this state to write the railroad legislation. Do they then wish the factory legislation to be written by the factories? Have the people of Alabama displaced one set of special interests, only to enthrone another?"

He did not know if the manufacturers could defeat the will of the people, but Murphy advised them not to try. Industry was only beginning in Alabama, and they had "the greatest opportunity ever given to the industrial leaders of any people, the opportunity to start free from the factory abuses which have clouded the industrial development of every modern state." They could "annex this industry to the moral enthusiasm of the South," or they could "lay its foundations in abuses which will make its whole future history but a record of accusations upon the one side and of apologies upon the other."

Seeing the impressive appropriations for education under Comer's leadership, Murphy questioned the exclusion of thousands of children from schools by factory employment. If the legislature failed to enact a child labor law, four years would intervene before another opportunity would present itself. He wrote the legislators: "That will be the day of *other* children. The opportunity to help *these* children is here today; it cannot return; it will pass with them and with you."[99]

Spurred by Murphy and the Alabama Child Labor Committee, the second session of the 1907 legislature passed a law which the National Child Labor Committee considered "the most effective child labor law that has thus far been enacted at the South." It brought the minimum working age "squarely up to twelve years; reduced the maximum number of hours for children under 14 from 66 to 60 hours; prohibited work from 7 P.M. to 6 A.M. for those under 16 and permitted only 8 hours of night work for those under 18." Particularly important was the requirement that child laborers under 16 attend school eight weeks a year, "the State's first acceptance of the principle of compulsory attendance."

Murphy regarded the law as "the high water mark of such legislation in the manufacturing States of the South" and particularly liked the provisions dealing with night work and education. Although Tennessee and Louisiana had higher age limits, they had fewer cotton mills. Of course, he noted, those familiar with the laws of older manufacturing states would recognize the inadequacy of the Alabama law. "But the enactment of the new law, under conditions of peculiar difficulty" was evidence of a "steadily increasing local sentiment." As in the case of all social legislation, it represented "the common feeling and conviction of the people at its minimum, rather than at its maximum" and came as the result of popular campaigns that had taken one-hundred children out of the mills for every one taken out by the law. The law was essential, however, and needed to be strengthened "in order to permanently hold the gains of agitation."[100]

Success in Alabama and North Carolina in 1907 strengthened Murphy's belief that local forces could enact adequate laws and did not need federal aid. In a letter to *The New York Evening Post*, he declared that the Alabama Child Labor Committee had "never been more efficient than during the past twelve months."[101] He asked Villard to publicize the activities of the local forces in the state, without which he could have done nothing. "Should you refer to the matter in any way," he wrote in a typical gesture of self negation, "it may be born in mind that Dr. B. J. Baldwin, the Rev. Neal L. Anderson, D.D., and Judge J. B. Gaston are . . most important"[102]

After the victory, Murphy again turned to the national scene. Undoubtedly he played an important role in persuading President Roosevelt not to support the Beveridge Bill. In November, 1907, the President wrote Murphy that, in consideration of his advice, he had decided not to recommend immediate action. If the states failed to do their duty, he would then call for enactment of a law.[103]

In the interim, the National Child Labor Committee rescinded its endorsement due to the protest of Murphy and others and the failure of Congress to act. Robert W. deForest had opposed the original endorsement and sent Murphy a check for $50 to be used in the "anti-Beveridge Bill campaign." He now offered a resolution stating that since the trustees disagreed as to federal regulation, the endorsement of the Beveridge Bill should be withdrawn and members allowed to take individual positions. To soften the action and provide a face-saving feature, a substitute measure was presented. It noted that "wide divergence as to a national law" existed among those who favored regulation and stated that the committee would not take action on such a law until the results of a congressional investigation of child labor, authorized in February, 1907, and to a great extent due to committee activities, were known. It also provided the holding of action in abeyance until "the results of a more searching consideration of the whole subject point the way to action upon which we can hope to unite all forces now devoted to the cause of child labor reform." The committee resolved to devote its efforts in the meantime to the support of "wise state and local legislation" and other measures to suppress child labor, including efforts to establish a federal Children's Bureau. This measure was approved first by an 18 to 10 and then a unanimous vote of the trustees.[104]

Murphy was greatly pleased by the action. He believed the milder resolution was adopted to spare the feelings of Lindsay and a few others and that, as deForest stated, the committee had "voted squarely to rescind its resolutions of approval of the Beveridge Bill."[105] Owen R. Lovejoy gave a valid estimation of the trustees' action, stating that it bound the committee to take no position on federal controls until the members had time to consider all phases of the question. By this means unanimity should be attained, since no friend of the child could withhold support.[106] DeForest would have preferred the adoption of his original resolution, but the substitute "was unanimously adopted whereas the other would have been adopted by a two-thirds vote." With the adjournment of Congress, there was no longer a Beveridge Bill, and deForest felt "the attitude of the committee toward any further Beveridge Bill is assured." Therefore, in January, 1908, he urged Murphy to return as a member of the committee and told him, "You have won out, and there are no feelings to swallow."[107] Murphy was now too ill to consider returning and had to rest content with his earlier achievements, but the committee continued a stepped-up program of state activities and was influential in obtaining establishment of the Children's Bureau in 1912. It was not until 1914 that it again endorsed a federal bill, which was enacted in 1916.

As much as any man, Murphy had "pricked the conscience of the country alive to the existence of child labor as a shame and a curse to America." The public repudiated child labor to a great extent due to his efforts and those of organizations he aided in founding and guiding, and it came to be defended only by a few employers who felt dependent upon a perpetuation of an existing system.[108] Murphy did not adequately evaluate the need for federal controls, and some of his objections now seem quite shallow and naïve, but his career ended before the impact of the "Square Deal" and the "New Freedom" made federal regulation seem feasible and logical. Despite this, many of Murphy's warnings as to weaknesses and dangers in federal regulation remain valid and logical. His greatest contribution, however, was that of a social pioneer who perceived and attacked a major problem when few others recognized it or dared raise their voices against it.

4.

Race Relations

THE NEGRO QUESTION was at the heart of many Southern issues in the early years of the century, and, as he wrestled with Southern problems, Murphy was forced to continue devoting much effort and time to racial matters. Already inequality had been "effected by force and regulated by law."[1] Murphy, while advocating segregation, at least temporarily, rejected the imposed caste system, believing it to be intolerable in a democracy and a major factor retarding Southern development. Essentially a conservative, he felt that the achievements of the past must be the springboard for advancement and that the status quo should be challenged only for weighty reasons. Yet he was also a progressive, contending that society must be ordered so that all men would have the chance for maximum growth and development. Unlike most contemporary Southerners, he saw that self-limitation was the only valid limitation on any man's achievements. His philosophy was deeply rooted in Christian ethics and, as such, was as much a triumph of the spirit as the intellect.

Like the progressive of every age, Murphy found himself playing a dual role—appealing to the more enlightened thought of his own region, which he felt must be the major source of advancement, and seeking to remove the misapprehensions of outsiders who threatened progress by arousing local hostility. In all his endeavors, he relied heavily on Booker T. Washington, whom he frequently consulted before making a major address or submitting an important article for publication.[2] Although not always agreeing, they shared much the same philosophy and had a genuine respect for each other. "The best men of the South" had "a deep and grateful pride" in Washington, Murphy felt. He did not hesitate to acknowledge Washington's help in obtaining political preferment for his friends and wrote, "I cannot see how a man of the truest feeling can accept a favor of anyone, no matter what his condition or his race, and then feel in any way ashamed to acknowledge it."[3]

Murphy's moderation was a scarce commodity in the South of his time. Although lynching declined after 1900, the system of Negro repression was tightened as many otherwise progressive leaders aided the process. Negro disfranchisement was complete in many regions, and Washington reported that some Alabama registrars were notably unfair.[4] The convict lease system, which enriched a number of Southern industrialists, primarily exploited Negroes, whose lives were often brutalized and brief. The malodorous nature of the system was such that even the hardened Southern social conscience began to rebel. Louisiana ended it in 1901, and between 1906 and 1913 five other states did also, while much needed restrictions were added elsewhere. But where it continued to exist the Negro was victimized. Washington, noting that the state of Alabama netted $437,000 from leasing its convicts—three-fourths of whom were Negro—in a ten month period, felt that "an investigation would show that the colored convicts alone turn much more into the state treasury than the state spends every year for the education of the whole Negro population in Alabama."[5] Even when some reforms were instituted in the Alabama convict lease system due to court decisions, numbers of Negroes were given prison sentences for violation of contracts. "This simply means," Washington wrote, "that any white man who cares to charge that a Colored man has promised to work for him and has not done so, or who has gotten money from him and not paid it back, can have the Colored man sent to the chain gang."[6]

From every side fate seemed to be closing in on the Negro. J. W. Dinsmore, the Dean of Berea College, was especially concerned with the ending of economic opportunity and the exclusion of Negroes from one skilled occupation after another. With this in mind, he declared in 1909, "The mass of negroes are in a worse condition today than they have been since the days of slavery."[7] The Rev. Quincy Ewing well understood that segregation could not be confined to social affairs and reflected this in his criticism of Ray Stannard Baker's *Following the Color Line*. He believed Baker failed to get at the "kernel of the thing, which is simply the determination of the white South that the Negro must always be treated as an inferior being, and reminded of it in every possible way by political and social discriminations steadily insisted on."[8] This amazing position reached a crest and the height of absurdity in the political philosophy of Napoleon Bonaparte Broward. Like Montague, Aycock, Vardaman, and Hoke Smith, he was a Southern progressive and a racist who as Governor of Florida recommended in 1907 that his legislature memorialize Congress to acquire domestic or foreign territory to which all American Negroes would be moved after their property had been purchased by the United States government. He held that education would lead Negroes to feel they could obtain the highest positions in government and society.

Such paradoxes in liberal-racist thought were not confined to politicians. The educational statesman, Edwin A. Alderman, president at various times of the University of North Carolina, Tulane, and the University of Virginia, writing in 1908, glorified disfranchisement of the Negro as a "constructive act of Southern genius." He stated as fact, not prophecy, "that the negro race is declining in the south, and must continue to decline in relative numbers."[9]

Rare indeed were any who perceived, or much less attacked, the system of racial repression. One who did was a former Butler County, Alabama, Superintendent of Education and graduate of the University of Alabama, I. T. Little. In disgust he wrote Washington from Ackerville, Alabama, "All the so called missionary churches I have seen are trying to convert somebody in Africa, or China, when in America, these same churches are killing, extortioning, swindling the Negro at their doors." In his own school district, Negroes received approximately thirty-five cents per pupil compared to $15 for each white student.[10]

While such deplorable conditions as these emerged in the South, racist ideology, supported by Social Darwinism, thrived in the North. Here too emerged segregation that confined Negroes "to marginal occupations and marginal residential districts."[11] Shortly after retiring as President of Columbia University and Mayor of New York City, Seth Low wrote:[12] "I apprehend that the fundamental difference between the two sections is very slight. Race purity is as strong an instinct at the North as it is at the South; but, there being at the North so much larger a proportion of whites to blacks, this is maintained in the North by much less drastic measures than are believed by Southerners to be necessary in the South. . . ." Clearly a modern student of race is correct in concluding "that American thought of the period 1900–1920 generally lacks any perception of the Negro as a human being with potentialities for improvement."[13]

Murphy was pondering these developments in the spring of 1902 when a renewed attack of rheumatic fever forced him to convalesce for weeks in New York. But even this setback had its advantages, for he found time during his recuperation to clarify his views. When summer came, Maud and the children made a temporary home in Concord, Massachusetts, and he wrote one of his most influential addresses, "The Task of the South," which was delivered at Washington and Lee University in December. Much of the address was devoted to "The Problem of the Negro" and presented a well-formulated concept of education's role in dealing with the most urgent of Southern questions.

Initially, Murphy sought to rob the Vardamans, Tillmans, and other demagogues of their thunder by accepting separation of the races in schools and acknowledging that the Negro was the weaker race. At this time he defended segregation as a means of preserving the Negro's "wisest and strongest representatives—its leaders—who, under different conditions, would have been absorbed into the life of the race above them." Murphy's views were not severe or harsh considering the time and place. Concurrently the distinguished Northern historian, James Ford Rhodes, maintained the Negro to be "innately inferior and incapable of citizenship," while Harvard's president, Charles W. Eliot, stated that his school had 5,000 white students and 30 Negroes, and if it had an equal proportion or if Negroes were a majority it too might impose segregation.[14] Later Murphy modified his conceptions and came to hold that segregation can have validity only as it is self-chosen and imposed in such a fashion as to give equal rewards for equal ability.[15] Using a similar definition, many—including the United States Supreme Court—have contended that separation by its very nature brings inequality, a conclusion Murphy might also have reached had he lived and wrestled with the race question a bit longer.

Murphy was undoubtedly correct in attempting to allay fears of racial amalgamation as a first step in interracial cooperation. In his address he hastened to assure North and South alike that there was no danger in this area since the vast majority of both races were opposed to it. Least of all should education be feared as a menace to white society as Vardaman and others said.

> The only real peril of our situation lies not in any aspect of the Negro's wise and legitimate progress, but rather in the danger that the Negro will know so little, will do so little, and will increasingly care so little, that this great black mass of his numbers, his ignorance, his idleness and his lethargy will drag forever like a cancerous and suffocating burden at the heart of the South.

The only solution lay in the provision of the highest education every man could wisely use, regardless of race. "Where individual capacity exists, the only thing, the only right and wise thing to do with it is to equip it and to direct it." Capacity can not be destroyed, Murphy stated. "The repression and perversion of the capacities of our greatest Negro would have made him the most dangerous factor in Southern life."[16]

Statistically, as compared with the white race, the percentage of Negroes obtaining higher educations was declining. The major question was what type of education did the majority receive. Murphy strongly defended the Negro "common school," maintaining that its difficulties came from lack of support and resources, reflections of Southern poverty. He praised even the simplest school as "an institution of moral power in the life of every child within its walls," an institution which represented the disciplines of punctuality, order, silence, and association. Under the influence of Washington's philosophy, he held that the usual system of Southern education was ill adapted for the life led by the majority, and he maintained that industrial and agricultural education that would utilize "natural symbols and practical forms" were needed. By such means, perhaps the "best Negroes" could be induced to stop their flight from the soil and devote their talents to the enrichment of the South.

Murphy was appalled by those who thought the Negro was not fitted for factory employment because he quickly fell asleep when near the hum of machinery. These men were generally the same who ten years before had insisted that industrial and agricultural training was the only type of education the Negro should have. "The poor Negro! The man who would keep him in ignorance and then would disfranchise him because he is ignorant must seem to him as a paragon of erect and radiant consistency when compared with the man who first tells him he must work and then tells him he mustn't learn how!"

Murphy held only disdain for those who wished to keep the Negro back economically. The productive, efficient Negro was not to be feared, he said, and least of all should the economic error be accepted "that the volume of the world's work is fixed in quantity, and if the Negro does a part of it, there will be less of it for the white man. . . . Every laborer who is really a producer represents a force which is enlarging the market for labor." The productive Negro contributed to the economic well-being of all Americans.

Though Murphy defended the Negro's right to work, he did recognize that the Negro had weaknesses, but wondered which of these was "made better by idleness, hopelessness, and industrial helplessness." No Negro virtues would be destroyed "by right thinking,

DuBose Murphy
New Haven, Connecticut, 1908

DuBose Murphy
New Haven, Connecticut, 1910

The Trinkkuranlage, Bad Nauheim, Germany, 1912

DuBose Murphy en route to Europe, 1910

DuBose Murphy
Yale University, 1915

by real knowledge, by the capacity to see clearly and to work successfully." "God made him a man," he informed his audience. "We cannot and we dare not make him less." Yet if he were to reach his potential, one of the greatest tasks of American life lay before both the North and the South.[17]

Following its presentation, *The Task of the South* was issued in pamphlet form and received wide circulation. Professor Francis G. Peabody, of Harvard, praised it as containing

> . . . enough sound political economy and political ethics to satisfy an entire generation. One of my colleagues was showing another a Greek vase, and remarked, "Isn't it pretty?" To which Professor Norton replied, "Pretty? It is ultimate. It is the whole of art." One feels the same sense of conclusiveness as he reads Mr. Murphy's discussion, with its perfect balance of passion and power.[18]

Because of Murphy's prominence as a commentator on racial affairs, President Theodore Roosevelt summoned him to the White House following the nomination of a Negro to a Charleston office. The South Carolina senators exercised "senatorial courtesy" to block the appointment, and a furor arose throughout much of the South. Roosevelt's racial policies constituted one of the strangest and most vacillating aspects of his administrations. A Social Darwinist and believer in the Anglo-Saxon myth, he accepted without question the premise of Negro inferiority. Yet Roosevelt had a sporting sense of fair play and was head of the party which prided itself on liberating the Negro. The day he assumed office he wrote Washington asking him for advice on appointments. Washington called on the President on October 16, 1901, while en route to New York, and dined at the White House, unleashing an unexpected explosion of public sentiment. Though he never ate with Washington again, Roosevelt relied on his patronage advice, publicly acknowledging it. "What influence I have had with the President has grown out of the fact that I have not taken part in the general scramble in the direction of pushing individual candidates upon him, but have waited until he saw fit to consult me in regard to the fitness of men," Washington wrote. He sought "to bring recognition to Southern white men of the highest order, men of ability, character and generosity of judgment regardless of politics," in the belief "that this type of white men could help the Negro better than any other class," and thus he used his influence to have the Democrat Thomas G. Jones appointed federal district judge in Alabama. But Roosevelt soon became fearful of Mark Hanna's opposition for the presidency in 1904, and his appeal to the Southern Negro delegates. Therefore, until after the election he generally, but not uniformly, opposed the Southern "Lily Whites." Probably the two most spectacular aspects of his pro-Negro policy were the appointment, on Washington's recommendation, of Dr. William D. Crum to be Collector of the Port of Charleston and the closing of the Indianola, Mississippi post office when whites sought to remove the Negro postmistress appointed by President Harrison.

Roosevelt was gravely troubled by the opposition and asked Murphy for his frank opinion of Crum's appointment. Privately, Murphy told the President if he were a Negro he would defer the seeking of office until he had attained other rights. Memories of Negro office holding were too prevalent to permit this without difficulty until the Negro had demonstrated his fitness in other areas. "Wisdom and patience and faithful service must be for the time the Negro's way of advancement." Murphy felt if Crum would voluntarily withdraw, he would better serve the interest of his race and the country. Upon leaving the White House, Murphy refused to reveal the nature of his interview, stating to reporters only that it concerned the entire South.

Roosevelt was influenced by Murphy's advice, and, after the interview and using Murphy's name, he dictated a telegram to Washington, which urged him to have Crum accept another appointment. Murphy was surprised and embarrassed—particularly since the telegram was sent collect—but the President's secretary stated that this was necessary in order to keep the White House out of the affair. The strategy did not work, and Roosevelt gave Crum interim appointments until the Senate acted in January, 1905. Crum held the office until 1908, when President Taft, as part of his general policy of Southern appeasement, obtained his resignation.[19]

Significantly, the Republican platform of 1908 dropped its plank demanding enforcement of the Fourteenth and Fifteenth amendments. This reflected Roosevelt's reversal of policy, which became public after the election of 1904 but had been developing even before. Writing to Albert Shaw, February 3, 1903,[20] Roosevelt stated in a typical rationalization that he had appointed Crum in the belief that there would be no objections in Charleston and that the Indianola post office had been closed solely to uphold the law since it had become the scene of demonstrations. In an oversimplification he added, "I have deliberately thrown down the colored and white scalawag southern machines, so that if there is a contest for the nomination I shall probably have the delegates from most of the southern states bitterly against me." Shaw completely accepted Roosevelt's rationale, writing Governor Montague of Virginia,[21] "Roosevelt is the only President since the Civil War who has practically quit appointing Negroes in the South; I cannot quite see why there should be so much criticism."

After being "elected in his own right," Roosevelt adopted a very conservative racial position, actually reducing the number of Negro office holders. In a 1905 Lincoln Day address he called for racial purity, advocated industrial training for the Negro, whom he labeled a "backward race," and urged that racial contacts must come in such a fashion that white civilization would not be degraded. Professor Edwin Mims correctly wrote that Roosevelt was in sympathy with Murphy and such Northern liberals as Albert Shaw, Robert C. Ogden, Lyman Abbott, and St. Clair McKelway who held that "*segregation in school, church, and society is in the interest of racial integrity and racial progress.*"

In trips across Texas in April, 1905, and from Richmond to New Orleans in the fall, Roosevelt did all possible to propitiate the white South, including using references to his mother's Southern birth, but offered no new avenues of advancement to the Negro. On the contrary, at Tuskegee Institute he cautioned Negroes to avoid the professions.[22] But it was only after he had three companies of Negro troops, including several Medal of Honor winners, dishonorably discharged on the basis of circumstantial evidence following the Brownsville Riot in August, 1906, that the masses of Negroes were aroused to hostility as they had not been aroused by the action of any other president. In a masterful rationalization the President wrote Murphy:

> It is too melancholy that most Northerners—certainly most Northerners of my own political party—should have shown such morbid sympathy with criminals as they have shown in this Brownsville affair. Of course all I did was to act precisely on the principles which I have so often preached . . . and in this case no consideration of party expediency, no action of sentimentalists of demagogs [*sic*] could make me swerve a hand's breadth from the course I have mapped out.[23]

Many questioned the President's decision and interpreted his delay in acting until the day after election as a political scheme in which the Negro was sacrificed. Even the ever faithful Washington was disgusted, and Villard's contempt knew no bounds. He wrote, "The outcry against this act is astounding. . . . It is really disgraceful, but it is in keeping with Mr. Roosevelt's whole treatment of the army. So far as his administration of it is concerned, I can prove to you that he has been the worst President we have had in 25 years."[24]

Fortunately, Murphy did not believe that the solution of racial problems lay mainly in the political realm or he would have been more discouraged. He did not relish intervention in politics and was confident he could do more for the South and the Negro by working for industrial education and for such schools as Hampton and Tuskegee. Washington's practical, humane methods seemed to Murphy the best possible approach. He warmly agreed with Washington's statement: "If all the energy that has been spent in the North . . . in discussing the relation of the races had been spent in training the children of each race to useful work and to thrifty habits, the Negroes would now have fewer shortcomings to discuss and white men would have less time to discuss them." He agreed with Washington that, "A good rule of life is this—when you feel an overpowering impulse to indulge in this discussion, which is now more than a century old and somewhat threadbare, spend your energy in helping to train one child—white or black—to some useful work; and you will serve your country better."[25] Acting on this philosophy, Washington achieved such notable results that, after he became Ambassador to Great Britain, Walter Hines Page could say unhesitantly, "the work of this one man has been the strongest single influence toward taking the negro problem out of the region of angry controversy and into the region of useful, helpful work. He showed a way of hope and demonstrated its practicability."[26]

Whenever he could promote Tuskegee and Hampton, Murphy did so, and, as an articulate, white Southerner who was respected by leading men in both North and South, he was often asked to appear in their behalf. In February, 1902, he and Frissell were the speakers at a meeting in Boston's Old South Church to raise funds for Hampton. In his address, Murphy declared that the white South, obviously referring to its better elements which retained control only with difficulty, did not wish to prevent the education of the Negro child, and he praised Hampton's teaching methods as opening to the Negro the "fullest exercise of the individual capacity."[27] The presiding officer of the meeting, the venerable Edward Everett Hale, was much impressed. Following the session, in the dimly lit anteroom, Hale had difficulty with his overshoes until Murphy came to his aid. Without recognizing his assistant, Hale observed, "Good speech that Murphy made; good speech. Fine young man." Murphy frequently recalled this incident and his warm reception by the audience and the Boston press.[28]

On April 14, 1903, Murphy appeared in Tuskegee's behalf at a large meeting in New York's Madison Square Garden. The other speakers were Abbott, Baldwin, and Washington, and former President Grover Cleveland served as presiding officer. In a tribute to Washington, Murphy termed him "one of the greatest moral assets in the life of our country." While many Southerners, at times, disagreed with some of his policies, they could not deny that he had wrought "a great work in response to a great need"; his achievements were triumphs for all America. A great danger lay in the possibility of Negro failure; "where a race suffers moral and physical decay, where a vast life dies, no man may safely live." But he felt there was every indication that the Negro would not fail, due to institutions like Tuskegee and Hampton which put first things first. "Without abandoning any honest conviction as to the broader political or educational heritage of the race," they "taught in season and out of season the creed of thrift, the paramount importance of work, the joy of usefulness, the supreme distinctions of decent, sober and contented living." Murphy believed, "The Negro has many sorrows. He is entitled to many aspirations." Tuskegee and Hampton denied neither but constantly taught that "hate is impotent and that only patience is strong."

Murphy again sought to deal with the "smokescreen" of racial amalgamation, stating it found "its basis not in self-respect, but in despair." "This nonsense about social equality has got to be met somehow and somewhere," he later wrote, "and so far as I am concerned, I should like to meet it right at this point."[29]

Those "who would not keep the Negro at the storm center of political agitation should support the great Negro schools, which, instead of encouraging attempts at political dominion, sought to promote industry and the acquisition of property. Surely the time had come when a civilized state would no longer stress prohibitions but would open to the Negro at least "a very short list of the things permitted to him." Tuskegee helped in emphasizing the opportunities for employment, something at times denied in the North but available in much of the South. It gave Negroes the "assurance that they themselves may help to constitute the rehabilitation of their land." It taught them "that they may drink of wells which they themselves have digged; may eat of vineyards which they themselves have planted; may dwell in cities which they themselves have builded." This was emancipation indeed![30]

Murphy continued his interpretation of Southern conditions in a series of letters to Villard. When *The New York Evening Post* criticized Alabama and advocated federal action to attain Negro rights, Murphy protested, pointing out that 3,000 Negroes had voted under the new Alabama constitution. He agreed that more should receive the ballot and trusted that this was only the beginning. The "gradual admission" of Negroes would be "delayed chiefly by unjust and undiscriminating criticism from the North," he believed. Appeal to the Republican Party would also prove futile since in Alabama it refused Negroes admission to its state convention. Nationally it might reduce representation of the state in Congress, but it could only enforce wholesale Negro suffrage by the use of troops, an expedient for which no one was ready. Coercion would hurt the Negro most of all because an attempt to apply the Fourteenth Amendment would result in the destruction of the Negro school systems, he feared. The best prospect for progress lay in the development of a local sense of obligation, with recognition in the South that "the penalties which threaten from Washington are but a pale rumor of penalties compared with the penalties that arise within." He counseled *The Evening Post* to appeal to the best in Southern life, not the worst, confident that more could be achieved in this way than any other. "If you would give freedom to the deserving negro, first give the assurance of freedom to the Southern life that stands about him."[31]

Here as on other issues, Murphy's hopefulness betrayed him, and federal withdrawal sealed the Negroes' fate in the South for generations. Perhaps his association with old-line conservatives such as Judge Jones and former Alabama Governor William C. Oates misled him, and he failed to realize that the younger leaders were abandoning paternalistic attitudes toward the Negro. He overvalued reason and the strength of Southern Christian ethics as stabilizing and molding forces. Much of the South's tragedy in the twentieth century arose from failure to heed Murphy's counsel and that of men like him.

Murphy assumed much the same posture when, on June 16, 1903, *The Evening Post* charged that Southern solidarity prevented honest men from protesting cruelty to the Negro.[32] This came following the issuance of thirty-five indictments for peonage against eighteen Alabama men who had worked Negroes without pay. Murphy replied with a vigorous letter pointing out that Judge Jones' court had conducted the investigation and brought the indictments. He felt it unfair to condemn Alabama courts for not doing what federal courts previously had been unable to do. The unfortunate position of some

Negroes was similar to that of New York City immigrants—an illiterate and lowly people were always in danger of "becoming the prey of brutality and greed." While this did not excuse apathy, an entire state or region should not be condemned. "In company with hundreds, indeed thousands of other Southern men," Murphy never ceased to speak out against injustice and cruelty. "I have publicly and repeatedly protested against any suffrage test that should not bear evenly and justly upon both races," he wrote. "Such a course has involved neither eccentricity nor martyrdom."[33]

When *The Evening Post* adamantly used the peonage cases to illustrate that the South should never have been left to solve its own internal problems, Murphy replied that the South had never been given this advantage. Northern "intrusive censure" and "political threatenings" had kept the region constantly on the defensive and had partially neutralized "the forces of self-criticism and of local responsibility." He hoped that the appointment of Judge Jones indicated a new approach by the federal government.[34]

In July the cases went to trial, and, after a number of convictions, Murphy sensed "a slight disposition, upon the part of certain interests in the State, to 'call a halt'" for fear of injuring Alabama's reputation. In a letter to *The Montgomery Advertiser*, he warned that this must not happen. He believed there were in Alabama, particularly by men of the upper classes, "more manifestations of genuine personal kindliness toward the negro than can be found in Boston or New York." Yet abuses also existed, and the real enemies of the state were not those who exposed mistreatment but who were the perpetrators of it. Cruel men not only gave the anti-Southern press something to write about but weakened rural life by driving Negroes from farms to cities, where they received greater protection. All guilty parties must be brought to justice, and, as they were punished, the case against the South would collapse.[35]

Murphy was not opposed to constructive criticism, even from the North, and he never allowed a belief in state's rights to destroy his national patriotism. He was pleased that there was such a thing "as a national citizenship and such a power in Alabama as a national court."

He commended *The Outlook* for its editorial on the cases, since it recognized "the local forces of self-correction." "Too often we find that when a Northern paper discusses wrongs at the North or at the West it criticizes the *wrongs,* but when it discusses wrongs at the South it criticizes the South." This makes evils "arising in the Southern States, issues not between Americans everywhere and the foes everywhere of a true Americanism, but crude and bitter issues between the North and the South. Such criticism reflects a Pharisaism which is the very soul of sectionalism—a Northern sectionalism as offensive as any sectionalism in our Southern States." The North as the North is a meddler in Alabama affairs, but the nation "has to do with every issue in Alabama that touches any national right of the humblest of its citizens." Murphy pleaded for "a criticism national in the exacting nobility of its ideals" and in its "moral vigor" but national also "in its intelligent . . . and constructive criticism."[36]

When Villard protested that *The Evening Post*'s editorials were fair, Murphy refused to agree since there were ten editorials dealing with Southern wrongs to every single editorial on the wrongs of other sections. Moreover, the difference was qualitative as well; those dealing with the South were vindictive and bitter. Their treatment of the peonage cases was used by defense attorneys in an effort to prove that Judge Jones, Murphy, and others "were simply parties to a rabid attack by the North on the South." In reporting a Montgomery murder, *The Evening Post* seemed to "'write up' the life of a city on the basis of a single incident." Murphy protested, stating that he had lived in the South thirty years without seeing a shooting. "The only murder I ever saw was . . . on the main street of Emerson's quiet Concord." Reminding Villard that "The North is no longer the Nation," he urged him to broaden his vision.[37]

As a result of Murphy's correspondence, *The Evening Post* declared editorially that *The Montgomery Advertiser* reflected the sentiments of most Alabamians in supporting Judge Jones. This pleased Murphy, who apologized for his zealous letters and explained that one of his major provocations had been *The Evening Post*'s habit of following its Southern criticism by an appeal, not for the Negro, but for the

Republican Party. He told Villard that Washington requested a race be "judged by its best," and he asked the same for the South. He knew there were many peonage cases in the South, and it was right that the press attack the evil, but not right to attack the section or its major political institutions. Judge Jones, the first Democratic federal judge in Alabama in years, was leading the fight against peonage. If in the previous thirty years the Republican judges had done a comparable job the evil would not exist. Pound the evil, he advised, "but give the Federal judges—the good old Republican orthodox sort—a little pounding too!"[38]

Murphy suspected that *The New York Evening Post*'s coverage of the Alabama situation was part of a larger political strategy, and, of course, he opposed federal intervention as self-defeating. He informed Washington, in confidence, "Mr. Villard admits that he is paving the way for the agitation for the enforcement of the amendments." He feared Villard had "wrought untold harm already" and that his success would "stampede the South against the Negro, and . . . cause untold wretchedness."[39]

In anticipation of an attempt to use federal power to insure Negro political rights, Murphy wrote, "Shall the Fourteenth Amendment be Enforced?" for *The North American Review*.[40] In it he repeated his often expressed opinion that only the qualified of both races should be allowed to vote, and that wholesale enforcement of Negro suffrage would enthrone the unfit and create bitter racial strife. "Ballot reform is not a reform by elimination only. It is a reform by addition of the worthy as well as by the elimination of the unworthy." He was happy to "hold in honor the Negro man who, after only forty years of freedom, is able to stand upon his feet before the white man's law and take the white man's test." It was a major responsibility of the church, school, and press to prepare an increasing number of Negroes to do so. The weakness in his program was the absence of an alternative if these agencies of Southern life failed to function as they should.

Undoubtedly Murphy's reasoning played some role in the increasing abandonment of the Negro to local Southern control. *Harper's Weekly*[41] found his arguments the strongest yet presented against the enforcement of the Fourteenth Amendment. Even in the heart of New England, *The Boston Evening Transcript*[42] concluded from his reasoning that if penalties were enforced on non-complying states, those individuals "now most affected would be more hopeless than ever." It praised Murphy for "devoting, we might say consecrating, rare gifts to the illumination of the problems of the South."

Many of Murphy's concepts were developed more fully in *The Present South*, a book of eight essays dealing with race, child labor, and education. Published in 1904, it reveals, perhaps more than any other work, his knowledge of Southern conditions, his breadth of view, and his broad tolerance. It presents an admirable philosophy whose only major weakness is unwarranted faith in the ability of enlightened Southerners to gain control and channel social developments. In the preface, Murphy disclaimed any intention of presenting a formula to resolve the South's difficulties. Great problems "are solved only in the sense that life becomes adjusted to them" or a working adjustment is attained. He saw the difficulties of the South "as phases of the essential movement toward a genuinely democratic order." Reflecting a view that motivated the Montgomery Conference on Race Relations, he held that diversity of ideas must receive expression, and little cooperation could exist unless concepts were tested by counter ideas.[43]

Murphy quickly acknowledged that the South's problems were essentially national ones which must have national solutions, without coercion of one section by another.[44] Drawing on the aristocratic tradition at its best, he contended the "Old South" must form "the real nucleus of the new nationalism." It was led, with a sense of *noblesse oblige*, by an aristocracy that assumed the Negro was inferior but improvable. If the masses of Southern whites truly wished to promote their own interests, they must choose leaders from this group— leaders able to instruct them and bring racial and inter-sectional peace. This was also the attitude of William Garrott Brown, who urged men of the upper classes to influence the public so that Negroes would gradually receive suffrage and other benefits as they were earned.[45]

Murphy, in a shrewd analysis, assumed that the central political factor in the emergence of the "New South" was the alliance, on the question of race, of the aristocracy with the masses of Southern whites, many of whom were voting for the first time. He failed to adequately acknowledge, however, that the aristocracy had abandoned many of its paternalistic attitudes to appease the whites. While the motive for this union was not ideal, he believed race to be a better unifying force than wealth, trade, property, family, or class. In this he disagreed with his friend, Bishop T. U. Dudley of Kentucky, who felt that race pride was primarily an excuse to keep the Negro menial.[46] This new society had a passion for education, and Murphy hoped the masses would acquire aristocratic ideas as they were educated; he trusted he could already detect a slowly lessening abuse of the Negro. He warned that economic dependency produces civil and political prejudice and urged that the Negro be given increasing opportunities to advance himself. The same attitude was well expressed by Trinity College President, John C. Kilgo, who wrote, "For a superior race to hold down an inferior one simply that the superior race may have the services of the inferior was the social doctrine of mediaevalism" and was unthinkable in America.[47] Murphy contended that the nature of democracy also demanded that there be no dependent classes, even as it required an enlightened electorate. In politics, standard tests for both races must be used. "If we are so morbidly afraid of the spectral possibilities of the negro's freedom that we must keep him ever in prison, then let us remember that on both sides of the prison door there is a man in duress," Murphy wrote in a modified version of a Washington simile, "for he who keeps a jail is hardly freer than his prisoner."[48]

Murphy felt that democracy was often misunderstood. With society as it was, democracy did not mean race fusion, loss of individuality in man, family, or race, nor equal political power for all at once. There was too much worry about the Negro's progress and the strength of his voice in government and society. It would be impossible "to keep the Negro in his place" as he obtained an education and wealth, both of which he was acquiring.[49]

To recognize the quality of the Negro and to correctly evaluate him was no injustice, according to *The Present South.* The "old time Darkey" was gone, and the South must not look for him. By the same token, in developing an education program, the South had to realize that, "The average negro child starts much farther back than the average white child. To recognize that fact and to educate as though we recognized it is not cruelty to the negro, but the fairest and tenderest kindness." He must have nurture and care and be enabled to develop race pride for his and humanity's sake.[50]

Racial problems and Negroes differed in every area of the South, and Murphy saw danger in generalizations. With the loss of control following emancipation, the masses of Negroes culturally declined before they began to conform to the ideals of white civilization. The brilliant achievements of a few Negroes offered hope that the vast majority would continue to develop. Murphy felt that the ability to create a stable home was the supreme test of civilization, and an increasing number of Negroes were accomplishing this. Unfortunately, white society often did not see this since contact was usually made with the Negro world at its worst.

Murphy as well as Washington considered the removal of white ignorance a major hope for improved race relations, and this spurred him to campaign for improved white education. At the same time, certain perverted Negro attitudes must be modified. The Negro must recognize he was not the only subject of prejudice, and he must seek to correct legitimate objects of criticism. In particular, Negro leaders must fight crime within the Negro community and help their own people make decent lives for themselves. And the white man must stop insisting on penalties which were too lenient or too severe and practicing the grave abuse of lynching.[51]

Murphy believed the school offered the best method to equip the Negro effectively to work the soil and labor in factories, essentials for full Southern development. Before 1870, education had been largely in the hands of the church and was aristocratic in nature, but as democracy emerged a democratic school system to educate everyone became essential. "Education brings its dangers," he wrote. "But the risk of making fools is of smaller import than the larger chance of making men."[52]

The Present South received accolades throughout the nation, and the press reviews were generally cordial. *The Outlook* declared, "Not since the close of the Civil War and therefore not since the South began to deal with its present problems, has there been a contribution of such importance to a clear understanding of those problems as that which Mr. Murphy has made." "It is impossible to overpraise such a book—to overestimate the effects of its poise, its sanity, its wisdom," wrote *The Louisville Post. The New York Tribune* found it "a valuable contribution to the literature of American statesmanship," while *The New York Times Saturday Review* praised Murphy's "coolness of judgment, sustained impartiality, and . . . constant regard for the teachings of history, science, and common sense." *The Southern Workman*, the Hampton Institute publication, was thankful that "a man brought up in the South and so thoroughly loyal to its traditions, has been able to state Southern needs so forcefully." The reviewer was most impressed with his nationalism, his indictment of white ignorance of Negroes, and his assertion that a permanent dependent class cannot exist in a democracy.[53]

The views of individuals were equally rewarding. Baldwin wrote Murphy,[54] "It is the greatest statement of the Southern Social and economic forces that has appeared. I was lost in admiration of your calm, clear, comprehensive statement." Washington stated, "It is refreshing as well as encouraging to find a writer who discusses the South and the race question with the temper of a judge and the manner of a scholar. . . . Nothing in the way of a 'review' can do the book justice."[55] The venerable Carl Schurz said he read the book "with the greatest delight. Your argument for negro education is overwhelming in power, and I can only hope that every intelligent person in the country might read it."[56] Secretary of State John Hay wrote that despite constant interruptions he read the book twice,

> . . . and I feel that I must, in common honesty, send you a word to let you know how deeply I am indebted to you for the

pleasure and profit I have found in it. I have read nothing referring to the vital question it discusses at all comparable with your book in vigor, fairness, and lucidity. I hope it may have wide circulation, especially among the young men of the South and of the North.[57]

Murphy was so pleased with Hay's letter that he sent a copy to Wallace Buttrick, Secretary of the General Education Board, who replied, "it is worth living and working for a life time to get such a letter. . . . I rejoice with you,—in fact . . . I am proud of you."[58]

Others did more than merely praise the work. In the summer of 1905, George Foster Peabody claimed "the privilege" of purchasing the first 1,000 copies of a paperback edition for gratis distribution.[59] Then, in recognition of the contribution made by *The Present South* and his other works, Yale University bestowed the honorary Master of Arts degree on Murphy at its commencement exercises, June 29, 1904. The citation referred to him as "a Southerner whom North and South alike are glad to honor," and continued,

> Known before as an able writer on religious subjects, his recent book on *The Present South* is a contribution to the discussion of the vital needs of that portion of our country, which is of unmatched and permanent value. As a crusader against Child Labor, his service has been national in character. . . . A constructive statesman and philanthropist who is rendering original, unique and powerful service to both white and black, in North and South.[60]

Murphy was delighted with the recognition he attained but was disappointed with the few letters received from Negroes. He lamented the fact that publishers did not send works to Negro newspapers and that many Negroes might feel that he, as a Southern white man, would not care to hear their views. He knew that there "were hundreds of colored men and women of intellect and good character upon whom we must depend for the expression of the best forces of negro life and feeling," and he resolved to communicate with them.[61]

Though Murphy may have failed to reach a large Negro audience, he succeeded in influencing many prominent Northern white men. Among these was Ogden, who avidly read *The Present South* and sent copies to "influential friends." Since 1900, and through contact with Murphy's philosophy, Ogden had come to believe much more strongly that federal intervention in the South would create more problems than it would solve. This view was sharpened and sustained by reading *The Present South*. He noted with satisfaction the great pressure being placed on President Roosevelt to keep the disfranchisement issue out of the 1904 presidential campaign. The President ignored the issue in his speech and letter of acceptance following the Republican convention, and Ogden concluded that the plank advocating federal investigation "was smuggled into the Republican platform without the knowledge of Mr. Roosevelt or even Henry Cabot Lodge."[62]

Ogden personally refrained from writing the President until after the election, but then he fully expressed his views. He commended Roosevelt for his silence on the plank, commenting that this had kept the issue out of the campaign. Had the question arisen, Ogden believed, it would have played into the hands of Southern demagogues and interrupted "the quiet power of the constructive educational work" being done in the South. Northerners advocating congressional action were "either mistaken or reckless," and in a phrase that could have been written by Murphy, he declared, "The vital solvent must come from the best South," a class of "splendid, patriotic and national men of statesmanlike quality." Slavery had harmed the poor Southern white as much as the Negro, and education offered the only solution to his racial bias. In the interim, prejudice must not be nourished by Northern opposition. Ogden feared enforcement of the Fourteenth Amendment would be "the Negro's undoing," and Negro punishment would follow reduction of Southern representation. The forced abolition of all education tests would see a "crowding of ignorant voters upon the registry and a dangerous demoralization of the suffrage." Ogden advised the President, "Philosophers, not politicians, are needed in the treatment of the Fourteenth Amendment."[63]

Roosevelt replied "his present feeling" was that Ogden was correct, but he could not speak for the future. He asked him to write Senator Warner Miller,[64] but Ogden considered Miller to be of insufficient consequence to "educate" on the matter. He believed him a demagogue, "not quite as bad as Vardaman or Davis of Arkansas, but . . . largely in the same class," and suspected his only interest in the Negro was notoriety and political support.

Immediately after the 1904 election, Washington also used his potent influence with Roosevelt to prevent punitive measures against the South. "The time is now here when we shall have to take a decided stand upon the question of reduction of Southern representation as a cure for our present ills," he wrote T. Thomas Fortune, editor of *The New York Age.* "In advising the President on the proposition I took the same ground as you take, that reduction of Southern representation will not help us, and he agrees to advocate that view of the case." Washington feared federal action would, in effect, be "legalizing a wrong done the Negro in the South" and would encourage such states as West Virginia and Indiana to disfranchise their Negroes. If Fortune would write strong editorials on the subject, he felt there would be little trouble in "getting the other Afro-American journals to assist."[65]

Ogden was convinced that there would be no action by the present or succeeding Congresses. "The point to which we should now address ourselves," he wrote Murphy, "is such control of the situation as to eliminate acrimonious discussion." To aid in this mission, he contacted a number of political leaders in New York and in the Congress. Moreover, he had a copy of Murphy's article, "Shall the Fourteenth Amendment be Enforced?" presented personally to the President by Shaw.[66] Although it cannot be said that Murphy's plea determined the President's policy, it does appear to have carried great weight, and Roosevelt wrote him, "I have grown accustomed to looking to you as one of the men to follow in reference to the Negro question."[67]

Unlike the President, *The New York Evening Post* paid little attention to Murphy's racial views, although it respected him as a social reformer. In a January, 1905, editorial, it praised him but at the same time criticized the President for not enforcing the civil rights amendments. This distressed Murphy, who feared the editorial would be misinterpreted by Southerners. He wrote Villard, "To put me in the attitude of being unfair to the South means the weakening of my influence *for the very ends* that *you* have at heart," and jeopardized the accumulated influence of years. "Deeply as I value your approval I would rather have you fight me than to have you praise me to the prejudice of my position among my people." He loved the Southern people, and, although they made mistakes, they were "sound at the core"; given the right leadership they would continue to improve. While respecting Villard's courage and many of his policies, Murphy considered his racial views untenable, writing, "I fear and fight the extremists of the North as frankly as I fear and fight the extremists of the South."[68] Villard replied that he believed "thoroughly in extremists, when their views are based upon the principles in the teachings of Christ."[69]

Another controversy arose when Murphy criticized A. B. Hart, Professor of History at Harvard, whom Villard had served two years as a student assistant. Hart had congratulated Murphy on *The Present South*, stating that it threw a "flood of light upon many of the different reaches" of the Negro question. However, he had recently returned from the South where he found conditions worse than anticipated, and, after visiting migrants to the Black Belt, he proposed to write a full account of Southern conditions. He enclosed four articles with his letter which he acknowledged were not "as moderate and careful of phrase" as Murphy's.

Murphy felt that Hart was a greater danger than Thomas Dixon. Dixon was a North Carolinian and had been a brilliant student at Wake Forest and Johns Hopkins before beginning a remarkable career as a Baptist minister, which attracted, among others, John D. Rockefeller. He resigned from the ministry in 1899 and in the next eight years wrote three of the most fabulously successful racist novels —*The Leopard's Spots*, *The Clansman* (which became the basis of the 1915 movie, "The Birth of a Nation"), and *The Traitor*.[70] Murphy had the utmost contempt for Dixon and believed all knowledgeable people were coming to share his views. But Hart was different since he held a responsible position, moved among gentlemen, and his well expressed opinions did much to make "the South feel more bitterly toward the North and toward the negroes." Murphy believed "that each section is chiefly concerned about the exaggerations of the other section rather than about its own," but the South had shown a greater tendency to criticize "its extremists" than the North.[71]

The work of extremists had its effect, and, in the spring of 1906, Murphy had never seen "the 'race' situation so bad. Our narrow people do not surprise me," he wrote. "The saddest phase of it, however, is the despair of our truest, broadest and best."[72] Due to changing Southern attitudes, Murphy advised Washington to spend two years "addressing gatherings of *both* races at the South" to present "the Tuskegee story." Washington did not fail to venture into the heart of opposition territory as time and resources permitted, and his combination of humility and common sense, and his flattery of the whites usually won the appreciation of his audiences. While he did gain good will for the Negro and was a force in the prevention of the division of educational funds by tax receipts from each race, he and his friends overestimated his long range influence as a speaker. For example, following a successful address in Macon, Georgia, he forwarded a laudatory editorial to Murphy and told him, "This illustrates the change of feeling I could bring about in most every section of the South, if I had the time and strength, and the institution had the money to permit me to do this kind of work." Murphy urged him to make a national appeal for financial aid and even cut some work at Tuskegee, if necessary. "I think the *most* important thing just now (even for the sake of the Institution) is the restoration and extension of your influence at the South. I say this because *you can do it*, you can now do a work for both races, for their better understanding of each other, and for our whole country that no other man can do."[73] Though unable to follow Murphy's advice fully, Washington devoted much time to his one-man crusades. One of the most colorful and successful came in Mississippi in 1908, where he directly challenged Vardaman's attack on Negro education. In spite of some newspaper appeals for whites to stay away and warnings that his life was in danger, he drew large, responsive crowds. He so thoroughly discredited Vardaman's pleas to end appropriations for Negro schools that they were never used effectively again.[74]

In 1907 Murphy's concern with Southern leadership induced him to write "The Task of the Leader," which he submitted to Washington for approval before publication in *The Sewanee Review*.[75] In this he revealed his contempt for many of the new business leaders who had turned on the Negro and formed an alliance with the poorer whites, and he made a romantic appeal to the legendary Southern aristocracy to save society. Murphy felt the "burden of intelligence and character" required the former planters to lead the South in all its affairs. This demanded an altruism rare to humanity, but the Southern aristocracy "possessed the deeper qualities of reserve, magnanimity, of a well-considered patience" equal to the task. Praising the aristocracy, he wrote:

> Between the mental attitude of the man who was born to the knowledge of the negro as a slave, and the attitude of mind in which there is a simple and evident pleasure in a worthy negro's economic independence and industrial success, in which schooling is claimed for his children and a free suffrage is welcomed for the man, there is a transition full of a certain heroic significance. Some may read it a triumph for the North; others may read in it a triumph for the negro. But there are those who may not fail to read in it—as they take acount [*sic*] of the deeper values and struggles of our human nature—an even larger triumph for the spiritual resources of the South.[76]

Murphy maintained that the aristocracy must lead the Southern people to a democratic way of life and believed the result would be much happier than if democracy came as "the artificial, unstable product of mechanical and coercive processes." He questioned, is "a forced democracy democracy at all?"

The Southern racial problem was not a strange phenomenon. In many ways it was a form of class conflict, prevalent in all areas at all times, and it was intensified by the relative strength of divergent groups. Although self-interest demanded racial tranquility if industry were to be attracted, education flourish, and society progress, the solution of racial problems could never be trusted to self-interest. Magnanimity, adaptability, and a sense of proportion were also required. These aristocratic virtues could never predominate in a society dominated by a new middle class unless the moral strength of aristocratic leadership could be accepted and emulated by the more numerous group. Murphy hoped this would occur and that as a result "a more reasoned and more consistent policy" implementing aristocratic ideals would emerge. While having faith in the "Old South," he urged the Southern leadership to respect the opinion of mankind everywhere, "knowing that no people can ever wisely stand outside of the context of its century and civilization." Although it would protect white children from immediate contact with inferior Negroes, it would also insure "that the weakest and lowliest of every race shall have in the interest of all, not a hothouse chance, not opportunities without grievances, but the best chance which can be wrested from that fate which has bound us to a common soil."[77]

Undoubtedly Murphy ascribed qualities and degrees of virtue to the Southern aristocracy that it never possessed. In his romantic appeal an entire stratum of society was called upon to become altruistic and sacrifice itself for the common good. The historian may well question if this has ever occurred. Equally important, he failed to realize that the old aristocracy was dead, and those who most effectively kept vigil at its altar were stripped of the economic and political power to do what he asked. He was nearer to an accomplishable goal when he called on the new middle class to accept aristocratic leaders and emulate aristocratic virtues, since the myth of the Southern aristocracy proved irresistible to the new, aspiring classes. Yet they had no intention of self-renunciation of power, and those former aristocrats who rose to leadership did so by acquiring bourgeois attitudes and principles.

Despite weaknesses, "The Task of the Leader" was a noble appeal, and it correctly diagnosed many of the South's ills even if its remedies were unattainable. Washington was one of the first to congratulate

Murphy on it, writing, "Your impressive analysis of Southern conditions and your clear-cut ambitions, which are intended to benefit all of the people of this section, have always enlisted my cordial approval." Even Villard expressed accord with the article and asked for additional copies.[78]

While dealing with race relations, Murphy was suddenly confronted by a specific issue in 1907—the suggestion that a separate Negro episcopate be created in the Episcopal Church. He believed its establishment would be a departure from the traditional custom of the church and a serious mistake. He developed his views fully in a letter sent to a member of the House of Bishops, in which he averred that the Negro's condition was an impermanent one, and that it would be a grave error for "any branch of the Catholic Church [to] meet a temporarily abnormal situation by organic provisions which must be permanent in their effect." All true friends of the Negro hoped to see him adopt the higher standards associated with the best of white society; to segregate his religious leadership could only serve to perpetuate the conditions the Church must try to minimize.

Murphy suspected that much of the support for the proposal came from those who wished to see the Negro fail. They wanted something less than full diocesan Negro bishops—either missionary, assistant, or suffragan bishops chosen by someone other than the Negroes themselves. Here was the plan's great weakness. Would any man worthy to be a bishop be content with such a status for himself and his people? "The Church of the past has known something of 'suffragan' bishops, but not of the permanent establishment of a 'suffragan' people," and it could not now afford to become more reactionary than the state. "Why go to these elaborate plans merely to put our race discriminations into a new and more obnoxious form?"

Murphy's concept of the Catholic faith enabled him to see the proposal's danger to the white man as well as the Negro. "There is not a white man anywhere who does not know that his own Church would be a smaller and shallower inheritance if it fixed its limits short of the limits of humanity, and if it were forced to conceive of its offices and its privileges in the terms of class." He pleaded for acceptance of the

Negro as a full-fledged member of the Body of Christ instead of attempting to hide the problem by making "a scapegoat of the organization we have inherited." He felt recall of the role assumed by another chief minister to an alien people should resolve the question. "Imagine St. Paul as a 'suffragan' or as a modern 'missionary bishop,' holding his jurisdiction at the discretion and under the limitations enacted by another race, and representing a vague constituency of the ecclesiastically disfranchised!"[79]

Influenced by Murphy, the General Convention of the Episcopal Church wisely defeated the proposal. He wrote, "Much of the muss has been due to a sheer lack of intellectual capacity; so many men can see around *one* corner; so few men have the statesmanship to see around two." Upon reflection, he added, "The brazen self-appreciation in that sentence would be humiliating if it were not so amusing!"

Although his livelihood was earned in the ministry and later as an officer of the Southern Education Board, "an inordinate amount" of Murphy's time over the years was devoted to racial matters. For his era and region, he wrote and spoke intelligently, effectively, and progressively on the subject, although he was mistaken in his faith in white Southern fairness and ascribed more power to aristocratic leadership than it possessed. Much of his time and energy was spent in personal conversations and letter writing known to but a few. "I sometimes wonder if it pays," he wrote, "and yet as I look back, in detail, and note the changes here and there in policy and expression on the part of our journalists and public men, I think that no work has counted more deeply. . . ."[80]

5.

The Southern
Education Board

As HE DEALT with the race question, constitutional reform, child labor, and other issues, Murphy came increasingly to believe that a lack
of adequate education was the principal factor in all Southern problems. He knew from the census of 1900 that 1,176,976 of 2,472,895
Southern white children between the ages of five and twenty were not
in school, and that the South's 262,590 young (10 to 19) native white
illiterates were a national disgrace.[1] One-fifth of Southern white children were completely illiterate, and the percentage of Southern illiteracy was as great in 1900 as it had been in 1850. Distressingly, there
was little hope for improvement since one-fifth of the white children
and one-half of the Negroes never attended school; approximately the
same percentage was illiterate. Of 217 counties in the nation in which
20 per cent of the white men of voting age could not read and write
in 1900, 212 were in the South.[2] John C. Kilgo, President of Trinity
College, described Southern school attendance "as a sort of pastime,
a good thing to do when nothing else may be done."[3]

Yet only through education could a skilled working class be formed
and farmers taught creative production—essentials if the shackles of
Southern poverty were to be removed. Only through education was
there hope that the democratic system would function properly—that
the voice of the demagogue would be stilled and all Southern people
enabled to participate intelligently in their own government. As S. C.

Mitchell, President of the University of South Carolina, asserted, "Industrialism and democracy are twins."[4]

Knowledge of the need for Southern education was not a twentieth century development. Schooling was one of the freedman's passions, and the establishment of state school systems was one of the most important achievements of Reconstruction. Unfortunately, the Redeemers did not have equal enthusiasm, and through the failure to provide leadership they allowed many of the promising beginnings of the immediate post-war years to be lost.

Despite this, determined efforts to improve conditions were made by forces in both the North and South, with much of the Northern interest concentrating on the Negro. As early as 1867 the international financier, George Peabody, elder cousin of George Foster Peabody, contributed one million dollars to aid Southern education; known as the Peabody Fund, it was augmented by another million in 1869. At first the Peabody Fund concentrated on grants-in-aid to local primary schools, and, in its earlier years, an historian estimated that it "produced in effect ten times its financial value on the public school system of the South." In the late 1880's, however, due to a great extent to the convictions of former President Rutherford B. Hayes, the Peabody Fund chairman, much effort was devoted to higher education. The Slater Fund, founded in 1882, was under Hayes' chairmanship from its inception, and in 1891, when the Peabody agent, J. L. M. Curry, became the Slater agent also, the two funds were closely coordinated. The results achieved were commendable but not outstanding. The moneys available were limited and provision was made for expenditure of their principals within two to three decades. Moreover, until 1891 the Slater Fund diffused its appropriations to so many schools that little was accomplished. Particularly unfortunate was the Peabody Fund's acceptance of the "Jim Crowism" from earlier years, and Curry, although an advocate of the older paternalistic Southern racial views, favored those Negro schools specializing in manual training.[5] It is ironic that the stated goal of the Slater Fund, "Universal Suffrage, Universal Education" was becoming impossible to attain due to Negro disfranchisement at the very time the philosophy became more widely accepted in both North and South.

Perhaps this situation could have been avoided had there been federal aid to Southern education before the repressive legislation of the 1890's was enacted. A golden oportunity was lost when Congress defeated four Blair Bills between 1881 and 1890. Had the Blair Bill been enacted, apportioning allocations on the basis of illiteracy, the South would have received a majority of the funds and a tremendous educational stimulus. Although Southern opposition to the measures increased in the late 1880's, as Allen Going has shown, the proposal "was acceptable to the dominant leadership of the lower South, where the largest Negro concentration existed." Generally, the Redeemers were for the plan, but it was killed "by a combination of border and northern Democrats, by agrarians, state right southerners, and ultimately by Republican leadership."[6]

No one realized more than Murphy the titanic problems Southern conditions posed for those who wished universal education. Eighty-five per cent of the South's people lived in rural areas, and, to further complicate matters, they were often scattered over such large districts and so inadequately united by poor roads that the unit cost of quality education was many times that in Northern cities. Segregation enormously increased difficulties since it required the maintenance of two school systems; however, in reality, the education given Negroes was incomparable to that given whites. Omnipresent Southern poverty was also a basic difficulty. At the end of the Civil War, Massachusetts alone had half as much taxable property as the entire South. Proportionately, Southern states spent more on education than other states, but their efforts were insufficient. Alabama and the Carolinas gave 50 per cent of their state revenue to education, but expended only $4.50 a year per pupil, while the national average was $21.14.[7]

While fully cognizant of these conditions, Murphy knew that the Southern states must do more, both state-wide and in local districts. In the 1880's George Washington Cable had made the same contention. When informed that the Southern states allocated more per capita and that Massachusetts had seven and one-half times the per capita wealth of North and South Carolina and Arkansas, he replied that this only demonstrated that Massachusetts should spend more.

Subtly, he suggested that comparisons should be made between agricultural states of similar population. This would reveal that Arkansas, though the poorest Southern state and with a greater proportion of children in the population than North or South Carolina, spent almost twice as much per capita, even though less than two-thirds of her children were in school. Equally revealing, he pointed out that Iowa, with taxable property two and one-fifth times that of Arkansas, expended five times per capita that of the Southern state. After considering the sources of school revenue, Cable concluded "in such a State as Iowa or Kansas the burden, from 4 to 11 times as heavy per capita as in any Southern State, falls more wholly on the tax-payer than it does anywhere in the South." He assumed that much of the explanation for the situation lay in Southern racism, and Murphy completely accepted his criticism of those who opposed Negro education and sought a division of educational appropriations by racial tax contributions. They failed to recognize that society is one and that public education is a "paying investment" of the taxpayer.[8]

At the end of the century it was obvious that little could be done to improve Southern education without "the liberalization of opinion," as Walter Hines Page described it. Like Murphy, he had unbounded faith in the average Southerner, and he referred to the "common country people" as the "better class of people." Since the publication of his famous "Mummy Letters" in 1886, Page had been attacking the reactionary leaders of Southern society—the ministers, politicians, and editors—who failed to provide the leadership the masses needed.[9] In 1897 he delivered his renowned lecture on "The Forgotten Man" at the Normal and Industrial College for Women in Greensboro, North Carolina. In its eloquent plea for the freeing of the masses of Southern whites and especially Southern women from ignorance and poverty, it became a classic appeal that did much to inspire the Southern education revival.

In choosing to set forth clearly his diagnosis of Southern ills in his native North Carolina, an area he loved despite its weaknesses, Page chose a state on the brink of an educational renaissance and one where determined efforts had been made since the early 1880's to arouse the people to response to educational needs. Some date the state's progress from 1881 when Edward P. Moses inaugurated a graded school system in Goldsboro, but the true founders were at that time undergraduates at the University of North Carolina. The handsome, articulate, urbane Edwin A. Alderman, the crusading, ambitious Charles B. Aycock, and the energetic, popular Charles D. McIver, at times referred to as a "steam engine in breeches," formed a cordial triumvirate. Progressive on all except the racial issue, they were worthy disciples of Page and of Josephus Daniels, whose *Raleigh News and Observer* was the herald of a new era in the state. Following graduation, all three men devoted much of their lives to public education. Aycock served a term as Superintendent of the Wayne County schools, was chairman of the Board of Trustees of the Goldsboro Graded Schools throughout much of his career, and was elected Governor of North Carolina in 1900 on a platform promising a revolution in the state's education system. Alderman and McIver were to a great extent responsible for the stimulation of public sentiment making Aycock's election possible and, even more significantly, they developed a technique which was to become the basis for the Southern educational awakening. After holding public school positions, they concluded that teachers must be imbued with professional zeal and the public aroused to education's needs. For three years, from 1889 to 1892, they conducted five-day teachers' institutes and addressed mass rallies throughout the state. As a result, appropriations for schools were modestly increased, denominational efforts to cripple public higher education were withstood, and in 1892 the Normal and Industrial College for Women was established with McIver as President. Alderman held the college's newly established professorship of education until he became President of the University of North Carolina in 1896.[10]

While the North Carolina triumvirate was continuing its struggle at home, a national movement arose that was to utilize its leadership and methods. From his Alabama pastorate, Murphy watched this trend with great interest, little realizing that within a few years he would become one of its principal leaders. Plans for the movement were laid in 1897 by the Reverend Edward Abbott, Rector of St. James' Church, Cambridge, Massachusetts, after conferring with Hollis Burke Frissell. Distressed by the conditions he had seen in the

South and impressed with the results of the Lake Mohawk Indian Conference, which sought to utilize the forces of philanthropy to aid a minority group, he proposed that a similar gathering in behalf of Christian education be held at Capon Springs, West Virginia, in 1898. As a result, thirty-six educational leaders, half of whom were clergymen, gathered to discuss Southern needs in the First Conference for Christian Education in the South. Frissell, as Chairman of the Resolutions Committee, presented a realistic report calling for national support as a public duty to aid in the education of the "needy of both races." He thanked Northern philanthropists for their aid, but cautioned that coordination and cooperation among Southern educators were essential if quality education was to be achieved. Stressing that "thoroughness in elementary education is of the first importance," he urged immediate steps be taken to provide longer school terms, qualified teachers, and industrial education.[11]

In 1899 Frissell's leadership attracted to the Second Capon Springs Conference on Christian Education in the South Northern philanthropists and Southern leaders who were to direct the education revival for the next decade and a half. Among the Northerners were George Foster Peabody, Albert Shaw, and Robert C. Ogden, who was elected Vice-President. The venerable dean of Southern educators, J. L. M. Curry, led a group of distinguished Southerners and was elected President. He presented a "Survey of the Field," which was well supplemented by an excellent paper analyzing the cooperative relations of various agencies dealing with Southern educational work given by G. S. Dickerman, a Connecticut Congregational clergyman working at Hampton Institute.

The 1899 conference initiated a new approach to Southern education problems. Realizing that confrontation through the churches was too narrow, it dropped the name Christian from its title, becoming simply the Conference for Education in the South, and, in a momentous decision, resolved that the education of the white race in the South was "the pressing and imperative need." Thus at the very beginning the Negro was relegated to a secondary role in the Southern educational awakening. Certainly the humanitarians at Capon Springs did so in the belief that ultimately this was the only way the Negro could be helped, but they were mistaken even as the progressive supporters of the "Atlanta Compromise" were in the political realm. There was no mistake, however, in the conference's belief that Northern philanthropy should be increased and steps taken to prevent its improper use. It proposed coordination of the leading funds and that grants be made only on the basis of accurate information. To further this goal, Dickerman was employed to investigate educational conditions, under Curry's guidance, and report the following year.[12]

Murphy planned to attend the 1900 conference and began preparation of a paper for presentation, but illness intervened. At this meeting his friend Ogden was elected President, a position held until his death in 1913, and the secularization and expansion begun earlier were accelerated. Much of the progress was due to Dickerman's exhaustive address, which outlined the need for Southern elementary schools and urged a concentration of forces to establish and expand them. Ogden accepted the report and continued the theme in a plea for "the education of the plain people throughout the Southland." He proposed to "urgently" bring the issue "before the business men of the South as a business proposition."[13]

Ogden as president converted the conference into a much more effective organization. Sensing that a small gathering at Capon Springs would be too isolated to generate enthusiasm, he moved the 1901 meeting to Winston-Salem, North Carolina, and brought a special train of Northern philanthropists as guests. Many Southern professional educators made their first appearance, and Ogden's vision of a cooperative effort began to function.

Among the Southerners present were McIver, Alderman, recently chosen President of Tulane University, and Charles W. Dabney, President of the University of Tennessee, who, encouraged by Frissell, had come to obtain the establishment of an information and propaganda bureau, which he had tried unsuccessfully to found within the Southern Educational Association.[14]

The basis for successful intersectional cooperation was laid through a public renunciation of major concern with Negro education. This came in an address by Dickerman in which he held that Negro education prospered most "not where the negroes are most numerous, but where the whites are in the majority and have given the community something of an intellectual character." Thus by focusing on white education, he proposed to eventually aid the Negro. On much more solid ground, he contended that the best public schools were partially supported by local taxation levied by an awakened local opinion. To obtain this, he suggested that Southern men lead the educational revival and that Northern aid be increased but kept in the background. "The men on the ground are in the foremost place. They know the situation. They are familiar with conditions. They have sharpened instincts to sense the meaning of things that would be a snare to others. [Being] In agreement with them is strength. We have to wait for these master spirits of the South to bring in the new order. . . ."[15]

It is amazing that men like Dickerman, who had a genuine concern with Negro advancement, formulated this policy. Undoubtedly they overestimated the strength of Southern racial moderates such as Murphy and Page, and it was perhaps inevitable that they would make the same compromise with the white South which political leaders so warmly embraced.

Provision for the conference's further organization was made at Winston-Salem and reflected both the racial policy of the group and an acceptance of the strategy succeeding in North Carolina. By resolution the Conference for Education in the South authorized the choosing of eight men, including the president, to form an executive board, which came to be known as the Southern Education Board, whose main duties were:

1. To conduct a campaign of education for free schools for all the people, by supplying literature to the newspapers and periodical press, by participation in education meetings and by general correspondence; and

2. To conduct a Bureau of Information and Advice on Legislation and School Organization.

The board was authorized to "raise and disburse funds, to employ a secretary or agent, and do whatever was necessary to implement its functions."[16]

Recognizing the importance of the project, Ogden moved cautiously. In August an informal group of members met at Morris K. Jesup's Bar Harbor home; included were Ogden and a number of Southerners. They concluded that much energy and time were lost through lack of coordination of philanthropic agencies and that generous gifts would be available if Southern conditions were publicized. On September 13, 1901, Frissell conferred on the meeting's results with McIver and Dabney in Greensboro. These three then traveled to Asheville and met with Curry, who had been detained by family illness. All agreed that the Southern Education Board members should be officially appointed and that a New York session should be held in November to meet with representatives of the Peabody and Slater boards.[17]

Ogden appointed Curry, Dabney, Aldermen, Frissell, McIver, Peabody, and Wallace Buttrick, an Albany, New York, Baptist clergyman later to be the secretary of the soon-to-be-formed General Education Board, to the Southern Education Board, which began a week's session on November 4, 1901, in Ogden's office. It elected Ogden, president, McIver, secretary, Peabody, treasurer, and Albert Shaw, William H. Baldwin, Jr., and Walter Hines Page as additional members. Interspersing its meetings with luncheons and dinners at the city's most exclusive clubs, the board in earnest sessions quickly transacted much important business. It held informal meetings with representatives of the leading educational funds and received assurance of their cooperation. It elected Curry general supervisor of administration, and to aid in obtaining its main goal, the arousing of public opinion, it established a Bureau of Investigation and Information under Dabney and a Campaign Committee composed of Curry, Dabney, Frissell, Alderman, and McIver to direct campaigns to arouse popular support for education in specific states.[18] A budget of $40,000 was adopted for both 1902 and 1903, $12,000 for use by the Bureau of Investigation and Information and most of the remainder for campaigns in Virginia, North Carolina, Georgia, and Louisiana. It was specifically decreed that no money would be given any institution or school, "but it shall be expended exclusively for the purpose of stimulating public sentiment in favor of more liberal provision for universal education in the public schools of the South." Dickerman and Booker T. Washington were appointed field agents at salaries of $1,000 a year,[19] and Ogden was empowered to select an executive secretary "who should be his assistant and personal representative wherever the President should desire to use him."[20]

Ogden, believing the board's work to be primarily "educational evangelization," felt that the executive secretaryship was the position he had been seeking for Murphy in which they could work together to implement their common ideals, so he offered him the job at a salary of $3,000 a year. "I hesitate to place any argument before you in favor of this work, as the interests of your own life and family are so deeply concerned that I am not disposed to advise until requested," he wrote, but since Murphy was the only man he knew that was suited to the job, he could "create his own place" and would be "the de facto President."[21]

The position offered the opportunity to work with Ogden in behalf of the whole South for which Murphy had longed. He was aware that the South, with 25 per cent of the nation's people, received only 3 per cent of educational contributions, and he knew that initially the board could obtain a minimum of $100,000 a year for Southern schools from Northern philanthropists. Moreover, he thought that wealthy Southerners would share their resources and that the masses could be awakened to their responsibility of providing adequate tax revenue. He agreed that emphasis must be placed on the education of middle and lower class whites and that the Southern Education Board afforded the best means of uniting the resources of all America in the endeavor. Therefore, he presented his resignation to a called meeting of St. John's vestry on November 27, 1901. Closing his successful three-year rectorship and taking up the new work involved many sacrifices and, after much soul searching, he stated that he did so as "my best response to God's will, and to the needs of our church and our country." Wherever he might be, his intense concern and prayers for the "noble and historic parish" he had come to love would continue. "No priest ever had a more loyal people. May God help me to pay back something of this debt."

The vestry, which had always worked in harmony with Murphy,

accepted his resignation with great reluctance and aptly described him as one whose interest in others made him "marked among men." The Bishop of Alabama, the Rt. Rev. Richard W. Barnwell, summarized the attitude of the parish and diocese when he characterized the resignation as "a calamity."[22]

In resigning as Rector of St. John's, Murphy did not abandon Montgomery. He always considered it home, returned as often as he could, used it as his permanent address on all his stationary, and enrolled his sons from Montgomery when they entered college. But his new job required him to go East at once, and he was given an office in Ogden's New York building where the two could easily confer. Maud and the children spent the winter of 1901–1902 with his mother in San Antonio and moved to Concord, Massachusetts, in the spring. Since Murphy's time was valuable and his health poor, they moved to New Haven in 1904 for a five-year residence. The two-hour train trip from New York was more convenient than the difficult journey to Concord, and, an additional inducement came when William Lewis Elkins, Murphy's second cousin and the Director of the Yale Observatory, insisted they live in his empty house purchased for use after retirement. Elkins and his wife, who lived in a university residence, were the Murphys' closest friends, and they thoroughly enjoyed being neighbors.[23]

When he assumed his new duties, Murphy gave a rationale for his action in a newspaper interview. Pointing to illiteracy, he proclaimed that backward people "constitute in large measure the neglected wealth" of the region. He foresaw, with proper leadership, that the whole country would become aware of the South as an area for educational investment and proclaimed that no finer sentiment existed than that of Northern philanthropists who came to its aid. They were "attempting to do personally what the nation has not done officially," and their motive was not " 'Charity' but 'Patriotism.' " He assured his readers that the work of the Southern Education Board was based on three assumptions: (1) In educational work, exclusive concern with the Negro was a mistake. The North should not draw a racial line any more than the South; (2) Southern men who knew conditions should develop the educational policies for their area; (3) The fundamental work must be done with the masses of white people. The federal government freed the slave but did nothing to prepare him for his new life. The presence of the Negro reduced money for white education and primarily accounted "for the backwardness of education among our poorer classes." Now Northern philanthropy combined with Southern leadership offered a good chance of success.[24]

Privately, Murphy assumed his new responsibilities "with some misgivings," as he had little educational experience per se, but his broad cultural background, conciliatory manner, personal friendships, and knowledge of men ideally fitted him for the position. Embarrassed by the laudatory nature of some newspaper accounts, he said, "I hope no member of the Board will think they are the result of any wish of mine. Our daily journals personalize and vulgarize so much of all they touch that 'publicity' is not an unmixed blessing."[25]

Murphy's fears were not unfounded, since some members of the board felt the newspaper release had been unwise. For this reason, Frissell was most pleased when a fine tribute was paid Murphy at the December meeting of the Southern Educational Association.[26] Henceforth Murphy remained singularly free of criticism throughout his board career. He carefully avoided overstepping his authority and even refused to instruct Washington on his duties when asked, referring him to Curry or Ogden. He and Ogden cooperated fully, and, while Murphy did not repress his views, he never attempted to modify Ogden's desires once a decision had been made.[27] The strong willed but unselfish Ogden dominated the board as he did the conference by the strength of his personality and the confidence he engendered. To him Southern education became a holy cause to which he devoted much of his time and a share of his $100,000 yearly salary. His main weapon "in all his record of achievement was absolute self-forgetfulness," wrote Alderman. "I have never known a man intimately who won such fine pleasure and happiness through complete self-surrender." Page concurred, declaring that he knew no one else "who had such a genius for helping others and for inspiring men to help one another."[28]

The obstructions and limitations the movement encountered were distressing to Ogden and Murphy. "The very little good South; the very broad prejudiced South; the radical North, little understanding the true conditions" were all factors. Ogden doubted if there were one hundred men in the United States who were sincerely interested in the Southern question. Although not personally prejudiced, as evidenced by his entertaining Washington as a house guest through the years, he completely accepted the philosophy that the Southern Negro must wait for advancement until the white South had been enlightened. Like Murphy, he could not conceive of repression continuing as the masses were educated. He did not foresee that education would simply provide a more sophisticated rationale for segregation. "We cannot meet the views of our colored friends and must be content to be greatly misunderstood for the sake of the greater usefulness," he advised Villard. However, he was distressed by what he felt he must do. For fear of offending the white South, he consistently refused to invite Negroes to the annual conferences, and of this he wrote, "I am greatly ashamed, but, nevertheless, it is worse than useless, at present, to quarrel with conditions we must accept because we cannot control."[29]

Southern misunderstanding and distrust of the educational movement was also a heartbreaking development. In part it sprang from dislike of Northern intrusion, a condition Murphy anticipated and which the board tried desperately to avoid by weighting its membership heavily with Southerners, by having campaigns constantly under Southern direction, and by a capitulation to Southern racial views. Ogden's plush, annual train excursions to the conferences, whose expenses he bore, were the only means he knew to inform and interest Northerners in Southern education, but they aroused jealousy and bitterness. The situation was not helped by journals like *The New York World*, which headlined (April 28, 1901) an account of one trip, "Men of Millions to Redeem the South." *The Charlotte News and Observer* (August 20, 1904) described the Ogden odysseys as invasions, and *The Manufacturers' Record* compared them to a "minstrel troop." The latter journal consistently furnished the most bitter opposition, which Ogden was unable to explain by "any theory consistent with sanity, or sincerity." Undoubtedly much of the opposition arose from Murphy's role and came from those forces which detested his efforts to control child labor. Ogden pointedly blamed "vested moneyed interests" that were seeking "to maintain the frightful conditions of child labor that prevail in some (not all) cotton mills." He scorned the use of the term "Ogden Movement" and declared, the "whole Southern educational movement comes from the superior and patriotic class of Southern people." Their role was completely ignored by such critics as *The Charleston News and Courier*, but formed the basis of much of the support given by such newspapers as *The Columbia State* and *The Raleigh News and Observer.*[30]

In all the attacks made on him and the board, Ogden demanded that no replies be made, and his commands were followed.[31] Instead, he preferred that Murphy and others present the positive aspects of its work. To further his preparation for this endeavor, Murphy, in January, 1902, visited Dabney at Knoxville, McIver at Greensboro, and Frissell at Hampton. Afterwards, much of his time was taken in selecting speakers for the April conference to be held in Athens, Georgia. In the interim, he, Ogden, and Baldwin discussed means to enlarge the scope of the board's work in the fall.[32]

The hope for all Southern education was greatly heightened in early 1902 by the organization of a new board that was a direct outgrowth of the educational movement. John D. Rockefeller, Jr. had attended the 1901 conference, where he was converted to the idea that Negro education depended on education of the whites. Following this, he interested his father, who had just established the Rockefeller Institute for Medical Research, in the plight of Southern education. Continuing to discuss the issue with leaders of the Southern board, on January 15, he met with Baldwin, Curry, Peabody, Ogden, Buttrick, and Jesup at Jesup's home and planned the establishment of a money-raising organization. In February the General Education Board was created, with Baldwin, Buttrick, Curry, Ogden, Page, Shaw, Rockefeller, Jr., D. C. Gilman, and Edwin M. Shephard as members; Baldwin became chairman and Buttrick executive secretary. The largely identical membership of the Southern and General Education boards insured the closest cooperation between the two. In 1904 Ogden became chairman for a year, and he was succeeded by Frederick T. Gates, the Baptist cleric and adviser who had persuaded the elder Rockefeller to start the University of Chicago in 1890. Buttrick became an incessant traveler—visiting schools, conferring with educators, and earning the affection of innumerable Southerners for himself and the General Education Board.

The General Education Board's function, to promote education through the provision of funds to worthwhile endeavors, was complementary to those of the Southern board, which sought to arouse public sentiment in both North and South. Many of the general board's gifts were "recommended and urged by the members of the Southern Education Board; probably not one of them would have been made over the protests of the Southern Board," Murphy wrote. The genius of the General Education Board's grants was their incentive to local initiative since they were contingent on local efforts. As Murphy expressed it, both boards existed "not because of what the South has failed to do, but in order to recognize and to meet what the South has done," and, he might have added, to stimulate it to do much more.

In its early years, the General Education Board's grants were small and of an exploratory nature; by the fall of 1903, $286,000 had been donated to teacher training and to rural and industrial schools. Thereafter, contributions to a wide variety of efforts increased rapidly; the Southern Education Board alone received $100,000 over a twelve-year period for operating expenses. By the time the last major grants were made in 1960, $136,491,002.05 had been appropriated from the income and $187,703,918.78 from the principal of the numerous Rockefeller contributions. The general board did not become a clearinghouse for gifts from other benefactors as the Rockefellers had hoped, but their contributions were great enough to make it one of the most important factors in shaping the Southern educational renaissance.[33]

At the time the General Education Board was being organized,

Murphy was again ill and was forced to spend several weeks as the guest of friends at the Grace Church rectory, New York. By April he was able to attend the 1902 Athens conference, to which he journeyed on the Ogden train.[34] It proved to be one of "mutual congratulations" over the organization of the two boards, and a revivalistic atmosphere prevailed throughout the meeting, from the singing of the opening song, "Blest Be the Tie that Binds." Announcement was made of fifty $50 scholarships to the Georgia State Normal School by the General Education Board and of a $40,000 gift from George F. Peabody to the University of Georgia Library. Encouraging reports were received from the district directors. McIver, speaking on the renewed campaign in North Carolina, outlined the goals being sought—consolidation of weak school districts, improvements of buildings, and adoption of local school taxes. His committee had furnished materials to every newspaper in the state and contacted every minister asking that sermons be preached in behalf of the crusade. District conferences were planned and speakers recruited to rouse the populace. Alderman, calling for all to join in the battle for taxation and Negro education, assured his audience that the Southern board wished to try nothing new but sought only to aid the forces at work.[35]

Following the Athens meeting, Murphy and Washington obtained $600 from the General Education Board for an Alabama educational conference, and Murphy went straight to Montgomery to direct the project. He appointed committees and guided them in preparation of the program, the first of many such programs of inspiration and education staged by the Southern Education Board.[36]

After the Montgomery conference, Murphy gave addresses in Birmingham, at the Alabama Polytechnic Institute at Auburn, the Alabama Educational Association, and presented the commencement sermon at the University of Tennessee. The Knoxville invitation revealed Dabney's high regard for Murphy, on whom he relied heavily for advice and as the author of the Bureau of Investigation and Information's most successful pamphlets. In April, 1902, Dabney confided that his work was proving difficult and that it was taking "all the love and patience" he could summon "to bear the trials and overcome the difficulties that arise out of the prejudice of people." Murphy urged him not to despair, stating, "All great enterprises are beset by trivial oppositions and ours is not an exception. Every expression of narrowness is just another argument for the education and the best education of all the people."[37] Dabney's bureau was under the immediate direction of Philander Priestly Claxton until the end of 1902 and Charles L. Coon until 1904, when its functions were assumed by the General Education Board. It issued 15,000 to 25,000 copies of biweekly circulars, and from March, 1902 to February, 1903, *Southern Education Notes* were distributed to newspapers throughout the South. Beginning in May, 1902, a series of well prepared and highly informative bulletins were published which did much to make known the facts regarding conditions.[38]

Among the best was *A Statement Concerning the Southern Education Board*, a reprint of Murphy's December newspaper interview. Another was *Progress Within the Year*, his description of the Summer School of the South, at Knoxville, an institution partially endowed by the General Education Board and organized by Dabney to attract students from throughout the South and to inspire them with the ideals of universal education. Students flocked to the campus as to a convention, and, although a number did not attempt the examinations required for credit, many teachers were indoctrinated for the new crusade. Alderman and McIver served as faculty members, and Page and Buttrick visited the school. As early as February, Murphy agreed to give a course in history, literature, or philosophy and to conduct the daily "platform exercises." His health forced him to limit himself to a visit, presiding at chapel for a week, and giving an address on modern poetry.[39] The school, the largest of its type in the world, enrolled 2,019 students. Philanthropy and the relative poverty of the South enabled it to have excellent teachers, zealous to advance the cause of learning, and the low registration fee of five dollars, the only charge for attendance, opened it to all interested white persons. Caught in the zeal of the movement, on July 4 the students solemnly met and adopted resolutions urging campaigns for local school taxes, consolidation of schools, the use of merit alone in teacher appointment, and the inclusion of agricultural and mechanical training in the school curriculum. Murphy believed that the "essential forces" of the school and the Southern Education Board were alike and wrote, "I have never witnessed anything finer in American life."[40]

Following his Knoxville stint, Murphy attended the Chattanooga meeting of an older, less effective organization than the Conference for Southern Education, and one at the time widely believed to be dominated by textbook agents—the Southern Educational Association. Following this he returned to New York, Concord, and the Massachusetts coast for the remainder of the summer of 1902. After several months of travel he had to rest a great deal, but all the while he gathered materials and organized plans for the work to be done. "I am trying to observe the earnest and wise advice you gave me," he wrote Peabody, "but I warn you that if I succeed in establishing a reputation for indolence and self-indulgence, I shall tell people who to blame!"[41]

The vacation was interrupted only by the summer meeting of the Southern board, the first of many hosted by Peabody at Abenia, his summer home on Lake George. At the sessions, Murphy, on Peabody's motion, was elected a member of the board and played a leading role in the meetings. He and Buttrick reported on the work in Alabama and, with Ogden, were authorized to convene a meeting of county superintendents in the state. All concurred in the selection of Richmond as the next annual conference site. Murphy was so impressed with Peabody's hospitality and his home that he produced a poem, "At Abenia," to celebrate the virtues of the board's retreat.[42]

In the fall, Murphy completed plans for the Alabama superintendents' meeting, including an address by Curry.[43] Next, he attempted to change the newly adopted board seal, a picture of Jefferson around which were the words "Preach A Crusade Against Ignorance," since he felt it embodied a negative approach. He was unsuccessful because the board felt the seal was distinctively Southern and that the use of Jefferson's picture would help with Democratic politicians.[44] Following this, Murphy delivered a major address on "The Task of the South" at Washington and Lee University in Lexington, Virginia. Although dealing extensively with the Negro problem, it was also a statement of the role of the Southern Education Board at the end of its first year, aimed at enlisting Southern support and overcoming criticism. As such it received wide publicity and did much to clarify the board's mission.

The Tuskegee philosophy permeated Murphy's thought, and he contended that for the white masses, as well as the Negroes, common schools must be provided which included practical, agricultural training applicable to everyday life. He chafed under the contempt sometimes expressed "for the poorer and humbler" whites, "an uncorrupted stock full of native vigor and native wit," declaring, "The fact remains that the merchant who scorns him is usually the first to ask his trade and that the politician who derides him is always the first to seek his vote." Since little immigration came into the region, it was fortunate that the poor whites possessed great potential. If the South was to flourish, they had to be educated and become effective producers and consumers.[45]

Murphy assumed that the vast majority agreed on the "necessity and policy" for white education, yet he warned a danger lay in the assumption that a work everyone agreed upon would be done. "There is in mere agreement no real dynamic of social progress. There is little moral power in the universal affirmation that two and two make four." Recognition of the immensity of the problem and the motivation of the people to action were the first responsibilities of the Southern Education Board. To those who through embarrassment sought to overlook the problem, Murphy asserted that Southern illiteracy, "due to historic and formidable forces," was no disgrace. "There would be disgrace, however, in a policy which would now perpetuate it by concealment and which would feed its indifference upon the husks of a flattering and senseless optimism."[46]

To those who opposed outside aid and cooperative effort, Murphy replied that these were essential if the South's educational needs were to be met. The sons and daughters of the wealthy benefited from philanthropy as they used the buildings and endowments of Harvard and Vassar. Why should the poorer people be deprived of similar benefits? Surely, if any children could rightly claim such aid it was those of the rural South, whose energies had been diverted by poverty, thinness of settlement, and "intense preoccupation with the problem of the Negro."

Murphy deplored the fact that the federal government freed the Negro and gave him the ballot before attempting to educate him. Under paternalistic influence the white South had taken up the task, and, as inadequate as it was, it had spent four dollars for every one contributed by Northern philanthropy. Under the circumstances, Northern investment in Southern education was not "the extension of 'charity'," as some proud critics claimed, but was "the acceptance of obligation." The Southern states must increase their local taxation for education, but, realizing that they lacked the resources to do the job, Northern philanthropy must also be obtained. But Murphy knew this would be insufficient also, and, overwhelmed by the needs and opportunities, he stifled his strong state's rights conscience and urged federal aid. "Our children are the nation's children," he stated. "In their potential citizenship lies the social and political forces which are to have a part in the making of their country's government, in the shaping of their country's destiny," and he concluded that a "national response" to their needs was fully warranted. He contrasted the annual federal expenditure for education in Alaska of $17.45 per child with Alabama's $4.42 and wondered how long such favors would be bestowed on non-voters and withheld from residents of Alabama and other states. The government must realize that, "To enlarge the lot and to increase the inspirations of the children of these United States . . . is the supreme duty of our national capacities and of our national self-interest." Later he argued that the South should protest the millions of dollars spent on armaments and public improvements while the government allowed "paper theories to stand between the vast resources of its wealth and the human appeal" of its children. "A democracy which imposes an equal distribution of political obligation must find some way to afford a more equal distribution of educational opportunity." Until it did, Murphy rejoiced that generous men were trying to do "what the nation has not done officially," and were "proving that a true citizenship has a duty to the nation." They recognized that "all education is but philanthropy; and philanthropy is but humanity believing in itself and its God."[47]

Although the other members of the board did not accept Murphy's plea for federal aid, they were pleased with his success as a speaker and as their representative. Peabody reflected their views when he said, "if nothing had been accomplished by the Southern Education Board beyond the discovery and utilization of its secretary this achievement would justify us in regarding the past year as a success."[48]

Undoubtedly gratified by his reception, Murphy returned to Concord for the Christmas holidays and was in New York by January, 1903, for the week-long annual meeting of the Southern Education Board. The University Club, Philadelphia, entertained the group, and Ogden staged a dinner at the Waldorf-Astoria to introduce members of the board to 150 national educational leaders and acquaint them with its objectives. Murphy, Alderman, McIver, Buttrick, Baldwin, and Dabney gave addresses on the board's aims and methods. At board sessions, Murphy's salary was increased to $3,500 a year and, upon his recommendation, $1,800 was allocated the newly appointed field agent for Alabama, Dr. Joseph B. Graham.[49]

At the conclusion of the meetings, Murphy rushed to Montgomery to complete plans for the late January superintendents' conference. After a similar meeting proved successful in Virginia, he and Ogden felt the future of their movement depended on the same results in Alabama. Ogden especially was "extremely anxious" due to the intensity of hostile feeling on the race question, but all went well. When Curry became ill, Murphy obtained Alderman as the principal speaker, and the county superintendents seemed genuinely impressed with the board's program. Under the circumstances, Ogden wrote Alderman, "your speech, as reported in the paper at hand this morning, comes to me 'like the shadow of a great rock in a weary land.'" Apologizing for this emotional response, he stated, "I cannot, nor would I if I could, divest myself of a very deep feeling in the cause that binds us together."[50]

Murphy did not present a formal paper at the Montgomery meeting but preached on the board's work at St. John's Church. In the large audience was Dr. B. J. Baldwin, President of the Montgomery Educational Association, who was so impressed that he devoted the rest of his life to the board's work. Murphy obtained permission for Baldwin to use the title "Associate Field Agent for Alabama," and he did yeoman's work in the state after the early, untimely death of Graham. They became the closest of friends, and Murphy used Baldwin's office when he was in Montgomery.[51]

Murphy was at his best while dealing personally with men and articulating ideas, but he found that much of his time was consumed with tedious paper work. Due to his sense of duty and disciplined nature, he performed his job with meticulousness and ability, although, partially due to his poor health, he found the details grueling. Plans for the Richmond conference occupied most of his time from February to April, 1903. Stopping at Richmond en route from Montgomery, he conferred with the local arrangements committee and made plans for a special group of "Boston pilgrims" to attend the meeting. He checked the list of those to receive invitations, mailed out three to four thousand, and worked on the program. In most cases, probably after conferring with Ogden, he chose the title of the speakers' addresses and in his invitations gave an indication of what he expected. For example, in requesting D. Clay Lilly of Tuscaloosa, Alabama, to speak on "Negro Education from A Southern Standpoint," he suggested that Lilly repudiate social equality but hold that since non-education was "impracticable in a democracy" Negro education should be promoted under Southern auspices. Yet Murphy hastened to add, "I would not in any way attempt to outline the nature of your address."[52]

Before the conference was held the board was attacked as a pro-Negro organization because two Negro newspapers received announcements of the meeting, and a story was circulated that two board members had dined with Negroes. While deploring these attacks, Murphy sought to quickly silence them for fear that they would jeopardize all the board's work. The intensity of Southern feeling may be judged by the tone of his explanation. He declared that the Negro newspapers would never have received the announcements had he not been kept from the office by his son's illness. Furthermore, he labeled as "scarehead" the story that portrayed board members imitating President Roosevelt in dining with Negroes when in reality two Northern members of the board had been joined only after dinner by Negroes for discussions. Murphy had spoken vigorously in behalf of Negro education and was appalled at the foolishness with which "the press and stump" dealt with the question and at Roosevelt's bad judgment in playing into the most reactionary hands by dining with Washington. To clarify the issue, he scheduled a conference paper by "some representative Southern man" not connected with the Southern or General Education boards and found the ideal person in Chancellor W. B. Hill of the University of Georgia.[53]

The Richmond conference, the largest to that time, received heartening reports of school consolidations in Virginia and of the organization and activities of the Women's Association for the Betterment of Public School Houses in North Carolina, two developments that were later to be encouraged elsewhere, as well as reports from campaigns in a number of states. The Bureau of Investigation and Information had excellent reports available on conditions in Tennessee, North Carolina, and Louisiana, and those on Alabama and South Carolina were near completion. These revealed, as Dabney told the conference, that the great impediment to educational progress in the South was "the absence of efficient social organization" in the "almost completely unorganized" rural communities. While the clergy had "done much to instruct the people," they had divided them into so many sects that the church was largely useless as a center of life. Dabney contended that "the consolidated, public industrial school" was the most hopeful institution around which the rural South could organize. His assistant, P. P. Claxton, who in 1911 was to begin a decade's service as U. S. Commissioner of Education, presented a portrayal of a model country school, which included "a small farm and a teacher's home, with a principal to make the school a growing country life institution."[54]

The entire program was well received, and Murphy was honored by an appointment to the Committee on Organization.[55] He needed this recognition because immediately before the conference he had asked the Bishop of Alabama to depose him from the ministry for other than moral reasons. He had come to feel that he could work more effectively for Christian ideals outside of the priesthood. Much of the South was virtually organized on denominational lines, and perhaps Ogden was correct in believing that Murphy resigned in order "to bring his influence to bear without prejudice upon the great mass of the Methodist and Baptist population." Murphy did not hesitate to take this action although he knew many would misunderstand. Dickerman, a fellow cleric, comprehended the situation fully and extended his deepest sympathy, assuring Murphy that a heavy personal cost was the usual price exacted of anyone who attempted to do anything for humanity. Ogden said that he did not "know a greater illustration of civic self-sacrifice."[56]

Murphy continued to arouse support for education through a series of important addresses in the spring and summer of 1903. He gave the commencement address at Montgomery's Girls' High School, spoke to the Nashville Chamber of Commerce on "Commerce and the Common Schools," and presented a ringing Jeffersonian-type defense of academic freedom at the University of the South in an address entitled, "Culture and Democracy." Democratic government, he contended, must permit culture to flourish and have freedom to scrutinize the popular will. Only by this means can democracy be secure under "progressive and constructive leadership." As Murphy saw it, the university, sustained by popular support, is more than a propagator of common ideas; it is a conservator of the noblest ideals of the past and a watchman for new modes of their expression. He warned that culture must keep itself pure for the sake of humanity and could not do this if freedom of thought and expression were repressed in the university. Academic freedom is a prerequisite for intelligent action, and political freedom will not endure if it is destroyed.[57]

Following the Sewanee address, Murphy made a quick visit to the Summer School of the South, which enrolled 2,150 students, the largest enrollment in United States' history, and gave an exuberant endorsement, which Ogden declared was of "unusual value" due to his "clear and calm judgment."[58] He attended the sessions of the National Education Association in Boston where, on July 10, he delivered a major address, "The Schools of the People."[59] Before this distinguished forum, he spoke in the national vein characteristic of his writings and presented Southern educational problems as national problems requiring national solutions.

Public education in the South was both inadequate and progressive, Murphy held. Though far from achieved, everywhere an attempt was being made to provide free schools for all, an effort supplying "one of the great unifying and constructive forces" in Southern life. Although innumerable problems intervened, many were being alleviated through road building, the development of industry, school consolidation, the levying of new school taxes, and, Murphy incorrectly hoped, a tendency to establish the same educational qualifications for voting for both blacks and whites.[60] Although the need was great and resources limited, Murphy was not despondent since, unlike New England, the South was gaining on illiteracy. Southern poverty itself provided "a teaching force of broad ambitions, of real culture, and of true and generous refinement," and "the educational enthusiasm" of the Southern people was increasing. But time would be required for broad gains to be registered. "The nation must be considerate with the South, and the South must be considerate of herself," he advised, while urging both national and Southern interests to recognize that the removal of illiteracy was not enough. "The school must stand rather for a larger and larger measure of trained intelligence, of controlled and sobered will, of sound, resourceful and efficient life." It must realize a duty not only to culture but to citizenship, and teach the people when challenged by crime, lust, and hate to be motivated not by vengeance, but by thoughts "of what is due to their civilization, their country and their children." It must "help men to see that liberty of government means there is no liberty except through being governed; that being governed and being governable are largely the measure of our distance from the jungle." Only in this way could education elevate the nation to its greatest potential.[61]

In all his activities, regardless of their tedious nature, Murphy was attempting to promote this end. At the Abenia meeting in August, 1903, he helped persuade the board that Birmingham was the ideal site for the 1904 conference. Much of the remainder of the year was required to edit and publish the *Proceedings* of the Richmond conference; all addresses had to be verified since the stenographers inserted their own interpretations when they did not hear correctly.[62]

While editing the *Proceedings*, Murphy also wrote and rewrote *Alabama's First Question,* a pamphlet for general circulation which was a plea for a constitutional amendment on taxation and for enactment of local school taxes; taxes of one mill or less (ten cents per $100) were permissable under the state constitution of 1901. No other Southern state had such a limitation, and Murphy demanded that it be removed. "To prohibit the people of a county from levying upon their own property—if they chose to do so—for the education of their own children seems to be both un-democratic and un-American," he wrote. In the interim, he urged the levying of the highest taxes possible under the law to relieve the distressing conditions in Alabama. Although since 1880 Negro illiteracy had been reduced from 80.6 to 54.4 per cent and white illiteracy from 25 to 14.8 per cent, new jobs could not be created nor immigrants attracted unless conditions could be further improved. In 1900 Alabama still stood forty-fifth among the states in its percentage of literate people. In eight counties, 20 per cent or more of the white men of voting age were illiterate, and almost one-sixth of the state's native whites, a number greater than the population of its sixteen largest cities, could not read nor write. Many of the state's cities had relatively good schools, but only 7.5 per cent of the people lived in incorporated towns of 8,000 or more, and every child must *"have its chance"* regardless of where he lived. To those who found satisfaction in the fact that the state gave a larger percentage of its income to education than other states, Murphy replied that this was not sufficient and that the real solution lay in additional local taxation. Alabama schools relied almost exclusively on state revenue, a practice legally necessary before 1901. In New England, however, educational revenues came almost entirely from local sources; in Massachusetts less than one dollar in every hundred came from the state. The same plan was working in Mississippi which, with more Negroes than Alabama, was able to reduce its white illiteracy to 8 per cent.[63] The same could occur in Alabama, Murphy predicted.

> It is a method almost universally adopted throughout the country; it deepens interest and responsibility by more largely making the support of the schools a point of local pride; and, inasmuch as the people always closely watch the use of money they themselves directly contribute, it is a method of support which insures the largest measure of efficiency.[64]

Murphy gave his personal touch to the Alabama educational movement when he came to the state in March, 1904, to complete plans for the next annual conference to be held in Birmingham. He found that Dr. J. H. Phillips, Birmingham Superintendent of Schools, had done a splendid job in perfecting the local organization, and Murphy was able to choose a director for the state campaign and devote most of his time to it. "*Something* must be done—and with the small amount of money at our command I know of nothing else to do," he wrote.[65] Spurred by his efforts, two-thirds of Alabama's counties responded within a matter of months. Equally important, a strong grass-roots sentiment for education was stimulated; this enabled B. B. Comer, when he became governor in 1907, to take heroic steps, for the first time converting Alabama educationally into one of the most progressive Southern states.

Racial attitudes were the greatest disappointment in Alabama. Murphy had never "seen so much sentiment against the negro"; Tuskegee and Booker T. Washington were never so unpopular. "Poor fellow," he wrote of Washington, "I am glad he does not see—and cannot see—the situation as it is."[66] Because of these conditions and to avoid demagogic attack, he intervened to prevent the Ogden party from visiting Talladega's Negro college, which had been added to the itinerary when an excursion to the State Normal School at Florence proved impractical. "The substitution of a negro institution in your itinerary will cause not only disappointment but deep resentment and humiliation," he advised Ogden, and, embarrassed, added, "I *know* our people, and I would be faithless to you if I kept silent." Alabama was in the midst not only of an educational campaign but also "the hottest sort of a political campaign." No action should be taken which would endanger the board's work, and Murphy felt an attack on Ogden "would 'drive to cover' men all over the state on whom we—and the negro—*must* depend for fairness, and patriotism." Ogden heeded Murphy's advice and rearranged his schedule, worrying less about the Negro than his group. "The worst fear I have about this is that the slow running may make a dull time for our party," he stated. "We will have to amuse them as best we can."[67]

Murphy became ill in Alabama and, to his disappointment, was unable to function normally during the conference, but he was pleased at its results. Ogden praised him in his opening address, noting that his and Buttrick's utterances were having incalculable national influence. Strong support was given to those forces seeking increased local taxation, particularly in an address of Sydney J. Bowie, who used many of the arguments from *Alabama's First Question*. Finally, in gratitude for his leadership, the conference elected Murphy vice-president.[68]

For months after the Birmingham meeting, Murphy was too ill for much work, but the ever generous Ogden gladly gave him "freedom from responsibility" to recuperate. By August he was well enough to attend the Abenia meeting, where he vigorously contended for an expansion of the board's operations and proposed that it consider federal aid as the only feasible solution of the critical Southern situation. Although he again portrayed the urgent needs, limited resources, and the logic of national aid to Southern children, he could not convince the conservative Yankee businessmen and Southern educators of the correctness of his position. Finally, as a face-saving device, they passed an innocuous resolution proposing that a study be made to consider the effect of expanding the board's propaganda activities.[69]

Despite his presence at Abenia, Murphy was not well enough to edit single-handedly the *Proceedings of the Conference*, and most of this work was done by Dickerman. With the coming of cooler weather, Murphy's strength began to return, and on November 25–26 he attended the convention of the Association of Colleges and Preparatory Schools of the Middle States and Maryland held at Princeton. Here, speaking on "The Public Function of the Public School," he again contended that in a democracy the public school must be "a nursery of citizenship." It must teach men "not merely how they are to relate themselves harmoniously to an established order, but how they themselves are to establish the order. . . ." Stressing the significance of teachers' personalities, he urged that salaries be increased to attract more men and better instructors into the profession and to hold them. He pleaded for a clearer concept of the school's role and for women teachers to assume more outside civic responsibilities. Only when the masses of people became aware of the school's purpose could results be expected.[70]

To illustrate his contentions, Murphy turned to the South. Here, one was struck "by the civic prominence of the teacher," who played a key role in public life. University presidents were "not only teachers but publicists" and were consulted on major state legislation. The same role was assumed on a lower level by the simplest grade school teacher in the smallest town as the masses became conscious of the need for education and were willing to sacrifice for it. Although problems were "absolutely prodigious," the "gospel" of education was being preached to the people, and they were responding, even though Negro prejudice still existed and presented the greatest challenge to be overcome. The defeat of the plan to divide educational taxes on a racial basis more than any other development indicated that the average Southerner had been converted to a belief in universal education and offered hope for the future.[71]

Following his Princeton address, Murphy's attacks of fever became progressively worse, and he was forced to omit many duties. He presented his resignation as vice-president of the conference, feeling Peabody's appointment would be of greater utility, but Ogden refused to receive it. Additional appreciation for his work came in March, 1905, when the board raised his salary to $5,000 a year, and, to Murphy's pleasure, authorized the holding of a superintendents' meeting at future annual conferences, henceforth one of their most useful features.[72]

Despite pain and weakness, Murphy prepared the program for the 1905 conference, to be held in Columbia, South Carolina. He importuned worthwhile speakers to appear and obtained space on Ogden's special train for many. In inviting Thomas Nelson Page to speak on "The Work of the University in the South," he confided to Ogden, "I earnestly hope he will steer clear of the negro question, as I think he has a very limited perspective in reference to that subject." In early April, however, Murphy's condition worsened; he abandoned plans to attend the conference and asked Buttrick to complete the final details of the program.[73] From one standpoint, these developments may have been fortunate. Ogden's special train was wrecked in the yards at Greenville, South Carolina, May 3, 1905, killing four trainmen, shaking up the passengers, and injuring a number, including St. Clair McKelway, editor of *The Brooklyn Eagle*. In Murphy's condition the shock of such an accident could have been fatal.[74]

The conference itself was notable not only for the first superintendents' meeting, but for the addresses of J. H. Phillips and W. B. Merritt, State School Commissioner of Georgia. Phillips first clearly focused attention on the need for high schools in his address, "The High School in the Public School System of the South." Merritt, speaking on a favorite Murphy theme, "The South and the School," contended that the school was the one agency that could furnish a solution to racial problems and tensions and again enable the South to play a constructive role in national life. "Racial adjustment is the distinctive task which has been set for the South," he declared. "We may fail in other things and escape notice; but not so in our dealing with the millions of Africans living among us."[75]

Ogden was grieved that Murphy could not attend and characterized him as "a philosophical statesman" to whom the whole country owed "a debt of gratitude which will never be fully expressed and cannot be paid."[76] But he and Peabody attempted to pay part of this debt in the summer of 1905 by sending him, at their expense, to Bad Nauheim, Germany, to take the baths and follow the famous spa's health regime. Earlier Murphy perhaps would have refused their charity, but, because of his dedication to the vital mission in which he was involved, he dared not let the sin of pride impede the recovery of his strength. Unfortunately, the relaxing treatments and splendid diversions of Nauheim did not produce notable results, but Murphy felt the journey was most worthwhile; he did become the fast friend of a gifted, sensitive physician, Dr. Theodor Schott, who became his principal medical adviser for life. At the end of the summer when he departed, he resolved to return the following year, more to consult Schott than to receive treatments.[77] Back in New York, Peabody insisted that his personal physician be available whenever needed. Murphy consulted no New York doctor whose perceptions were "so clear, so well balanced and so far reaching" as Peabody's physician, and none was of greater comfort to him.[78]

Murphy was unable to prepare the program for the 1906 conference, called to meet in Lexington, Kentucky, despite the best of care, and, hoping a warmer climate would help, he spent part of the winter in Montgomery and the balance with his mother and sister in San Antonio. In January, 1906, the board, meeting without Murphy, elected Dickerman to membership and asked him to serve as Associate Secretary for one year to relieve Murphy's mind from worry. Ogden missed Murphy greatly, particularly in preparing the progam, writing, "I often long for your counsel and initiative."[79]

In spite of a bout with flu in February, 1906, Murphy recovered sufficiently to return to New York in April for an informal meeting which discussed the conference's future. Ogden had come to question whether it had reached the limits of usefulness and should adjourn. Peabody had suggested that it either be reduced to a gathering of 150 to 200 leaders or be moved to a Northern city. Either would eliminate the need for the special trains that had been objects of criticism of such opponents as *The Charleston News and Courier* and *The Manufacturers' Record*. Murphy's strong defense of the prevailing arrangement may have preserved the conference. By careful scheduling, he argued, many areas of the South could receive stimulation and be aided in major educational advancements. Conceding that the conference was not working "as directly for Negroes as some desired," he pointed out that strong addresses in favor of Negro education had been given at each meeting, "and the indirect benefit was very great." Realistically, he correctly predicted that the unfortunate reaction against Negro education would continue, but he trusted as white schools improved so would the Negro schools. He did not urge more direct action for fear of alienating the whites, an unfortunate position in which his colleagues concurred with troubled consciences. He did not show such tolerance for a non-racial aspect of discrimination, however. The wealthier Southern people in conference cities had concentrated their care on Northern visitors "while Southern people were entertained in lowlier quarters or in boarding houses," thus negating one of the purposes for the meeting. To insure maximum results, Murphy strongly urged that greater hospitality be obtained for Southern guests and, of course, that Ogden remain as president.[80]

The conference continued in traditional fashion, and 2,500 people crowded the Lexington auditorium to hear Ogden focus attention upon the rural school, "with its poorly trained, ill-paid teachers, struggling to impart some crumbs of knowledge to needy scholars." McIver and Alderman surveyed the work being done and the needs that remained, but the most remarkable address, perhaps the most significant in conference history, was that of Dr. Seaman A. Knapp of St. Charles, Louisiana, who pleaded for farm demonstration work as the hope of the South. The acclaim he received aided in the promotion of his remarkable career, which was to transform Southern agriculture and with it Southern life.

Born in 1833 in a Lake Champlain village, Knapp received a classical education and taught school until illness forced him West, where he became a successful Iowa farmer and a Methodist minister. Following stints as Superintendent of the Iowa Institute for the Education of the Blind and as manager of the Iowa Agricultural College farm, in 1883 he became the latter institution's president. In 1885 he moved to Louisiana, where for a decade he directed the recovery of a million and a half acres of marshland for rice and sugar production, establishing the Southwest as the rice capital of America. Always sensitive to the farmer's need of government aid, he was the instigator of the 1887 Hatch Act creating agricultural experiment stations, and in 1902 he became the United States Department of Agriculture's "Special Agent for the Promotion of Agriculture in the South." In 1903 in Terrell, Texas, he perfected his demonstration farm technique, which showed conclusively that proper cultivation could increase production in the presence of the boll weevil, and thus sought to raise the economic standards of entire communities. The government began to support his work in weevil-infected areas, but seeing its potential elsewhere in the South, the General Education Board began subsidization in non-infected areas in 1906, with a $7,000 grant. By 1914, when the government assumed this work on a national basis under the Smith-Lever Act, the General Education Board's contribution had increased to $252,000 annually; its total investment in the program was almost one million dollars.

Many became enthralled with Knapp's achievements. For the first time Walter Hines Page realized that there was a way to increase Southern production, and he proclaimed Knapp and his demonstrators "the right sort of revolutionists." Albert Shaw kept President Theodore Roosevelt informed of Knapp's progress; this led to the establishment of the significant Commission on Rural Life, which Page used as a means to publicize Knapp's ideas. Knapp's policies became firmly entrenched in 1913 when on Page's recommendation, David Houston, President of the University of Texas, was chosen as Wilson's Secretary of Agriculture.

Knapp's work had a major influence on the Southern educational movement. By 1905 it was clear that without the federal aid Murphy sought Southern poverty would continue to severely restrict educational progress. Therefore, the annual conferences and the General Education Board increasingly devoted their attention to all aspects of Southern life affecting economic progress. Notable was the functioning of the Rockefeller Sanitary Commission which, with a fund of a million dollars, between 1909 and 1914 did much to rid the Southern people of hookworm, one of their most debilitating diseases.[81]

While Knapp was obtaining a significant forum at Lexington, Murphy was in New York preparing to sail for Europe, again at Peabody and Ogden's expense, and he departed before Ogden's special train returned.[82] In his absence, the group at the Abenia meeting continued to discuss Negro education and in its frustration took mild actions which were mainly defensive in nature and had slight long-range effect. It recommended each state (1) publish the facts regarding the collection and distribution of school funds; (2) allocate a place on the convention program of county superintendents for collecting information and suggestions regarding Negro schools; and (3) within a year secure a meeting of leading representative Negro teachers for consideration of ways to improve Negro schools. The board authorized the preparation of an article demonstrating the work done by Southern men for Negro education, and assigned the task to Dickerman; the article appeared in 1907.[83]

Murphy's sojourn at Bad Nauheim proved more profitable than that of the previous summer, and he returned in the fall hoping to resume much of his former work. Some of his colleagues felt that he was almost well, but his appearance improved more than his true condition. Ogden realized the extent of Murphy's heart damage, however, and wrote the details to Dickerman, who "had not supposed that his condition was so serious." Yet Murphy was able to attend a December meeting of the board, where he was elected to its Campaign Committee, and to hold a planning session with Dickerman for the next conference. Following this, he left for the South—spending a month in Montgomery and the remainder of the winter in San Antonio.[84]

While in Alabama Murphy again assumed the leadership in the state educational movement and laid plans to carry the fight into the three counties that had defeated a one mill school tax and the seventeen counties which had not voted on it (forty-six had approved). Much of his work was with a voluntary organization of fifteen men, known as the Alabama Education Commission, whose plans for statewide organization Murphy directed in the hope that the 1907 legislature would submit a constitutional amendment to the people permitting additional local taxation for schools. He knew if success were to come that it was not too early to prepare for the hard fight. Representatives from the state Federation of Women's Clubs, who were working for rural school house improvement, so impressed him by the formation of subsidiary organizations in each county that he promised them a $300 grant for rail fare and buggy hire. Murphy had never underestimated the power of women since his earliest years as a parish administrator, and experiences in Alabama confirmed his views of their importance in the educational crusade.[85]

Even while he was in Montgomery Ogden continued to consult Murphy, and as late as the December board meeting, plans continued to be made for the now traditional conference in Nashville. But McIver's sudden death and the charge in Virginia that the board was a partisan of Governor Andrew J. Montague led Alderman, the Chairman of the Campaign Committee, to insist that, at least for one year, a smaller meeting be held. The necessity for this was confirmed by Ogden's illness and probable absence, but Murphy still opposed the change unless Nashville should withdraw the invitation, feeling it would be regarded as "a retreat." Finally, Ogden concurred with those who wished a smaller gathering, trusting that "real conference and practical discussion" might prove feasible. He called the meeting for Pinehurst, North Carolina, while conceding that many would consider the change a "surrender to 'The Manufacturers' Record' and other ignorant or prejudiced influences." As always when Ogden reached a decision, Murphy cheerfully accepted it and, feeling much better himself, agreed to present a paper on the board's work. He urged Ogden to be prudent in his convalescence and assured him, "You were never so precious to us as now."[86]

At Pinehurst, Murphy, reviewing the achievements of the Southern Education Board, found the success of such "a composite of personal forces" almost miraculous. It had no charter, constitution, or by-laws. Moreover, he stated, "It has a Treasurer to whom it owes much more than has ever been paid in, a Secretary who is often ill and sometimes out of town, a President who presides over it and over whom it sometimes has the assumacy [*sic*] to preside; and yet things get done." He believed that due to the ability, cooperativeness, and dedication of its members more had been achieved than "if there had been more machinery and less freedom."

At first the board had devoted much of its attention to unearthing facts regarding Southern education through its Bureau of Investigation and Information, and this caused some resentment until people came to realize that publicity about illiteracy and backward conditions were not criticisms unless people were indifferent to these problems. As a result, a partially aroused citizenry did produce changes, and Murphy felt that the Southern Education Board was responsible for much of this. As he expressed it:

> That the facts are known; that there is some general appreciation of their compelling force; that they can be admitted frankly and discussed publicly—even by the candidates for public office—marks a distinct achievement of our public opinion within the past ten years. This Board—I need hardly say—has been by no means the sole agency of so marked a change. But the change is here; and that we have labored for it, in season and out of season, lies broadly upon the pages of our history.[87]

Of the several specific, onerous problems which the board considered, none was greater than that of the status of the teacher. Washington knew a Negro teacher at Snow Hill, Alabama, who received a contract for $7.50 a month for five months to provide the only formal education received by two hundred Negro children, and the board knew of many instances where salaries of $25 to $40 per month for three to five months prevented attracting able teachers. Those heroic souls who responded to the teacher need could not live on their wages or study to equip themselves for greater service. The board not only sought to inform the people of these conditions but its campaigns were designed to correct them. "The need was all but desperate" and "the struggle has constituted the most aggressive and unyielding element in our whole program of agitation," Murphy stated. The Campaign Committee, composed exclusively of Southerners, carried the struggle to the county and district levels, hoping to persuade the counties to impose self-taxation before seeking a state referendum on increased taxes. The board expended about $25,000 a year on this portion of its program; no institutions received grants, and speakers were paid only their expenses.[88]

In spite of limited funds the board's campaigns succeeded, and in the board's first five years of operation the Southern states increased their annual appropriations for education by $14,000,000. But this success was not easily obtained. "The struggle for money has involved a struggle for ideas," Murphy declared, and the task of enlightening the masses—"especially through the long summer months when the Southern farmer has the leisure and the mood for public question—is a burden involving sacrifices of which the woman of ease or the man of the office has seldom dreamed."

The board found one of its finest allies in the School Improvement Associations, groups of women first organized in North Carolina and Virginia, utilized by Murphy in Alabama, and with board support organized throughout the South. "The agents of the community are the women of the South," Murphy found, and the School Improvement Associations did not confine themselves to their stated purpose of visiting and improving school houses. Rescuing the rural schools from isolation and oblivion, they aided the board in the creation of a "fellowship of opinion, a sort of moral tradition" which demanded improved public education for all. As a result, a new concept emerged in many areas of the South; it held education to be the key to progress, and the board succeeded in obtaining more support to advance the cause.[89]

In addition to Murphy's paper, the Pinehurst meeting featured an address by Dr. Seaman A. Knapp. Again, he contended that a more prosperous Southern life depended on increased earning power of the farmer, and he estimated that, given the right training, the average Southerner could earn five times his present income.[90]

Optimism over Southern conditions was in harmony with Murphy's apparent returning health in the spring, summer, and fall of 1907. In July a doctor assured him that his heart was the best it had been in five years, and he found it possible to resume much wider activity in educational affairs. He advised Booker T. Washington on selections for the Jeanes Board, a new agency endowed with one million dollars by a Philadelphia Quakeress, which concentrated on subsidizing model teachers, and for the Slater Board; composed a moving seventy-first birthday tribute to Ogden; and journeyed with enthusiasm to Abenia for the August board meeting.[91] Here, he agreed to go to Arkansas to arrange for the use of a $600 appropriation and presented the report of the Alabama School Improvement Association. He related with delight that Governor B. B. Comer, whom he had opposed on the child labor issue, "through the work of some members of the Southern Education Board had been converted to the one mill tax idea," and had since proved a friend to education. Genuine progress was being made in Alabama.

Like Hamlet's ghost, the question of Negro education re-emerged as the members of the board began to realize that the increase in white education was not bringing the improvement in Negro training they had envisioned. Since he was the board's Executive Secretary, Murphy attempted to justify the position it had assumed, although he was not satisfied with it. The even less contented and usually more outspoken Page held that most conference papers on the subject were a rehash of those written in the 1850's and 1860's, and urged the board to have scientific studies of Negro life and education presented as a prelude to greater aid to Negro education. Murphy, explaining conference policy, stated he had consistently sought to have it deal explicitly with the question, but he knew that, illogically, popular opinion held the conference responsible for all its spokesmen; he had acted on the principle "that unless the question could be handled by the right man in the right way, it were better to ignore it." At Athens, Governor Charles B. Aycock, Hoke Smith, and H. St. George Tucker had given "sympathetic, vigorous and helpful addresses" favoring increased appropriations. Chancellor W. B. Hill had dealt with the subject in the "happiest way" at Richmond, and Bishop C. B. Galloway of Mississippi had made a warm emotional appeal in Birmingham; the latter speech was published in pamphlet form and widely distributed by Ogden and the Slater Board. "The situation was particularly critical in South Carolina because of the attitude of the Charleston 'News and Courier,'" and when Murphy failed to obtain Bishop Warren A. Candler to address the Columbia meeting, no adequate paper was presented. Surprisingly, the Connecticut-born Dickerman, who prepared the Lexington and Pinehurst programs and who came to the board from Hampton, did not arrange for treatment of the Negro education issue—another indication of Northern humanitarians' acceptance of the Southern approach.

Murphy still believed that a strong statement in behalf of Negro education should be given at every conference, but warned, "The subject, just at this stage of our public feeling, presents a magnificent opportunity for a calamity." There was value in scholarly reports such as Page suggested but except for Georgia, which listed Negro land holdings and educational appropriations separately, statistics were almost impossible to prepare. At the same time, Murphy knew the South well enough and sensed its problems sufficiently to see the continued usefulness of the old-time oratory and emotional appeals. "Our chief need is . . . not for cold scientific fact, but for right feeling," he wrote, in urging that speakers like Hill and Bishop Galloway be retained. Though the board might be unable to present a full report on economics, it could do much "to put crude demagoguery to shame, and to establish sound and Christian standards of just thinking and true feeling on racial matters." Murphy knew many persons, including a number of legislators, who cared nothing for statistics but who could and must be interested "in the elementary human principles that must always determine the right relations between man and man and between class and class." Forever the cleric, he declared, "We need science, but we need right conduct more."

Although Murphy, Page, and the Northern board members would have welcomed a concerted effort, Alderman objected, holding that "a crusade for Negro education" would jeopardize the success being achieved for the whites, and the board reluctantly accepted his views. Once again the Negro had been sacrificed, this time with less justification since the fallacy of board policy was becoming clear. Louis Harlan, an historian who has carefully studied the racial aspects of the board's work, appears correct in concluding that the philanthropists who supported the General Education Board and the Conference for Education in the South miscalculated in believing the "upper class wing of Southern racialism because it spoke the language of conservatism, would be their effective partner in protecting Negroes." On the contrary, the philanthropists were converted and practically abandoned the Negro.[92]

Disappointed but still dedicated to the board's mission, Murphy left New York in the early fall of 1907 for a delightful trip to Nashville, Sewanee, Little Rock, Fort Smith, Memphis, Birmingham, and Montgomery. Although some localities were unaffected, in many regions he found remarkable headway had been made in the campaign to promote white education. Yet two areas of critical weakness existed —money was voted unwisely and poorly administered. Similar conditions "usually attend any social development," but Murphy feared a reversal of sentiment would come unless there was wise coordination and unification. In Alabama, where there had been a 30 per cent increase in the salaries of county superintendents, many went for months without visiting schools in the apparent belief that the clerical function of holding teachers' examinations and issuing licenses was their only duty. Everywhere the high school and consolidation movements were making progress, but, again, poor administration was nullifying many gains. Often care had not been given to acquiring teachers and equipment and maintaining new schools, and, especially in Black Belt areas, consolidation had led to the destruction of inadequate schools without making adequate provisions for displaced pupils. These conditions, largely attributable to the newness of public education in the South, required the citizenry to gain some knowledge of administrative matters, and the Southern Education Board, "free from any sort of factional alliance," was the logical agency to inform them.

Murphy's tour convinced him that more than ever "rapidly developing enthusiasm for white education is bearing sharply and adversely upon the opportunities of the Negro." Everywhere resentment against the Negro intensified, and his schools were "hampered and impoverished where . . . not actually abandoned." If the railway rate issue had not emerged to dominate " 'big' politics," Murphy feared the race issue would have. As deeply as he deplored injustice to the Negro, he foresaw a greater menace in the establishment of an educational system "on a thoroughly undemocratic basis." He knew, "The moment one class starts out to cheat another, it inevitably ends in cheating itself," and that democratic America would not tolerate such conditions.

Probably because he had concurred in most board decisions, he did not censor it for failure to demand equal educational opportunities for the Negro.[93] Instead, with a typical forward-looking approach, he held that the board must help correct educational inequalities by exerting a "modest, tactful" influence that politicians and the press could never muster. As a beginning, he recommended that the board engage a professional journalist to conduct a continuous campaign designed to change Southern opinion on Negro education through the constant issuance of releases to newspapers. Care must be taken, however, to prevent the work from assuming a crusade aspect, which would offend more than it would convert.

Undaunted, Murphy realistically evaluated the board's work. On the positive side it had exerted a powerful influence in overcoming provincialism, and by competition had even forced the Southern Educational Association to become something more than the agent of textbook companies. "In helping the movement for 'more money' we have aided the South in assembling the raw materials, the stone and mortar, for the building of an educational system. But the nature of the building from its very foundations is still to be determined," he wrote.[94]

An example of the kind of appeal Murphy envisioned was contained in his article, "Progress in Southern Education," published in the January, 1908, *Tradesman*.[95] Though not in the least neglectful of white education, it stressed that Southern progress depended on the development of markets and intellectual leadership among all the people. The true statesmen were those who recognized "that the political influence of the south is not to be advanced by merely negative devices of resistance, but by the south's intelligent and positive contributions to the great national decisions."

Murphy believed universal education could be best advanced by holding the 1908 conference in Memphis, one of the South's largest and most cosmopolitan cities, and, although Ogden and other board members favored Nashville, he began preliminary arrangements resulting in its selection.[96] In early December, 1907, he attended an Atlanta planning meeting for the conference, and participated in joint sessions of the Campaign Committee, the Association of State Superintendents, and the newly established Professors of Secondary Education in state universities, a General Education Board project.[97] Following this, he hastened to Old Point Comfort, Virginia, for the December 9–10 meeting of the board, where he reported on plans for the conference, entered vigorously into discussions of the board's work, and was appointed with Page to prepare a statement summarizing the board's conception of its work in the light of the meeting.[98] S. C. Mitchell, now President of Virginia's Co-Operative Education Association, wrote Murphy, "I had really never so much admired your spirit, the balance in your judgment upon these delicate points, and your large statesman-like views" as at Atlanta and Old Point Comfort.[99]

The last day of the meeting, Murphy became seriously ill. Physicians put him to bed immediately, nurses attended him constantly, and Maud rushed to his side from New Haven. He recovered sufficiently to return to New York in a few weeks, but the episode convinced him that he must relinquish his duties.[100] January 28, 1908, he wrote Ogden[101] asking an early acceptance of his resignation. By sheer willpower, however, he continued his duties until May 1, successfully seeing the Memphis conference to completion. In the interim, he visited Montgomery, spent part of the winter with his ill mother in San Antonio, and returned to Montgomery to accompany the Alabama delegation to the conference.

The program was a rich one, highlighted by an address by Lord James Bryce, the British ambassador, and featuring a return to the earlier practice of individual school superintendents presenting reports at the meeting. Under his direction, a resolution was adopted imploring "improvement in county supervision as the strategic point in the entire educational system" and another urging the development of high schools to unite the elementary and collegiate systems. Dickerman was much impressed and wrote, "Mr. Murphy seems to have done his work exceedingly well notwithstanding the painful infirmities with which he has had to contend." Murphy was able to get through the conference, however, only by taking large quantities of stimulants, and at its conclusion, he wrote Ogden:

> I am now too deeply tired—too tired down in the depths of me—to make possible any immediate planning. And yet I do not in the least regret it. Life would be meaningless indeed without the acceptance of difficult conditions: I wanted the Conference to go to Memphis. I believed it would open to us the gateways of continued usefulness and would create opportunities that would demonstrate that there is a future for both the Conference and the Southern Board. Having assumed the obligation of advising the step, my responsibilities were clear, and I would have been utterly wretched had I permitted myself to avoid the practical issue of my own advice.[102]

Following the conference, Murphy, in a seventeen-page letter, summarized his views for Ogden,[103] urging fundamental reforms that would democratize the conference and make it even more a people's movement. He advised the centering of all activities in a headquarters hotel, the abandonment of private entertaining, and the creation "from our vague Conference constituency [of] a responsible membership that take an increasing part, not merely in the bearing of financial burdens, but in the election of officers and in the determination of policy." All those who had attended a meeting should be made electors of the organization by paying one dollar as annual dues. By this means, $1,000 or more could be raised each year, and, more significantly, a sense of responsibility created among the rank and file. Murphy thought many would contribute to an organization they helped manage, and he urged that the sense of mystery surrounding the conference be dispelled, beginning with an opening of its books. "Again and again, Southern men have said to me that they have regarded the anonymous character of our support as the most disquieting element in our situation," he wrote.

In politely criticizing policies originating with Ogden, Murphy did not neglect his own failures. At Memphis, to appease his critics, he had attempted to hold emotionalism down. This was a mistake, and the ever present critics were quick to note a general lack of enthusiasm which had permeated the gathering. Moreover, the program was overloaded with professional educators and neglected the concept that every man is a teacher—a principle on which the conference had always relied.

Although Murphy abandoned his secretarial duties after the Memphis conference, the board refused to act on his resignation before January, 1909, and continued his salary until then. He attended the Abenia meeting in August, 1908, and advocated, since many had no idea what a campaign entailed, that some state superintendents be sent to Tennessee to accompany Claxton in the vigorous campaign he was conducting. As in the past, he counseled closer school supervision and the gathering and dissemination of facts regarding Southern education. To those who contended that all who worked with the board should be paid, he replied that the money could be better spent in circulating pamphlets informing the people of Southern conditions.[104]

In the fall of 1908, Wicliffe Rose assumed many of Murphy's duties; he was appointed Executive Secretary in 1910. Murphy called a meeting to plan the 1909 conference for November in Atlanta, and attended although he was confined to his room in the Piedmont Hotel.

> The trouble does not seem to be climate . . . so much as the old foe "fatigue"—though it seems to me I have done so little for two years but submit to the most loving care and the most lavish coddling that a man could possibly have from his family and friends. How weary of myself I have become and how humiliating it all is—when I realize what I ought to be able to do.[105]

In a letter to Rose,[106] Murphy again revealed his desire that the conference become an independent, self-supporting organization as quickly as possible. He believed Ogden privately held this view also, yet Murphy knew the organization would keep close to Ogden since "we are all so conscious of the ultimate and absolutely paramount relation of his personality and his judgment to all that we do." Murphy's national views were reflected in his wish that the conference, as the only national organization recognizing the layman's role in education, change its name to the Conference for Public Education.

At the Atlanta conference, Murphy was appointed Chairman of the Committee on Program and Policy for the next conference, and he presided over planning sessions in New York in December. In January, 1909, he attended the regular board meeting and read his letter of resignation, which was reluctantly accepted.[107] In a letter to Ogden,[108] he expressed his pride in the board's achievements:

> We have helped the South to meet the problem of local revenue for local schools. While these funds are still inadequate, the spirit of self-help and of social achievement is upper-most. That this Board alone has wrought the change no man would say; that the change—without this Board—could or would have been wrought so generally or so soon every man must say who has any adequate personal knowledge of the facts.

Much remained to be done even though Southern schools were finding an initial answer to their money problems in state and local taxation. Despite advances, they stood in almost the same relation to the schools of other sections as they had in 1890. "In the most vital point of an education investment (its actual power to command the services of a good teacher)," Murphy believed Southern funds were less effective than in 1890. Furthermore, incompetent supervision threatened to destroy the advances made. As continued racial excesses indicated, "The need for the wise education and direction of our public opinion has never . . . been so great as now, and the South has never been more responsive to the tradition of disinterested service which this organization has attempted to represent." His concern for the board and conference prompted him to attend their meetings long after he was physically able to do so, and his heart was as much in their work after his retirement as before. He attended his last board meeting in February, 1910, in New York.[109]

Murphy's resignation as Executive Secretary in effect terminated his leadership in the Southern Education Board. Many sensed this, and expressions of regret and appreciation came from throughout the country. S. C. Mitchell declared he had demonstrated a grasp of fundamentals most others lacked. "You have impressed yourself upon a national cause, and you will live in the influences you have started." *The Montgomery Advertiser* lauded Murphy's ability to hold the confidence of Northern philanthropists as well as Southern educators and business and professional men. He seemed to organize each conference "with such tact, such a knowledge of men and delicate perception of local conditions, that it may be truly said that much of the astonishing advance of the cause of popular education in the South has been indirectly the fruit of his work."[110] The Vice-Chancellor of the University of the South, B. Lawson Wiggins, first became interested in popular education through Murphy, to whom he wrote, "You have done a great work for the country and especially for the South." He pledged, "In my own humble way I am going to continue to advocate the policies which you have so well formulated."[111] James H. Dillard, the new head of the Jeanes Foundation, stated, "I cannot think of the Southern Education Board apart from you. There must be some way to keep you with it without specific work."[112]

Words of praise eased retirement, but Murphy found it difficult. Repeatedly in letters to friends he summarized its advantages, chief of which were time and freedom for writing. "So many of the officials of the Southern Board are identified with State institutions that it has been difficult to do much without embarrassing them, (even the University of Virginia is almost absolutely at the mercy of every passing Legislature)," he confided. "So I am glad, in this sense that my *official* connection with the Board closes on May 1st" [1908]. Moreover, he expected to write with much greater facility after retirement. "I compose rapidly and easily under conditions of mental repose," he stated, "but sustained excitement and the consequent nervous exhaustion mean the paralysis of whatever productive power I have." As his boys prepared to leave for preparatory school, he looked forward to returning South, where he believed his work would have greater influence and he and Maud would be happiest. They preferred Montgomery, but felt it too far from the center of literary activity and so they increasingly thought of Richmond as a future home.[113]

Financial worries troubled Murphy as he faced retirement because he had found saving money impossible, and he was concerned with his and Maud's support as well as their sons' education. He wrote:

> I wish so much I could get upon some basis which would spare me the necessity for exhausting detail (not that I have been physically able to do very much, either) so that my strength can go into the task of writing. I have now won a position from which I can gain a hearing, and I long to do toward the creation and direction of a sounder public opinion, North as well as South.[114]

As a solution, Murphy and a number of his friends decided he should apply for a pension to the Carnegie Foundation for the Advancement of Teaching. This worthy foundation arose when Dr. Henry S. Pritchett, President of the Massachusetts Institute of Technology, mentioned to Andrew Carnegie while visiting at Skibo, his retreat in Scotland, that college professors had no retirement system. In a few months Carnegie gave ten million dollars, the income from which was to be used for pensions, and Pritchett became the administrator. (By 1915 demands became so great that no new pensioners were taken on, and the fund assumed the administrative cost of the newly founded Teachers' Insurance and Annuity Association.)[115] Since Murphy had never taught or served as the head of an educational institution there was no precedent for an award to him, but he had strong advocates. Ogden cordially endorsed the application, although, due to interruptions, in two visits to Carnegie he was unable to mention the subject. Booker T. Washington had better luck, however, and discussed the issue with Carnegie at length. With this support, in October, 1908, the Executive Committee of the foundation, whose members included Woodrow Wilson and Nicholas Murray Butler, voted Murphy a pension of $3,000 a year. Pritchett explained that the scale of grants called for an annual award of $2,900 in cases of those whose salaries were $5,000. A stipend of more than $3,000 had never been granted, and the foundation did not feel they should give Murphy more than this sum, also received by well-known college presidents. In making its award, the foundation stipulated that it did so in recognition of Murphy's "distinguished national service to education." "No one action of the Carnegie Foundation has brought me greater pleasure than that which was taken in your case," Pritchett assured Murphy. "It would not only have pleased you, but would have been a compensation for much toil and discouragement which you have endured, if you could have heard the estimate of your work expressed by the members of this Committee."[116]

As news of the foundation's action spread, Murphy's friends and associates were delighted. Dickerman wrote Ogden, "it is a most worthy bestowal on one who has merited such recognition for superior work in the cause of education." J. J. Joyner, President of the Association of State Superintendents, could not find words to express his pleasure, but told Murphy that the foundation's action would meet "with the universal approval" of his "hosts of friends throughout the South."[117]

The pension and warm greetings which came to Murphy eased his distress in relinquishing his official duties. They confirmed his belief that he had played a key role in the education revival in the South, and that he had attained a position from which his writings could continue the work he had begun. The distinguished Harvard professor, Francis G. Peabody, succinctly concurred when he wrote, "No other Southerner has, I think, contributed so much sanity, foresight and idealism as you, and all who watch this dramatic evolution of a new social consciousness in the South are permanently your debtors."[118]

6.

Retirement Years

In retirement Murphy did not abandon his interest in the improvement of race relations, education, and child labor in the South, but, due to poor health, he was forced to rely on his writings as a means for propagating his ideas. Consequently, some of his most brilliant published works appeared the year following his retirement.

In 1909 many felt that inter-racial relations in the South were deteriorating with no apparent hope for improvement. Murphy considered the entire question in an essay entitled, "Backward or Forward?,"[1] in which he admitted that the scathing attacks on the Negro had resulted in a repression he hoped would not come, but, assuming much the same attitude as Washington, he still found reasons for encouragement. Though exposed to much of the seamy side of Southern life, Washington could still write, "I feel that we are going to have these seasons of friction and depression which are going to be followed by longer seasons of friendship and progress and encouragement." As late as 1911 he declared, "More and more I find that when one gets down to the heart of the white people and colored people here in the South that matters are not so bad after all."[2]

While not denying that Southern developments challenged an optimistic attitude, Murphy rejoiced that the South was no longer "just the land of the negro question." The overwhelming significance of the Negro problem was receding, and the region was coming to concern itself with all the issues of American life. This indicated the

South was going "forward rather than backward," though racial friction was great. Antagonism had increased since 1900 in both North and South, and Murphy ascribed much of it to professional race haters who found profits in spreading their venom among both whites and Negroes. "It pays only because there are ignorant voters, with crude and irresponsible antipathies to be interpreted and represented," he wrote. "The haters of race have thus become the refuge of the political charlatan," who in the North introduces bills to pension ex-slaves and denounces evils no one seriously intends to rectify, and in the South raises unwarranted fears against the Negro and the North.[3]

Ironically, the number of friends to the Negro rose as unjust attacks were made, but estrangement appeared to be growing. Much of the chasm seemed to be due to the movement from racial interdependence to partial independence.

> The impulsive realization of a partial freedom leads to an eager straining at the remaining ties, a straining which chafes the still fettered limbs, inflicts suffering, rouses resentment and impels blind retaliation. Each man is free enough to understand—or misunderstand—his rights, but not quite free enough fully to perceive his duties. . . . Each is likely, in view of their bitter common history to attribute the miseries of his condition to the partner in bondage rather than their common fate.

Murphy felt that strife was "always temporary, incidental" and that the races must move to a third relationship—one in which each recognized the need for cooperation with the other. As Henry Watterson, the most eloquent of Democratic editors, wrote in 1908, their interests were "parallel and identical."[4] They shared a common soil, country, and humanity and must learn that harmony was in the best interest of everyone. "Almost everything has happened that could have happened to make the situation difficult," Murphy wrote, including "memories of slavery, of war, of reconstruction, of political alienation." But he trusted that as these receded and the percentage of Negroes in the Southern population declined that racial irritation would decline also.

Yet more than history and geography were involved in racial friction, and Murphy's sense of Christian brotherhood and knowledge of human nature led him to conclude:

> ... these two races have had, as yet, little adequate knowledge of each other, it being impossible for any human being to know any man whom he does not respect. The average white man has too often failed to respect the negro who has been great enough to work worthily with his head; the average negro has too often failed to respect the white man who has been great enough to work worthily with his hands.

This was the result of a "false psychology" based on a "defective experience." It was "a race friction partly because it is something else . . . like almost all our racial irritations." Mankind, to retain its "repose of mind," preferred to group humanity in traditional classifications. When confronted by a Negro who did not fit the stereotype, whites were disturbed and reacted adversely, not from hatred, but from shock and discontent with the need for reappraisal. The finest leadership was needed to help each race learn of the other.

Murphy failed to realize that the situation he described could never be corrected in a segregated society and that it would grow worse as the caste system hardened. A perceptive observer noted this in 1940, immediately before World War II inaugurated challenges which broke the stratification. "Steadily and, of late years, rapidly, the relations between the white and black races in the South have diminished," he wrote, with a corresponding decrease in inter-racial crime and a breakdown in communications and understanding.[5]

As in other cases, Murphy's diagnosis was brilliant, but his fear of hindering progress by offending Southern sensibilities prevented his presentation of an effective program. Instead he urged patience and education. However, he did recognize that, "Where the instinctive moods of the people, which should be calmed and informed rather than inflamed, are aroused by the intentional appeals of the selfish, our condemnation cannot be too great." Progress must not be delayed either by unconcern or overzealousness. Clearly perceiving the vital significance of Southern race relations on national and international life, he wrote:

> There is not a Japanese in the United States who has not felt
> the subtle tug and pull of the situation on the Pacific [Coast];
> there is not a negro in America—or for that matter in the
> Western world—who is not affected in his relations to the
> white community in which he lives by the adjustment or mal-
> adjustment of race relations at the South.[6]

"Backward or Forward?" was well received. Among the most trea-
sured encomiums was one from Washington, who wrote Murphy:[7]
"It is fine. It seems to me the best thing you have ever written." Cordially agreeing that everything possible had arisen to dissolve the relations between the races, Washington was heartened by the cooperation
that existed.[8]

The approval given his articles and his evolving racial views encouraged Murphy to write another book. Even before *The Present
South* appeared in 1904, he had begun work on another volume of
essays dealing with child labor, race relations, and education in the
South, and tentatively entitled *Southern Issues*. As he studied and
traveled, he became increasingly aware of the "South as a vital and
necessary part of the nation, sharing in the nation's life and progress,
making characteristic contributions to the nation's growth," and he
changed the title to *Issues, Southern and National*.[9] Eight of its fourteen projected chapters were completed, but since seven of these had
appeared, in whole or in part, as articles in leading journals, they were
rewritten and their statistics updated.[10]

In the proposed introduction to *Issues, Southern and National*,
Murphy again expressed nostalgia for unselfish aristocratic leadership.
"The new rulers of the South are bringing their curse as well as their
blessing and experience does not show that increasing wealth necessarily makes men more ready to help the weak and upbuild society
at its basis in the common people." At least for the first generation,
experience indicated that the new, wealthy bourgeoisie was most selfish. As a result, "our industrial bourbonism—child labor—race hatred
—[were] coincident with prosperity."

Even though its new leaders failed, Murphy trusted that the South
was not committed to a policy of repression and that aristocratic lead-

ership would still make its weight felt. "Class discrimination forced against one element in [the] population will react against all," he warned.

> Repression [is] utterly futile; the force which will hold the negro to himself must be found from within. We cannot control the passage underground (vice) by which the negro will desert his racial standpoint; he will pass down and through these, if he has no enduring basis in himself (in his own racial heritage) for sufficient and satisfying life. All that gives him essential opportunity and deeper satisfactions of manhood will be likely to hold him to his own destiny.[11]

As he worked on *Issues, Southern and National,* Murphy became increasingly aware that race permeated all Southern questions and, before dealing with a multiplicity of issues, a consideration in depth of racial conditions in the South was needed. For that reason, he temporarily abandoned *Issues, Southern and National* to write *The Basis of Ascendancy.* By early 1909 the manuscript was complete, but finding a publisher was difficult. *The Present South,* although it received wide acclaim in "long and important reviews" and many editorials, had not proved a financial success.[12] Because of this, the Macmillan Company would not fulfill their verbal agreement to take Murphy's next book; Doubleday, Page and Company and another firm also refused. "Made desperate with the long waiting," Murphy "declined to peddle it around any more; my whole heart is in it and I cannot but believe in its future." Therefore, he turned to Longmans, Green and Co., publishers of *The Larger Life,* who agreed to issue *The Basis of Ascendancy* at his expense. It was published on this basis, even though he could ill afford the seven to eight hundred dollars this entailed since his income had been reduced with retirement and his sons were now away in school.[13]

The Basis of Ascendancy was an attack upon repression as an absurdity in a free society. While still accepting the Washington philosophy that economic power was essential as a first step to other rights, the work was a plea to the whites to extend "security, opportunity and hope" to the Negro so that he could attain his maximum development. The themes first presented in *The Present South* were developed much more fully here, especially Murphy's disgust with unfair white regimentation. Yet he still clung to the hope that with right leadership the white South would reverse its policy and give the Negro his due.

Murphy believed that a valid national spirit was essential if the South was to be just to both the Negro and the white South, and he was much less harsh in his scrutiny of Northern interest in Southern affairs. Over-concern with race had denationalized the South, and the rest of the nation was fulfilling an historic role in seeking to bind it to itself. Before 1865, Murphy felt, the South had sinned against freedom in the name of property, and the North had done the same after the war in the name of government. Although he was aware of increasing Southern repression, he still feared hasty or harsh national action would increase the strength of Southern reactionaries, a conclusion that is hard to defend since their policies were being appropriated by many of the Southern liberals. In seeking to expand the area of Southern freedom, he urged the North to apply only "gentle coercion," realizing that the problem could not be solved in one or two generations. Concurrently, he felt that the South must work to make itself a vital factor in national life, recognizing its greatest contribution to the nation would be in demonstrating how two dissimilar races could live together in peace and prosperity.[14]

If Murphy's methods were inadequate, the same was not true of his goals and intentions. As he had so often done, but now more forcefully than ever, he pleaded that the Negro be given a larger role in Southern life. Self exclusion, not race or class proscription, could be the only exclusion possible in a democracy. A democratic nation simply could not tolerate repression. These conceptions compared favorably with those of George Washington Cable, the most eloquent defender of equal rights, who had written, "Outrages will never cease against the blacks as long as they are held in a degraded civil status by legal and conventional abridgements of their civil rights."[15] Murphy also held that the South must recognize that the rest of the free world would come to the Negro's defense in proportion to the degree that he was repressed. For the first time, he scolded the South for its super-sensitivity. Conscious of coercion from the "community of freedom," it reacted adversely to the outside challenge, but it must learn to know itself psychologically and control these reactions. It must recognize that power and growth would come from cooperation with the forces of the age, and that its own prevailing attitude was out of step. "The fundamental issue is not what we will do with the ne-gro, but what we—with the negro as the incident or provocation of our readjustments—will do with our institutions." Even with these advanced ideas, Murphy still held that the Negro could be granted his civil, political, and industrial rights without social integration and race amalgamation. The concept of the coexistence of segregation and equality seems absurd today, but it did not seem so to many enlight-ened Northern men of Murphy's time or to such Southerners as Henry W. Grady, who held that segregation "was instinctive and 'would assuredly develop' in any community where there were large numbers of both black and white."[16] The question of segregation had been so firmly and absolutely settled in Murphy's day that to have attacked it would have been to forfeit his entire program. As John C. Kilgo wrote in 1907,[17] "there are inherent differences between the two races, and . . . these differences have settled certain social questions. These phases of the question are settled except with a few who do not seem to know it. All that remains to be done is to see that the negro has a fair chance to develop himself. . . ." While accepting many features of segregation, Murphy challenged its caste nature and demanded that the Negro have fair opportunities.

In 1909–1910 another brilliant Southerner who devoted his career to advancing both Negroes and whites, Howard W. Odom, was writ-ing his doctoral dissertation, *Social and Mental Traits of the Negro*. He, too, accepted segregation, but, though never specifically repudi-ating the work, he grew into a firm defender of full equality. Had Murphy lived out a normal life there is reason to believe he would have gone through the same metamorphosis.[18]

In *The Basis of Ascendancy*, however, Murphy contended that the development of the Negro's manhood to the fullest extent afforded the best opportunity for each race to retain its integrity, and that Negro acceptance of proscription would constitute the greatest menace to the South and nation. It would indicate a lack of manliness and potential development and would open the possibility for the creation of an American helot class—an impossibility in a democracy. As the first step in the prevention of this and his inclusion in American life, the Negro must be given the ballot, but reasonable voting tests should admit only literate and stable individuals. The validity of every voting qualification could be tested by one question, "Does it exclude from suffrage in order finally to proscribe or in order finally to include?"[19]

Murphy's friendship with many leaders of the old order and his awareness of Populist abandonment of the Negro made him thoroughly distrust the more radical Southern leaders. The hope that the South would choose the road of inclusion, in Murphy's opinion, continued to be in the triumph of aristocratic leadership. He argued that part of the responsibility for this rested with the Negroes themselves; they must not give support to the coarser white elements who would destroy the gains that were being made. Only a sense of nobility would prevent whites from reacting injuriously to Negro provocations, protect Negro life and property, and extend opportunities for development. The ballot alone would not give the Negro protection. "With it or without it the political status of any social group will tend to conform substantially to its general economic and social position in the life of the State." For that reason, as quickly as possible, aristocratic influence must raise the Negro to a position of independence. Murphy doubted that enough chivalry existed in any class to adequately protect a helpless one for very long, and he urged that maximum aid be given the Negro to become self protective. This was the same opinion George Washington Cable had expressed twenty years before when he wrote, "Humanity—even Christianity—has never yet produced a *class* of people so noble, so wise & so good, that it will not oppress, if it has the power, any distinct class below it toward which it does not cherish a spirit of fraternity or of which it becomes in any way afraid."[20] Since this was true, Murphy held that "the basis of ascendancy" could not be one of exploitation or repression but was an intangible honor given in recognition of merit. Respect and esteem were instinctively bestowed on those groups which as stewards did their utmost to aid all people.[21]

At the time of his writing, Murphy believed the Negro, generally, to be unequal to the white race. Like John Spencer Bassett, he felt "the race is evolving its status out of barbarism slowly, indeed, but surely."[22] With education and opportunity, the Negro would improve and make greater contributions to society than ever before. Meanwhile, the race must not be judged by its members in the process of being educated, or have inequality externally imposed. "A discrimination put into the law is a discriminatory law; a discriminating law, in a democratic society, is not a law, but a revision of the law at the command of the majority," Murphy warned.

While pleading for an end of legal discrimination, Murphy, following the trend of the times, overemphasized the significance of race. Next to a man's humanity, he felt his race was the deepest thing about him. In the most plausible application of this theory, he predicted that a sense of identity among Negroes everywhere would become increasingly important and that Negroes in Africa would look to United States Negroes for leadership and aid. Envisioning a kind of American Negro "Peace Corps" which would aid Negroes everywhere with fundamental problems, he trusted that the younger generation of Negroes, seeing their development lay in service, would never despair. If this proved true, the world problem would hold the key to the American race question.[23]

Murphy correctly attributed much domestic difficulty to the deplorable race aggression by segments of the white community, an attack upon the weak by the strong which was totally indefensible. Unscrupulous politicians had learned that this policy struck a responsive chord with underprivileged whites, and, having disfranchised many Negroes, turned to other intimidations. Murphy believed the remnant of the older aristocracy, with the aid of the commercial and professional classes, had checked this movement in many areas and could do so elsewhere. Unless it was done, mistreatment of Negroes would soon spread to the whites. "The law which does not protect the weak, will not—and in the end cannot—protect the strong." Much discrimination probably arose from white people's lack of self confidence; a sense of adequacy and removal of hate offered the best hope for the development of both races. Also, knowledge of poor and illiterate people would demonstrate to the white masses that many qualities they disliked were not distinctly Negro and that many grievances were not peculiar to the South.[24]

Murphy and Washington believed it was most important that the Negro be taught to accept responsibility and educated to be able to assume economic power. From economic dependence on cotton alone, he must be trained to become a more productive force in Southern life and learn to respond to intelligent Negro leadership, which could do much to make him self-reliant. "The supreme question is not the date of arrival but the right direction of our progress," Murphy wrote. As long as the Negro, as a race, was constantly rising, his absolute position in relation to the whites was relatively unimportant. But the Negro problem could not be neglected and should be welcomed as a means for the South to develop its noblest capacities. "It was through the negro in our experience that the South once lost her mastery. It may be that through this same strange, waiting, baffling factor in her life, her ascendancy, in higher forms, may again return."[25]

In writing *The Basis of Ascendancy*, Murphy told Washington,[26] "I have exhausted every power at my command to 'knock out' once and for all the whole philosophy of repression." He emphasized to Villard[27] that in refuting repression he was criticizing a faction and not the whole South. The anti-Negro element was not completely dominant anywhere, and there were many encouraging signs. Hoke Smith had been rejected in his bid for re-election as Governor of Georgia, and Jeff Davis' candidate for governor was defeated in Arkansas, although Davis stumped the state for him. "My new book is the expression of the fundamental policy (as I understand it) of the progressive and ascendant forces of the South," Murphy declared in an obvious exaggeration of Southern enlightenment written in an effort to impress Villard. As such he was most concerned that reviews of it not depict him as siding with the North.

> The steadily increasing influence of my former book at the South among my own people is one of my deepest joys; this new book is much 'stronger meat'; but the South is ready for it if we can help our general public to understand that I have not made an attack on the South.

The work's reception was all Murphy desired. *The New York Times*[28] agreed with him that the South must work out its problems:

> When, therefore, a Southern man of extraordinary ability, of wide experience, of lofty aims, and of great sagacity, discusses the problem of his people and his class soberly and sincerely in a spirit with which the best men of all sections and of each race can heartily sympathize, he certainly renders a very great service to all concerned.
>
> To one who meets Mr. Murphy as a writer for the first time there is some possibility that the singular brilliancy of his style will obscure the soundness and solidity of his thinking.

The New York Times hoped *The Basis of Ascendancy* would be read by every Southern white man, all interested Negroes, and those in the North who thought on the subject.

The Commandant of Cadets at Hampton Institute found the book to be "the fairest and most perfect statement from every viewpoint of the situation in general." It handled delicate questions so well he wondered if they were delicate. Wickliffe Rose believed it "a triumph in the way of presenting a highly technical theme in a form which . . . will be quite clear to the layman."[29] Washington stated,[30] "I am sure that no book that I have read in recent times has given so searching and so clear an analysis of the situation as it exists in the South today." Although there were details with which he might not agree, he could say it came "as near being an accurate and, I might even say scientific statement, as any book I have yet read on this subject." At first he wondered if the title was misleading, but, he wrote Murphy, "you have done me and many others who are interested in these matters a personal service insofar as you have stated in general terms the underlying ideas and principles upon which the South must proceed in order to solve the race problem." He felt the work's value to be enhanced by its Southern authorship, and declared:

> Better than all else in the volume is the note of optimism and good will, which inspires its readers with the belief that earnest men of both races by getting together can not merely solve their problem but they can convert a condition that has sometimes seemed to be a danger in America into an influence that is useful and benevolent to both races.

Equally warm praise came from S. C. Mitchell, President of the University of South Carolina, and others from the white South. Mitchell could not find words to express his joy, and he wondered if God had shut Murphy in to continue work of this type. He confided, "All I can say is that I admire you and love you unspeakably for what you are in your own personality and for the vast service that you are rendering to our country."[31] Peabody found the book "the most sane and prophetic word which has been spoken on a theme which many people have regarded as complicated or obscure, but which, as you point out, is essentially a matter of the simplest ethics." James H. Dillard, President of the Jeanes Foundation, wrote Murphy, "long after you and I have passed away, and even more than at the present moment, [your books] are going to be blessed influences."[32] *The New York Daily Tribune* in its critique described Murphy as "a philosopher with a strong practical side. Such a writer if not destined to be a leader of the masses is likely to be recognized as a leader of the leaders. He shapes the issues and so exercises a subtle and controlling influence."[33]

Ogden received, in a private letter, the most perceptive adverse criticism of the work.[34] In seeming to accept the belief that the Negro had a distinct psychology, it contended, Murphy made him something less than human. Concurrently, he showed insufficient appreciation of diverse cultures in inadequately acknowledging that civilization is like a river fed by many streams. The author also indicted Murphy's doctrine of gradualism and his Washington-inspired defense of the South with all its injustices as the best home for the Negro. Everywhere in the South he found Negroes disfranchised "who could meet even the one sided requirements of the election laws in that section," while throughout Latin America at least twenty million Negroes enjoyed the same economic, social, and political positions as their neighbors.

The major public castigation of *The Basis of Ascendancy* came from *The New York Evening Post* and apparently arose from the unfortunate choice of its title, which was misinterpreted. The criticism was particularly galling to Murphy because *The Evening Post* had given excellent cooperation in the child labor movement, and the paper was held in high esteem in much of the East. For years Murphy had contested its handling of Southern affairs, a position in which he was not alone. Even Villard's uncle and close adviser, Francis J. Garrison, wrote him in 1906 that his editorials were splendid but invited Southern misunderstanding by unwise closing comments which implied "that the criticism and denunciation of Southern barbarity are sectional, instead of individual."[35] Perhaps Murphy prepared the way for an unkind review by challenging *The Evening Post's* Southern policy in March, 1909. At that time he wrote Villard:[36]

> During the past twelve months The Post has seemed to many of us more unjust and unreasoning than ever before in its undiscriminating attitude toward the South. I have kept silent partly because [I was] too ill to be much concerned with anything (such is the mere task of keeping alive & not a care to others), partly because I thought it all had a largely personal basis that might, with time, be modified; partly because it seems a pity for the friends of progress to contend in public.

For conscience and the Negro's sake, he solemnly protested that *The Evening Post's* editorial, "The Heart of a Class Problem," presented a false picture of race relations in the South.[37] Only an element in the

South regarded the menial Negro as the good Negro and opposed Negro progress. Only a small number of people supported Tuskegee because it turned out artisans and Washington because they felt his policies kept Negroes as "hewers of wood and drawers of water." After watching Hampton and Tuskegee for thirty years, anyone would find preposterous the contention that they existed to hold the Negro down. Murphy knew personally that a Southerner did not have to be brave to speak in favor of justice to the Negro. "So long as he observes the ordinary amenities of good sense and of neighborly behavior," he was "as free to think and speak and write as any man in any community of like size anywhere." Many of Murphy's Montgomery acquaintances had agreed with his views, while others disagreed, but he had found no greater intolerance than in the North. "No man could have for his neighbors a more generous or considerate or hospitable people." He questioned, "Is not the assumption that 'the South' is still justly baldly and literally a South of lynchers and Legrees the most terrible indictment we can bring against the negro, against the program of progress, against the whole policy of emancipation?"

Whatever its motive, on July 17, *The Evening Post* gave a caustic review of *The Basis of Ascendancy*, among other things charging, "Mr. Murphy's Ascendancy is the ascendancy of white over black at the South." It held that the work was "not so much left-over material as surplus philosophizing which Mr. Murphy *utilizes*." These charges stung Murphy to the quick since he felt they completely misrepresented his work. The entire book sought to show "that the only form of ascendancy possessing any validity or finality in a democracy is the ascendancy not of force but of service . . . How any man could read my book and yet not find that purpose in every page of it—I cannot see"; he concluded that the reviewer had read the title and leaped to a conclusion. Moreover, the charge of surplus philosophizing was equally hard to bear. "You yourself know how slowly and painfully I have to labor over all I produce," he explained to Villard. "Of course a man with a smashed heart may live along for many years in some sort of fashion; but facing the probabilities, I printed the Basis of Ascendancy first because I may not live to produce another. It is the most important thing I will ever do—or have ever done."

Murphy wondered how *The Evening Post* could praise A. H. Stone's *Studies in the American Race Problem*,[38] "full of its bitter pessimism supported by the shallowest 'economics' on the negro question" and be so critical of *The Basis of Ascendancy*. Washington rightly predicted what Stone's conclusions would be when he heard that the Carnegie Institute had commissioned him to make the study. "I think I have read with some care almost everything that Mr. Stone has printed on this subject," Washington wrote, "and I think I am safe in saying that without exception there has been but one conclusion to his investigations, and that is in plain words to damn the Negro."[39] Yet *The Evening Post* lauded his work and indicted *The Basis of Ascendancy*. Murphy had hoped for more courtesy from *The Evening Post* and its sister publication, *The Nation*, since they had been personally generous to him through the years and because they were "the two journals that talk most loudly and insistently of the Negro's status."[40]

Washington too interceded with Villard, writing that he could not believe the review had received his personal attention and asking that he see justice was done. "In my opinion and in the opinion of a great many others who have read it, it is by far the strongest, most philosophic and bravest work that has been spoken yet by any Southern man concerning conditions in the South."[41]

When Murphy protested, Villard replied that the review had distressed him more than any occurrence since his connection with *The Evening Post*, but when Murphy continued his criticism, he became angry. In early September, he returned one of Murphy's letters, asking him to reread it after a year and let him know if he thought it was written in the proper spirit. Murphy was shocked and replied by questioning the convictions of Villard's journals, particularly their praise of Stone and criticism of Washington. *The Evening Post* and *The Nation* "hate the South, and they will always flatter any Southerner who (justly or unjustly) turns on his people and rends them," he wrote.[42]

Perhaps it was due to his illness, which became progressively worse throughout the spring and much of the summer of 1909, or it may have been simply his keen disappointment at the misunderstanding that led Murphy to behave uncharacteristically and seek a retraction of the review. He felt this essential since *The Evening Post* had "an 'inherited access' to the educated public of the Eastern section of our country," and its misrepresentation would alienate much of the audience he hoped to reach. "I well know how hard it is to interest the public in any effort at fundamental thinking," he explained, and the added burden of influential misunderstanding was unbearable. Villard held his ground, however, writing Murphy, "Your hot Southern temper would have known no bounds of anger" if he had attacked the Southern Education Board or the South in the same manner in which Murphy had attacked *The Evening Post*.[43]

Conflict between Murphy and Villard was perhaps inevitable. Villard had supported the Niagra Movement, which, since 1905, had been seeking to overthrow the existing Negro leadership and obtain an immediate end to all racial discrimination. He personally authored the call for the larger 1909 meeting, out of which emerged the National Association for the Advancement of Colored People, which sought the end of all segregation and strict enforcement of the Fourteenth and Fifteenth amendments.[44] Villard's own racial views had undergone a liberalization since 1903 when he challenged W.E.B. DuBois to prove his assertion that the Negro press had accepted money to attack anti-Washington Negro leaders. Although he and DuBois had a personality conflict that proved troublous in the early years of the N.A.A.C.P., Villard grew increasingly weary with what he considered Washington's unwarranted concessions.[45] When Washington spoke of favorable aspects of the race situation during a European tour, Villard wrote him that had his grandfather done the same he would have hurt the cause of freedom. When Washington expressed elation over the appointment of a Negro in the U.S. Treasurer's office, Villard believed it was of "slight importance compared to the fearful needs of the race and the necessity for outspoken opposition to those who are steadily re-enslaving them to prejudice, both North and

South." Villard's opposition to Washington constantly increased, and he came to believe, "The great majority of the [Negro] men who have risen above the ranks consider him a traitor to the race."[46] Only Washington's charity and self-control preserved some degree of cooperation between the men. In 1911 he penned a moving tribute to Villard for inclusion in *My Larger Education* and in 1913 agreed to send a representative to an educational conference even though it was to be held at N.A.A.C.P. headquarters. At the time he stated, "If it will do the cause any good I am willing to plead guilty to the charge of cowardice and timidity." Even the vitriolic Villard could not hate a man of such temperament, although he felt compelled to oppose his policies and aid in the work of the N.A.A.C.P.[47]

Murphy completely opposed the new movement, as could be expected from one who felt that outside coercion would enable the baser elements to entrench themselves in the South and that the Negro's future depended on indigenous Southern developments. He underestimated the movement's strength but was disturbed by its existence. He never despaired until he received reports similar to those from the 1909 conference, he wrote Washington. "Not that they disturb my own faith, (all races have their silly element), but the task is made so much harder for everybody. Irrespective of the South, they do so much to injure the negro among the sensible people at the North." To Villard, Murphy wrote that in supporting the new movement his journals were "making Tillmans at the South by magnifying the cause of the negro with a program of bitterness and hate." He felt it highly significant that the two adverse reports he received of his book came from extremists at opposite ends of the political spectrum, the liberal *Evening Post* and the racist Tom Watson.[48]

While vastly concerned with racial affairs, Murphy spent much time reflecting on education, which he felt afforded the solution to many dilemmas. One of his finest statements dealing with the relation of education and government was written in letter form at this time to Peabody, who had it published and distributed.[49] No other words of Murphy so well expressed his educational philosophy with its strong overtones of Jeffersonianism or revealed more clearly the encompassing nature of his intellect. "I do not invest my money (primarily) in providing that principles shall be taught to my children," he declared, "but in the preparation and education of my children— so that they may themselves be fitted to understand and apply the principles which life (God) is always unfolding to us." In the United States, it seemed, the difficulty was not "the absence of well-advertised principles" but "the ever-broadening power of an untrained public mind: great masses of population trained indeed (in certain crude ways) to make money, but not fundamentally trained to use their faculties, to see life squarely, to appreciate its true satisfactions, or to accumulate its real wealth." He did not despair but felt "the overwhelmingly oppressive fact" must be faced that we have to deal with a public mind "which has been trained by its creature (the press) to believe conceitedly in its cleverness, but which possesses really almost no power of sustained thought about anything." It has few standards other than numbers and material gain.

Other nations had "uneducated multitudes," but Murphy thought the danger they constituted was infinitesimal compared to those of the United States. "Their uneducated multitudes do not govern, nor do they carry over the self-conscious assumptions of political procedure (the authority and finality of mere numbers) into all other procedures, into art, morals, literature, and religion." Having the right to rule, the mob assumed the right to judge in all the more important areas of life. Sensing this, almost everyone agreed that the masses must be educated, but few adequately realized "that democracy must be educated in order to live at all—in order to have fit and emancipating standards of law and right and beauty and religion, in order to have a world in which it, itself, will care to continue."

Murphy held that democracy, like government, was merely "the organized worship of power." Fortunately, in the United States another fundamental postulate—consent—existed. This implied persuasion as a necessary course of action and as a check on "the autocratic authority of numbers." In every area its influence must be strengthened through an education which elevated the standards of the masses.

> The capacity for *standards*, the training and nurture of respon-
> sive faculties, the discipline of apprehension and appreciation,
> are the work of education (elementary education)—a work
> performed under Judaism largely by the Church and the family,
> but handed over by us almost wholly to the State. —Yet how
> inadequately the State is responding!

Murphy believed in propaganda for peace, for more equitable taxes, and for free trade, but he felt they largely failed because their propaganda assumed that an unfinished work had been completed. "Our people are clever (in the newspaper sense). Our average of what we call 'popular intelligence' is astonishingly high." Yet its constructive results are meager in securing good government "and the deeper things of that sound public order for which government exists—the love of equity, the grace of loyalty, reverence, obedience, compassion." Americans loved to govern but found even self government to be an irritation because "there has been so little of the real discipline of education; a people may syndicate its universities and its newspapers, but there is no way in which it may syndicate a true basis for its social self-control or may extemporize a generous, gracious and luminous national culture."

The society Murphy longed for could never be achieved by merely educating its leaders. They would "be either corrupted or crucified unless the 'common people' are sufficiently trained to understand what real leadership is, and to see the difference between a Thad Stevens and an Abraham Lincoln, between a Hoke Smith and a Walter B. Hill, a Charley Murphy and an Edward M. Shepherd." Murphy knew such a task was a monumental one for the common school but one that could be done through "the co-operation of the Church, the home, the saner press—and all the educative forces of Society."

The vigor of Murphy's thought and the clarity of his expression concealed his intense suffering, and few guessed the stamina and determination required for his work. In hope of improvement, he planned to sail for Bad Nauheim in June, 1909, with his son, Du-Bose, as an aide, but when the time came, he was physically unable to go. In the early summer, he had "a severe surgical operation," after which his strength began slowly to return.[50] He confided to Peabody,[51] however,

> I am sensitive; but not unhappy. Physically, I am so much in distress that I say frankly to you that life is at times almost unsupportable. But mentally and spiritually I have not been so happy in many years. Life never seemed so interesting, so beautiful. Never think of me as anxious or unhappy. The longing to *work* never leaves me. I chafe under helplessness: but at heart I am not disturbed. In His own way and time He will take care of His world.

Part of Murphy's content came from a knowledge that those he esteemed most highly understood and appreciated him. At the time of his deposition from the priesthood, many were shocked and hurt. He believed, however, that he was doing God's will, and his devotion to the church remained unchanged. Through the years his motives came to be understood, a development wonderfully expressed in a letter from the Rt. Rev. Thomas F. Gailor, Bishop of Tennessee and former Chaplain of the University of the South. After meeting Murphy in 1908, Bishop Gailor wrote, "I want you to know how glad I have been to see you again and to be able to feel that the distinction you have earned has not changed the old simplicity of your Christian and Church loyalty." Gailor felt that those men who conceived and organized the Conference for Education in the South would live in the memory of their people. "The whole South realizes that a large share of this credit belongs rightly to you and that your earnestness and energy and great efficiency have actualized what otherwise would have been only a dream for many years to come. I wish to assure you of our wide-spread conviction that you have done a noble work for your people and for Christ."[52]

Murphy replied that there was nothing in the bishop's letter for which he was so grateful as his expression "concerning the relation of my work to the Church and to Christ." He had never thought that he left the priesthood for a higher vocation, but he pursued the course that seemed "the line of distinctive service." In doing so, he

turned down the presidency of Hobart College, which Peabody
agreed to aid if he would accept, as well as the rectorship of one of
the richest Eastern parishes. But his contribution appeared to lie in
the field of education. When he left the priesthood, Alabama had
approximately the same number of Episcopal clergy it had had in
1860. He wrote:

> I found many "causes" but there was one cause that weighed
> upon me night and day, partly because it had been ignored,
> partly because it was and is removable. . . this was the illiteracy
> or the semi-illiteracy of the masses of our rural population. A
> Church with a liturgy, a liturgical and educative Christianity,
> is almost as helpless with the semi-illiterate as with the illiterate.

Unlike some commentators, Murphy believed Christianity "was
from the first the religion of an educated people." The Jews "into
whose life the Lord came" were unlearned only in comparison "to the
standards of rabbinic erudition." Moreover, the church had always
stood as the propagator of "an educative faith." "I have longed to see
that basis for her work in the South," Murphy wrote, "to see her touch
the lives of our people as an educative force, for her sake as well as
their sake, —in the service of the common school as well as through
the university." He believed that higher education should come first,
but the time had come to move in the other areas where he had
worked, and, he told the bishop, "in seeing my work as a work for
Christ and the Church you have seen in it and have expressed concerning it the one thing I care most about."[53]

Another source of invaluable consolation to Murphy was the close-
ness of his family life. From the first days of marriage, Maud had
been a perfect wife—devoted, understanding, sympathic, competent.
Now as his sons, DuBose and Gardner, became teen-agers, their relationship with their father deepened and the love, tenderness, confidence, and respect they shared was unusual. Whenever he was home,
Murphy and his family did things together, although their activities
were limited by his health. When they were separated, they wrote to
each other, interspersing profundities with the trivia which is sig-

nificant only to those who love each other dearly. Murphy tried to guide his sons and encourage them to the highest achievement, but he always sought to impress them with his love, which was theirs regardless of what occurred. Thus, when they were considering Confirmation, in 1908, he told them it was "a wholesome and natural thing to do," the assumption of the responsibilities incumbent on every Christian. "But the chief thought about Confirmation is the thought of what God brings to us in it."

> Whenever we try to perform a real duty, the very act of doing the duty brings a new sense of strength. So, in Confirmation, in a still deeper sense, God's spirit answers ours, and our effort to bear our part in God's world is answered by a larger power to live truly and to work bravely. We confirm our vows, but God "confirms" and steadies us.

Yet Murphy did not pressure his sons to be confirmed. "Papa wishes it to be *your* doing, and if you make up your mind that you would rather wait another year, Papa will perfectly understand. He just loves, *loves* you so—every minute!"[54]

In 1909 DuBose was enrolled at the Hotchkiss School in Lakeville, Connecticut, and Gardner joined him within a year. Murphy's limited income would not have permitted his paying their tuition at this fine private school, but both were scholarship students who won many awards, much to his delight. He did regret that they had to be away when he was home for the first time in years, and this made their vacations even more precious. One summer when Maud was gone and Gardner was preparing for a short trip, he wrote him:[55]

> My dear Son:
>
> It is early and you are up stairs asleep and I am down stairs, where I have just had breakfast—and have put yours out on the table for you. In a few minutes I will wake you up and you can open the door of the closet and tell the alarm clock it is time for him to get up and dress—and clean his hands and wash his face, and look cheerful! But Papa's heart is thinking

of a darling boy who is going this morning on a little journey.
How *dear* you have been to me! You have been so unselfish and
patient and helpful—and your daddy loves you more and more
every day. Have a *good* time!

Papa E.G.M.

Interest in his sons led Murphy to a new career after retirement.
In 1908, he gave Gardner a subscription to *The Scientific American*
and, seeing his enjoyment of Henry Norris Russell's study of the
constellations, he became interested himself. He found a study of the
stars and planets fascinating and a calming diversion that could be
shared by his family and friends. As always, he sought more and
more information about his subject and, to his distress, found the
works available to be either dully technical or puerile. Therefore, he
decided to write *A Beginner's Star Book*, incorporating what he had
learned from many volumes and by observation. For three years, he
devoted hours to its preparation, including in it such "astronomy" as
he found interesting, but devoting most of his effort to a guide for
observation.

Since money was limited, he obtained a number of small telescopes
to facilitate his work by writing descriptions of them and their use
for instrument companies. In 1909 this led to his first published
work on astronomy, a description of what could be seen with a small
Warner and Swasey Co. telescope. It was entitled *By Starlight and
Moonlight* and sold for twenty-five cents.[56]

Due to his illness, Murphy had to do most of his observing from a
sitting position. Continually, he found that once he had an object in
view, it was lost while a chair was arranged for someone else to see.
He longed for an instrument that would allow simultaneous view-
ing by two or more persons. When this was not forthcoming, he
devised a multiple instrument which, by means of three tubes held in
parallel position by thumb-screws and wing-bolts, met his needs. It
was patented as the McKready Multiple Telescope, and, although
never produced in numbers due to an increase in the tariff on optical
goods, enabled him to enjoy many pleasant hours with his family and
friends.[57]

The entire family worked diligently on the *Beginner's Star Book*, preparing maps and charts and selecting illustrative photographs from the nation's leading observatories. G. P. Putman's Sons accepted the work for publication in 1912, after a leading importer of optical goods guaranteed the sale of the first thousand copies. To avoid reliance on Murphy's reputation in other fields, it was published under the pen name Kelvin McKready.[58]

The *Beginner's Star Book* opened with a discussion of "The Sky and Its Maps" and "The Stellar World," which treated star magnitudes and symbols, double stars, star colors, and nebulae. This was followed by chapters on "Learning to Observe," "Star Maps for Any Year," "The Solar System," "Some Instruments of Observation," "An Observer's Catalogue of Telescopic Objects," and "Star Distances, Star Motions, Star Magnitudes, etc." In a chart section, the right hand pages contained "Key Maps," fully labeled, showing the features of the region of the sky being described. On the opposite pages were "Night Charts," unlabeled maps of the same area presenting them as the observer would see them. Thus by stages one could move, without confusion, from the "Sky Map" to the "Night Chart" to the sky.

To Murphy's delight, the new work was well received. The Director of the Princeton Observatory, the man whose writings had first inspired Murphy, Henry Norris Russell, wrote, "I know of no book on the subject which combines so many good qualities." He praised the simple language, ease of use, "and *most of all, the thoroughly scientific spirit of the work.*" The President of the Astronomical Society of France, P. Puiseux, declared:

> Many authors have already undertaken to condense into a manual of small compass the knowledge useful to an amateur beginning the study of the sky. But never, we believe, has this intention been realized with so much success. . . . Each page reveals to us the trained astronomer, combined with the patient and lucid teacher.

Max Wolf, Director of the Konigstuhl-Observatory, Heidelberg, was equally laudatory: "The new points of view and the recent progress in science are by no means neglected, and the practical hints for the first use and for the treatment of instruments are extremely good." The Director of the Amherst Observatory, David Todd, expressed the opinion of many, writing, "The book is very practical indeed. It is the best book for the amateur with which I am acquainted."[59]

The critics' views proved correct, and the book was a decided success. Murphy was most pleased when a German firm agreed to publish an edition that appeared in 1913 under the title *Sternbuch für Anfänger*. The American version went through four editions, and as late as 1931 *Popular Astronomy* wrote, "Mr. McKready, in a delightful fashion, introduces the reader to constellations and planets, nebulae and clusters, by recalling his own early observational experiences." It advised the beginning observer that the work would prove "a great help."[60]

Much of Murphy's pleasure came from the congratulations of friends. Frissell wrote of his "delight" and vowed to use the book and not remain the ignorant man that he was. Edward Cary of *The New York Times* described it as "a little miracle, so clear, so well ordered & such a charming spirit." Abbott was amazed, stating, "If I were ever to write a book of Heroes and Hero worship you could be in it as one of the heroes I have known." He did not see how Murphy could do the work he did with his poor health. "You are a living demonstration of immortality; for your body could not conceivably generate the exhaustless energy which makes your abundant life."[61]

The dedication of the American edition was one feature not appreciated by many readers. It read, "To M. and D. and G., who have watched with me at the threshold." "This has, of course, a double meaning which none but my dear ones will understand," Murphy confided. "By the threshold I mean the threshold of the heavens— the heavens not of the stars alone but that other world which they suggest and at the door of which I have seemed to wait through these many years. At its threshold of the stars, my dear ones have watched with me, their love and care and patience sustaining me through every hour."[62]

During the years in which he was preparing the *Beginner's Star*

Book, Murphy made every effort to recover his health. In the spring of 1910, grieved by his mother's recent death, he took the "cure" at the sanitarium in Clifton Springs, New York, and after this made a "wheel-chair" journey to Bad Nauheim, accompanied by Maud, Du-Bose, and Gardner. Although little improvement was made, he remained confident that Dr. Schott and the Nauheim treatment offered his best hope of recovery. As Maud recalled, "In those respects in which it failed, he saw only unlucky incidents, and he was as eager as ever for another trial."[63]

After their return, and when he was not forced to rest, the friends of many years occupied Murphy's hours; they found such visits easier after the Murphys' return to New York to live. Ogden was as devoted to Murphy in retirement as when they worked together and, despite his own poor health, frequently telephoned him and remembered him in numerous ways. Adler, Washington, Dr. John Hodgson, an old Alabama intimate, and other friends called and found his mind as vigorous as ever and his spirit unquenched.[64]

Whenever they visited, Murphy's friends noted the quite pride and deep satisfaction he found in his sons' achievements. DuBose won the Chamberlain Entrance Prize in Greek at Yale in the spring of 1910, although he did not receive it because he waited until the fall of 1911 to matriculate. From his freshman days, he continued to excel in all things academic. Gardner consistently led his classes at Hotchkiss, graduating first in 1912 and receiving the Fidelity Prize, presented by the faculty to the scholarship boy who was most conspicuous in courtesy, thoroughness and punctuality. Murphy was confident that his sons had learned the value of work and how to choose "the real pleasures." As he wrote Gardner, "All the marks in the world are of less importance than this power over one's choices, the capacity for *selection*, among the interests of the moment. This *is* education." When Dr. DuBose came from Sewanee, Murphy's satisfaction was so great that he could speak of few things other than his sons. He confessed, "We talked boys and other things, and other things and boys, and then (just for a change)—boys!"[65]

Murphy's confidence in his sons was not misplaced. Both graduated

from Yale and served in the armed forces in World War I. Following study for the ministry, DuBose was ordained deacon and then
priest in the Episcopal Church. He served successfully in Dorchester,
Massachusetts, Starkville, Mississippi, and for eighteen years in Aus-
tin, Tyler, and El Paso, Texas, before coming to Christ Church in the
university town of Tuscaloosa, Alabama. Here for a decade and a
half he distinguished himself as a devoted priest and scholar. For a
number of years he served as Chairman of the Bishop of Alabama's
Board of Examining Chaplains, whose approval was required for all
men ordained in the diocese. Like his father, he wrote extensively for
the church press, well written works of meticulous scholarship that
enabled his ministry to extend far beyond his parish.

Gardner continued the study of psychology in graduate school and
received the M.A. from Yale in 1917 and the Ph. D. from Columbia
in 1923, where he taught until 1940. From 1940 to 1952 he served
as Head of the Psychology Department at the City College of New
York, and since 1952 has been Director of Research at the Menninger Foundation, Topeka, Kansas, one of the nation's most important
psychiatric centers. His extensive research and writings in the field
of personality have made him one of the nation's most respected
psychologists. Among his more important books are *Experimental
Social Psychology; An Interpretation of Research Upon the Socializa-
tion of the Individual*, and *Personality, A Biosocial Approach to
Origins and Structure*. Generations of college students have benefited
from his rich scholarship through study of his widely-used texts.[66]

Murphy's own scholarship received well earned recognition in the
spring of 1911 when the University of the South presented him the
Doctor of Laws degree, *honoris causa*. His achievements and intense
devotion to his alma mater led the Vice-Chancellor to write, "Of the
many loyal sons of Sewanee I do not know of anyone that I would
rather have seen honored than you."[67]

In the summer of 1912 the entire family again returned to Europe.
After a brief view of England, they made their way to the now familiar Nauheim where they settled down to the spa's routine. From

the first all went well. "We had a most delightful easy and successful journey and all is going famously with all hands," Murphy reported. DuBose and Gardner wheeled him to his baths, to the tennis courts, and the concerts. Dr. John Hodgson joined the group, greatly adding to its pleasure. By August, Murphy felt, "I am better in every possible way and if I can only get home without some absurd accident all will be most promising. . . . all goes happily and well."[68]

Upon his return in September, Murphy still hoped his recovery was underway. He walked in front of his apartment house, read a variety of books and articles, and tested new opera and field glasses. With Maud, he discussed plans for completing *Issues, Southern and National*, although he was never strong enough to undertake any additional writing. He closely followed developments during the political campaigns and rejoiced in Wilson's victory. In a statement reflecting his continued commitment to state's rights, he wrote, "Historically I think his greatest political service may prove to be his presenting a genial & fairly reasonable personality round which to organize the defeat of Roosevelt's assault on legitimate government. But he may have greater stuff in him."[69]

At Christmas time, the Murphys enjoyed a happier holiday season than they had known in years. By early January, however, Murphy was again desperately ill. "After more than two weeks of it," he wrote Gardner, "I am getting so *so* tired; but I feel the goodness and strength of your dear prayers every hour. Your sweet true love always reaches me, and always *will* reach me no matter where I may be."[70] His consciousness of the strength to be found in the Communion of Saints had grown as his health became more uncertain and as members of his family and friends died. "I find that each dear one who passes into the unseen reinforces the ties and deepens the reality of all who have gone before," he confessed. "As their numbers increase they seem to form a tender but imperious conspiracy, compelling us (though no compulsion be needed) to take account of them, to believe in them, to *live* in their confidence and rejoicing presence. And thus we grow not only to love them with a deeper wisdom, but to depend upon them and upon their love of us."[71] Sustained by such a faith, he faced death with serenity; in the intervals between attacks he insisted that plans be made for the future, and passage was booked for another summer excursion to Bad Nauheim. He longed for the beauty of spring and the privilege of being wheeled outdoors. But this was not to be. At two o'clock on the afternoon of June 23, 1913, Murphy died as gently as he had lived.

A private funeral service was held for his family and close friends in St. Agnes' Chapel and a public funeral in Trinity Church, Concord, where he was buried in Sleepy Hollow Cemetery.[72] In October, the Rev. William Norman Guthrie held a memorial service in Murphy's honor at his parish church, St. Mark's-in-the-Bouwerie, New York City. Bishop Gailor came from Tennessee to preach the sermon, and many of Murphy's friends remained for an "after-meeting" in St. Mark's Hall.[73] The trustees of the National Child Labor Committee called another memorial meeting for Sunday evening, December 7, at the Ethical Culture Society auditorium. In doing this, its secretary noted, "Aside from his practical services, Mr. Murphy deserves to be honored as one of the rarest and finest personalities that have in recent times appeared in American public life. . . ." Peabody served as chairman of the arrangements committee, which also included Adler, Buttrick, Caffey, Frissell, and Carnegie.[74]

The meeting was addressed by McKelway, Caffey, and Adler, three men of prominence who had known Murphy intimately and worked with him for years. McKelway recalled their work against child labor and Murphy's ability to overwhelm all rational arguments in its behalf. He compared Murphy's writing and speaking to that of Jefferson and Madison in their statesmanlike quality. Caffey, who had known Murphy in Alabama before he became nationally known, declared, "no unofficial statesman of our time, certainly none equipped with no resources save industry, eloquence and courage to present good causes, has in so few years, left such indelible, genuine marks upon his country's policies for social welfare." Adler found genius in Murphy's combination of the practical and the spiritual.

He spoke not merely as a politician, nor merely as a statesman, but as one having something of the quality of a religious seer. For while he did not withhold his pity from the oppressed, nevertheless, believing as he did, that injuries to the soul are more deplorable than any external injuries, he grieved with a peculiar solemnity of sorrow over the oppressor.[75]

The Southern Education Board[76] expressed its appreciation of Murphy in these words: "His vigorous years were a benediction to the weak and the oppressed; his later years spent in great weakness and suffering, were full of resignation, heroic effort and lofty endeavor, and were an inspiration to all who directly or indirectly came in contact with him."

Dr. DuBose declared Murphy came "nearer attaining national character" than any man "whose preparation for life was most closely associated with Sewanee." This was due not only to Murphy's residence in both North and South but also "it was temperamentally impossible for him to be sectional." He dealt with burning issues in a practical, scientific, and philosophical, as well as a Christian fashion. DuBose understood that Murphy left the priesthood in the belief that he would be able better to grapple with all-important issues. To be in contact with him, even briefly in his last year, "afforded the final and fullest revelation of the man—in his simple humanity as husband, father, and friend; sage; and," in DuBose's opinion, "as saint."[77]

The finest assessment of Murphy's career was given by *The Outlook*,[78] which recognized achievements he had strived to attain: "He became a leader not merely of Southern liberalism but of national progress in social welfare and in education" despite illness sufficiently severe to incapacite many men.

No man in this generation has succeeded so well in interpreting the South to the rest of the country. . . . Every child that is delivered by law from the oppressive toil of the factory owes a debt to Edgar Gardner Murphy. Every country school, especially in the South, that finds its resources enlarged will be in part under obligation to Edgar Gardner Murphy. Every movement in the approach toward a better understanding of the race problem in the South will feel in some degree the influence of the spirit of Edgar Gardner Murphy. He is one of those who will always be remembered as the makers of the new South and therefore of a new America.

Notes

Chapter 1.

1. Memoranda for biographical sketch of Edgar Gardner Murphy, Du-
    Bose Murphy Papers, in possession of Leonard B. Murphy, Abilene,
    Texas, collection hereinafter cited as DuBose Murphy Papers, Abi-
    lene; DuBose and Gardner Murphy, *Maud King Murphy, 1865–
    1957*, 13, hereinafter cited as D. and G. Murphy, *Maud Murphy*.
2. Maud King Murphy, *Edgar Gardner Murphy, From Records and
    Memories*, 5–7, hereinafter cited as Maud Murphy, *E.G.M.*
3. Burton J. Hendrick, *The Training of An American, The Earlier Life
    and Letters of Walter H. Page, 1855–1913*, 78–84.
4. W. Norman Pittinger (ed.), *William Porcher DuBose, Unity in the
    Faith*, vi, ix, 1–11, 14–16, 21–22, 26; Moultrie Guerry, "Makers of
    Sewanee: William Porcher DuBose," *Sewanee Review*, XLI (Octo-
    ber, 1933), 483–489; John S. Marshall, "From Aristotle to Christ, or
    the Philosophy of William Porcher DuBose," *ibid.*, LI (January–
    March, 1943), 148–155; Henry S. Nash, "Dr. DuBose's 'Gospel in
    the Gospels,'" *ibid.*, XV (January, 1907), 112–118; Murphy to
    Hollis Burke Frissell, May 23, 1900, Southern Education Board Pa-
    pers, Dabney Series, University of North Carolina, hereinafter cited
    as SEB Papers, Dabney Ser., UNC.
5. Maud Murphy, *E.G.M.*, 7.
6. Christ Church Bulletin, Lent, 1893, Gardner Murphy Papers, Topeka,
    Kansas, collection hereinafter cited as Gardner Murphy Papers,
    Topeka.
7. St. Paul's Church Bulletin, Edgar Gardner Murphy Papers, University
    of North Carolina, collection hereinafter cited as Murphy Papers,
    UNC.
8. D. and G. Murphy, *Maud Murphy*, 1–8; Maud Murphy, *E.G.M.*, 8.

9. *Ibid.,* 10–11; Maud to DuBose Murphy, February 15, (1914 ?), DuBose Murphy Papers, Abilene.

10. *Idem,* August 31, 1913, *ibid.;* D. and G. Murphy, *Maud Murphy,* 12.

11. Christ Church Bulletin, Murphy Papers, UNC.

12. "First Principles," *Homiletic Review* (January, 1893), *ibid.*

13. Christ Church Bulletin, Gardner Murphy Papers, Topeka; *Church News* (San Antonio), September, 1893, Murphy Papers, UNC.

14. *San Antonio Express,* August 3, 1893, *ibid.*

15. "Brotherhood and Brotherhoods," *St. Andrew's Cross* (September, 1893), *ibid.*

16. "Self-Fulfillment," *Homiletic Review* (October, 1893), *ibid.*

17. Murphy to Booker T. Washington, January 1, 1900, Booker T. Washington Papers, Library of Congress, collection hereinafter cited as B.T.W. Papers, L.C.

18. Murphy to Oswald G. Villard, June 29, 1909, Oswald G. Villard Papers, Harvard University, collection hereinafter cited as Villard Papers, Harvard University.

19. Clipping, *Laredo News,* Murphy Papers, UNC.

20. Murphy to Washington, January 1, 1909, B.T.W. Papers, L.C.

21. *Bishop's Junior Church News* (San Antonio), February, 1893, Murphy Papers, UNC.

22. Murphy to the Congregation of Christ Church Parish, September 5, 1893, *ibid.*

23. Murphy to Villard, June 12, 1909, Villard Papers, Harvard University.

24. Maud Murphy, *E.G.M.,* pp. 10–11.

25. *Chillicothe News,* May 14, 1894, Murphy Papers, UNC.

26. *Chillicothe News,* March 11, 1895, *ibid.*

27. *Chillicothe Gazette,* May 14, 1894, March 2, 1895, *ibid.; Chillicothe News,* March 2, 1896, *ibid.*

28. *Chillicothe Daily News,* February 15, 22, 1897, *ibid.*

29. *Chillicothe News,* January 12, February 1, 1895, *ibid.; Chillicothe Gazette,* February 8, 1896, *ibid.*

30. Clippings, Murphy Scrapbook, *ibid.*

31. *Chillicothe Gazette,* July, 1894, *ibid.*

32. *Chillicothe News,* January, 1895, *ibid.*

33. Notices of Convocations, Columbus Deanery, *ibid.*

34. Review of "Clerical Life and Work" (May, 1895), *ibid.*

35. *Churchman* (September 19, 26, 1896), *ibid.*

36. "The New American Saint," *Outlook,* LV (February 13, 1897), 487–488.

37. *The Living Church* (April 24, 1897), Murphy Papers, UNC.

38. *The Larger Life, Sermons and An Essay*, pp. x, 5–7.

39. *Ibid.*, x, 5–7, 11, 14–15, 22–28, 33, 43–44.

40. *Ibid.*, 63–64, 110–113.

41. *Ibid.*, 70–75, 111, 134–141, 148–159, 181–185.

42. Clippings, Murphy Papers, UNC.

43. *Sewanee Review*, V (October, 1897) 501–504.

44. *Words for the Church*, Preface, Introduction, 1–13.

45. *Ibid.*, 14–15, 20–22, 22–37.

46. *Ibid.*, 39–48, 59–90, 103, 114.

47. *Chillicothe News*, October 4, 1897, Murphy Papers, UNC; *Chillicothe Gazette*, October 4, 5, 1897, *ibid.*

48. *Chillicothe Gazette*, October 5, 1897, *ibid.*

49. Maud Murphy, *E.G.M.*, 15.

50. Clippings, Murphy Papers, UNC.

51. Maud Murphy, *E.G.M.*, 16.

52. Clippings, Murphy Papers, UNC.

53. *Outlook*, LVIII (February 5, 1898), 394.

54. *Churchman* (March 5, 1898), Murphy Papers, UNC.

55. *North American Review*, CLXVI (June, 1898), 751–752.

56. *Outlook*, LIX (August 6, 1898), 816–817.

57. *Papers, Addresses and Discussions at the Eighteenth Church Congress in the United States, Held in the City of Pittsfield, Mass., June 7, 8, 9, and 10, 1898*, 116–122.

58. Murphy to the Wardens and Vestry of St. John's, November 21, 1898, Murphy Papers, UNC.

Chapter 2.

1. Rector's Letter, February, 1899, Murphy Papers, UNC; Vestry's Statement to the People of St. John's, 1899, *ibid.*; Vestry to Contributors, March 30, 1899, *ibid.*

2. Rector's Letter, April, 1899, *ibid.*

3. Rector's Letter, August, 1899, *ibid.*; Maud Murphy, *E.G.M.*, 17.

4. Rector's Letter, August, 1899, Murphy Papers, UNC.

5. *Montgomery Advertiser*, February 15, 1899.

6. Rector's Letter, February, 1899, Murphy Papers, UNC.

7. Rector's Letter, April, 1899, *ibid.*

8. Rector's Letter, February, 1900, *ibid.*; *Montgomery Advertiser*, February 1, 1900.

9. Rector's Letter, June 6, 1899.

10. *Montgomery Advertiser*, June 6, 1899.

11. *An Episcopal Church for the Negroes of Montgomery, Alabama*, in Murphy Biographical Folder, Library, Alabama Department of Archives and History, Montgomery.

12. Bulletin, Church of the Good Shepherd, *ibid.*

13. *Church Record* (Tuscaloosa), November 1, 1900, Murphy Papers, UNC.

14. *Montgomery Advertiser*, n.d., *ibid.*; Clipping, Sermon before the Sunday School Association of the Arch-Deanery of Atlanta, January 18, 1900, *ibid.*; Perry Picture System advertisement, *ibid.* The Perry Co. owned the copyright to the pictures and chose to buy Murphy's lessons. Maud Murphy states (*E.G.M.*, 18–20) Perry was not seriously interested in the work and in a few years so neglected orders that sales ceased. Murphy attempted to buy the copyright but was refused.

15. Cited in Maud Murphy, *E.G.M.*, 34. Mrs. Murphy incorrectly gives the date of the ordination as 1901.

16. *Montgomery Advertiser*, October 27, 30, 1900; *Church Record* (Tuscaloosa), December 1, 1900, Murphy Papers, UNC.

17. *Churchman* (November 26, 1898), 775–776, *ibid.*

18. *Providence Journal*, January 19, 1899, *ibid.*

19. Page to Willa Alice Page, February 26, 1899, Page Papers, Harvard University; Harris to Page, August 14, 1900, *ibid.*; "Stirring up the Fires of Race Antipathy," *South Atlantic Quarterly*, II (October, 1903), 298; John E. White, "The Need of a Southern Program on the Negro Problem," *ibid.*, VI (April, 1907), 179; C. Vann Woodward, *The Strange Career of Jim Crow*, 2nd ed., 82–90, hereinafter, Woodward, *Jim Crow*, and *Origins of the New South*, 211–212, 352, hereinafter, Woodward, *Origins*; Paul Lewinson, *Race, Class and Party, A History of Negro Suffrage and White Politics in the South*, 83–85; I. A. Newby, *Jim Crow's Defense, Anti-Negro Thought in America, 1900–1930*, 13–16.

20. Southern Commission on the Study of Lynching, *Lynchings and What They Mean*, 8–12; William H. Glasson, "The Statistics of Lynching," *South Atlantic Quarterly*, V (October, 1906), 343–348; Moton, "The South and the Lynching Evil," *ibid.*, XVIII (July, 1919), 191–192; Carter G. Woodson, *The Negro in Our History*, 8th ed., 547.

21. Ewing to Cable, August 16, 1905, Cable Papers, Tulane University; Ewing to George Foster Peabody, June 5, 1903, Peabody Papers, L.C.

22. Arthur S. Link, "The Progressive Movement in the South, 1870–1914," *North Carolina Historical Review*, XXIII (April, 1946), 193–194; Oswald G. Villard to Hugh H. Gordon, Jr., August 28, 1906, Villard Papers, Harvard University; "The Georgia Atrocity and Southern Opinion," *Outlook*, LXII (May 20, 1899), 179–180.

23. *Montgomery Advertiser*, January 9, 1900.

24. Constitution of the Southern Society, Murphy Papers, UNC.

25. Philip W. Wilson, *An Unofficial Statesman—Robert C. Ogden*, 124–127, hereinafter, Wilson, *Robert Ogden*; John G. Brooks, *An American Citizen, The Life of William Henry Baldwin, Jr.*, 191–192, hereinafter, Brooks, *W. H. Baldwin*; August Meier, *Negro Thought in America, 1890 to 1915, Racial Ideologies in the Age of Booker T. Washington*, 100–103, hereinafter, Meier, *Negro Thought*; Francis L. Broderick, *W. E. B. DuBois, Negro Leader in Time of Crisis*, 65.

26. Manuscript from shorthand notes of the correspondents of *The Outlook* and *The Boston Evening Transcript*, Murphy Papers, UNC.

27. *Montgomery Advertiser*, January 11, 1900; *New York Evening Post*, January 20, 1900.

28. Brooks, *W. H. Baldwin*, 8, 19, 33, 41, 52–53, 101, 165, 192n., 206, 223; *Dictionary of American Biography*, I, 548, hereinafter, *DAB*.

29. *Ibid.*, VII, 36.

30. *Ibid.*, XIII, 641; Wilson, *Robert Ogden*, 20, 42–43, 58–60, 89–90, 124–201; Samuel C. Armstrong to Ogden, June 18, 1878, May 31, 1892, Ogden Papers, L.C.; Ogden to Armstrong, March 19, 1874, *ibid.*; Ogden to Rep. George D. McCreary, December 9, 1904, *ibid.*; Ogden to James A. Worden, September 23, 1903, *ibid.*; *Southern Workman*, XLII (September, 1913), 469–471. Ogden was also a leading member of the Board of Trustees of the Union Theological Seminary.

31. Maud Murphy, *E.G.M.*, 27.

32. *Philadelphia Public Ledger*, January 19, 1900, Murphy Papers, UNC.

33. Louis R. Harlan, "Booker T. Washington and the White Man's Burden," *American Historical Review*, LXXXI (January, 1966), 441–442; Washington, "My View of Segregation Laws," *New Republic*, V (December, 1915), 113–114; Donald J. Calista, "Booker T. Washington: Another Look," *Journal of Negro History*, XLIX (October, 1964), 240, 254–255; Richard Bardolph, *Negro Vanguard*, 87; Washington to Villard, November 16, 1904, Villard Papers, Harvard University; Woodward, *Jim Crow*, 82; Samuel R. Spenser, Jr., *Booker T. Washington and the Negro's Place in American Life*, 103, hereinafter, Spenser, *Washington*; Basil Mathews, *Booker T. Washington, Educator and Inter-Racial Interpreter*, 299, hereinafter, Mathews, *Washington*.

34. Murphy to Booker T. Washington, February 7, 13, May 30, 1900, Letters, Principal's Office, B.T.W. Papers, L.C.

35. *The White Man and the Negro at the South, An Address delivered under invitation of the American Academy of Political and Social Science, the American Society for the Extension of University Teaching, and the Civic Club of Philadelphia, in the Church of the Holy Trinity, Philadelphia, on the Evening of March 8th, A.D., 1900,* 3–9, hereinafter, Murphy, *The White Man and the Negro.*

36. Abbott to Katherine Coman, May 2, 1903, B.T.W. Papers, L.C.

37. Murphy, *The White Man and the Negro,* 10–14; Robert W. Winston, "An Unconsidered Aspect of the Negro Question," *South Atlantic Quarterly,* I (January, 1902), 265.

38. Murphy, *The White Man and the Negro,* 14–26; James W. Garner, "Lynchings and the Criminal Law," *South Atlantic Quarterly,* V (October, 1906), 333; Mathews, *Washington,* 295.

39. Page to Willia Alice Page, February 26, 1899, Page Papers, Harvard University; Cable miscellaneous ms., Scraps-File Folder, Cable Papers, Tulane University.

40. Murphy, *The White Man and the Negro,* 26–35; Chamberlain to W. G. Martin, August 13, 1904, Villard Papers, Harvard University; Donald J. Calista, "Booker T. Washington, Another Look," *Journal of Negro History,* XLIX (October, 1964), 255; Page to Murphy, April 15, 1900, Page Papers, Harvard University; James W. Garner, "Recent Agitation of the Negro Question in the South," *South Atlantic Quarterly,* VII (January, 1908), 15.

41. Murphy, *The White Man and the Negro,* 36–41.

42. *Church Standard,* March 17, 1900.

43. *Montgomery Advertiser,* March ? , 1900, Murphy Papers, UNC.

44. March 24, 1900.

45. *Montgomery Advertiser,* March ? , 1900, Murphy Papers, UNC; Maud Murphy, *E.G.M.,* 28.

46. Murphy to Albert Shaw, February 7, 1900, Shaw Papers, New York Public Library, hereinafter cited as Shaw Papers, N.Y. Library; Murphy to W. Bourke Cockran, March 8, April 2, 1900, Cockran Papers, New York Public Library, hereinafter cited as Cockran Papers, N.Y. Library.

47. Murphy to Washington, March 28, 1900, B.T.W. Papers, L.C.

48. Ogden to Page, April 5, 1900, Page Papers, Harvard University; Page to Murphy, April 15, 17, 1900, *ibid.*

49. Murphy to Cockran, April 11, 18, 1900, Cockran Papers, N.Y. Library; Hollis B. Frissell to Murphy, May 3, 1900, Southern Education Board Papers, Miscellaneous Series, University of North Carolina, hereinafter cited as SEB Papers, Misc. Ser., UNC.

50. Thomas M. Owen, *History of Alabama and Dictionary of Alabama Biography,* III, 798.

51. *Race Problems of the South—Report of the Proceedings of the First Annual Conference Held Under the Auspices of the Southern So-*

ciety for the Promotion of the Study of Race Conditions and Problems in the South at Montgomery, Alabama, May 8, 9, 10, A.D. 1900, 26–38, hereinafter, *Race Problems of the South.*

52. *Ibid.*, 41–55; Thomas F. Gossett, *Race: The History of An Idea in America*, 280.

53. *Race Problems of the South*, 58–77. See also MacCorkle's *Some Southern Questions* (New York, 1908). MacCorkle was not pleased with his reception at the conference. When the Southern Society wrote him to suggest someone to appear on the following year's program, he asked Washington to name a speaker who held his views. See MacCorkle to Washington, July 30, 1900, B.T.W. Papers, L.C.

54. *Race Problems of the South*, 85–94.

55. *Ibid.*, 107–113.

56. *Ibid.*, 152–155, 178–194. [For a fuller treatment see Barringer's *The American Negro; His Past and Future* (Raleigh, 1900)].

57. *Ibid.*, 194–216. Cockran was so impressed with Washington and the description he gave of the work at Tuskegee that after his return to New York he sent Washington a check, stating it was "but a faint indication of the deep interest I have in your work, and the high hopes I have built upon its success." See Cockran to Washington, May 14, 1900, B.T.W. Papers, L.C.

58. *Race Problems of the South*, 219–220.

59. Murphy to William H. Baldwin, Jr., May 12, 1900, B.T.W. Papers, L.C.; Murphy to Cockran, May 14, 1900, Cockran Papers, N.Y. Library.

60. Murphy to Washington, July 9, 1900, Letters, Principal's Office, B.T.W. Papers, L.C.

61. "The Montgomery Race Conference," XL (August, 1900), 630–632. John E. Milholland wrote Washington (September 13, 1900, B.T.W. Papers, L.C.) that the most interesting feature of the Conference for him occurred when Herbert "gushing over you wound up by asking the assembly if anyone present would welcome you as a guest to his household; and such was the cowardly, disgraceful spirit of the audience at the time that no one stood up to answer in the affirmative." He would have "given a thousand dollars to have been present just at that time. It was an opportunity for the stupidest man that ever faced an assembly to score a point."

62. Murphy to Cockran, June 5, 1900, Cockran Papers, N.Y. Library.

63. *Idem*, June 27, 1900, *ibid.*

64. *Idem*, May 14, 24, June 5, 13, 27, July 23, August 8, 15, 1900, *ibid.*

65. Murphy to Page, February 22, 27, 1900, Page Papers, Harvard University.

66. Murphy to Washington, July 9, 1900, Letters, Principal's Office, September 24, October 22, 1900, January 20, March 8, 27, 1901, B.T.W. Papers, L.C.; Maud Murphy, *E.G.M.*, 31.

67. *Montgomery Advertiser*, October 19, 1900, January 16, February 17, March 8, 1901; Murphy to Cockran, August 8, 22, 1900, Cockran Papers, N.Y. Library; Murphy to Albert Shaw, November 8, 1902, Shaw Papers, N.Y. Library; Murphy to Andrew Carnegie, n.d., *ibid.* In December, 1903, Murphy asked Washington to go with him to call on Carnegie; see Murphy to Washington, December 14, 1903, and Washington to Murphy, December 15, 1903, B.T.W. Papers, L.C.

68. Louis Ware, *George Foster Peabody, Banker, Philanthropist, Publicist*, vii, ix, 14, 23–30, 64–68, 80, 92–100, hereinafter, Ware, *Peabody*.

69. *Montgomery Advertiser*, October 6, November 12, 1901.

70. March 28, 1901.

71. *Montgomery Advertiser*, March 23, 1901.

72. Kenneth K. Bailey, "Southern White Protestantism at the Turn of the Century," *American Historical Review*, LXVIII (April, 1963), 625–626; Josephus Daniels, *Editor in Politics*, 102, 112–116, 230–231.

73. *Montgomery Advertiser*, October 19, 1900; *Church Record* (Tuscaloosa), December 1, 1900, Murphy Papers, UNC.

74. *Montgomery Advertiser*, December 6, 1900, January 13, February 7, 1901.

75. February 24, 1901, Murphy Papers, UNC; *Southern Workman*, XXXIII (June, 1904), 324.

76. Murphy to Washington, February 25, 1901, B.T.W. Papers, L.C.

77. Newby, *Jim Crow's Defense*, 143–156; Woodward, *Origins*, 321, 334–335; Albert D. Kirwan, "Apportionment in the Mississippi Constitutional Convention of 1890," *Journal of Southern History*, XIV (May, 1948), 238–246; William Alexander Mabry, "Disfranchisement of the Negro in Mississippi," *ibid.*, IV (August, 1938), 327–330.

78. David D. Wallace, "The South Carolina Convention of 1895," *Sewanee Review*, IV (May, 1896), 351; George B. Tindall, "The Question of Race in the South Carolina Constitutional Convention of 1895," *Journal of Negro History*, XXXVII (July, 1952), 300–303; Francis B. Simpkins, *Pitchfork Ben Tillman*, 302.

79. William Alexander Mabry, "Louisiana Politics and the 'Grandfather Clause,'" *North Carolina Historical Review*, XIII (October, 1936), 301, citing *The New Orleans Daily Picayune*, February 21, 1898; Washington to T. Thomas Fortune, November 7, 10, 1899, B.T.W. Papers, L.C.

80. William Alexander Mabry, "Louisiana Politics and the 'Grandfather Clause,'" *North Carolina Historical Review*, XIII (October, 1936), 310; Mabry, "Ben Tillman Disfranchised the Negro," *South Atlantic Quarterly*, XXXVII (April, 1938), 180; James H. Brewer,

"Editorials from the Damned," *Journal of Southern History,* XXVIII (May, 1962), 225–229.

81. Woodward, *Origins,* 321–349, 369–395; Josephus Daniels, *Editor in Politics,* 283–302, 307, 319–326, 363–368; William Alexander Mabry, "Negro Suffrage and Fusion Rule in North Carolina," *North Carolina Historical Review,* XII (April, 1935), 97–102.

82. Page to Willia Alice Page, January 12, 1907, Page Papers, Harvard University; for treatment of Montague's racism in Virginia, see William Larsen, *Montague of Virginia, the Making of a Southern Progressive,* especially 119–193.

83. *Alabama Journal* (Montgomery), April 15, 1901; *An Open Letter on Suffrage Restriction, and Against Certain Proposals of the Platform of the State Convention,* Fourth Edition, hereinafter cited as *An Open Letter;* Malcolm C. McMillan, *Constitutional Development in Alabama, 1798–1901: A Study in Politics, the Negro, and Sectionalism,* 249–260.

84. *Ibid.,* 261; *An Open Letter,* 1–7.

85. December 22, 1902, Shaw Papers, N.Y. Library.

86. *An Open Letter,* 8–13.

87. *Ibid.,* 13–18.

88. Newspaper clipping signed "Optimist," Murphy Papers, UNC.

89. *Alabama Journal* (Montgomery), April 18, 1901.

90. Owen, *op. cit.,* III, 1515.

91. *Montgomery Advertiser,* July 12, 1901.

92. *Ibid.,* June 26, July 12, 1901; Murphy to Washington, July 12, 1901, B.T.W. Papers, L.C. Murphy sent Washington copies of his letters, at this time and later.

93. Murphy Papers, UNC.

94. *Montgomery Advertiser,* July 12, 1901; citation in Maud Murphy, *E.G.M.,* 41.

95. "Progress in the South," *Outlook,* LXVIII (June 29, 1901), 475–476.

96. Murphy to Washington, October 7, 1901, B.T.W. Papers, L.C.; clipping from *Outlook,* Murphy Papers, UNC.

97. *Montgomery Advertiser,* April 2, 1901.

Chapter 3.

1. *New York Evening Post,* July 2, 1913; a portion of this chapter appeared in "Edgar Gardner Murphy and the Child Labor Movement," *Alabama Review,* XVIII (January, 1965), 47–59, and is used with permission.

2. Murphy, *The Case Against Child Labor: An Argument*, 23, and *Child Labor and Business*, 3; A. J. McKelway, "Reply to Miss Magruder's Article in *The North American Review*, October, 1907," Andrew J. McKelway Papers, Library of Congress, hereinafter cited as McKelway Papers, L.C.; McKelway, "Child Labor in Its Relation to Education," *ibid.*; McKelway, "Child Labor in the South," an Address before the American Association for the Advancement of Science, Philadelphia, 1907, *ibid.*

3. Broadus Mitchell, "Economics in the South," *Current History*, XXXII (May, 1957), 270; McKelway, "Fact vs. Superstition," McKelway Papers, L.C.

4. Bernard Mandel, *Samuel Gompers, A Biography*, 180–181; Murphy, *Child Labor Legislation, Review of Laws in the United States*, 1, 3–5.

5. Elizabeth Huey Davidson, "Early Development of Public Opinion Against Southern Child Labor," *North Carolina Historical Review*, XIV (July, 1937), 230–231; Robert G. Smith, "Mill on the Dan: Riverside Cotton Mills, 1882–1901," *Journal of Southern History*, XXI (February, 1955), 61–62; Jerome Dowd, "Child Labor," *South Atlantic Quarterly*, I (January, 1902), 41–43.

6. Maud Murphy, *E.G.M.*, 42; Benjamin B. Kendrick and Alex M. Arnett, *The South Looks At Its Past*, 127; McKelway, "Child Labor and its Attendant Evils," *Sewanee Review*, XVI (April, 1908), 215.

7. Elizabeth H. Davidson, *Child Labor Legislation in the Southern Textile States*, 20–23, hereinafter, Davidson, *Child Labor Legislation*; Davidson, "Early Development of Public Opinion Against Southern Child Labor," *North Carolina Historical Review*, XIV (July, 1937), 239.

8. *Montgomery Advertiser*, February 7, 1901.

9. Broadus Mitchell, "Two Industrial Revolutions," *South Atlantic Quarterly*, XX (October, 1921), 301–302; George T. Winston, *A Builder of the New South, Being the Story of the Life Work of Daniel Augustus Tompkins*, 2, 18, 22–23, 28–29, 33, 53, 56, 69, 72, 76, 95–96, 102, 116–117, 132, 146–147, 157, 165–167, 187–189, 241, 255–281; William P. Few, "The Constructive Philanthropy of a Southern Cotton Mill," *South Atlantic Quarterly*, VIII (January, 1909), 82, 89.

10. Clipping from *Birmingham Age-Herald*, Murphy Papers, UNC.

11. Murphy, *Child Labor in Alabama, An Appeal to the People and Press of New England With A Resulting Correspondence*, 6, hereinafter, *Child Labor in Alabama*.

12. Miss Ashby recounted rumors that both the Senate and House committees were "fixed" before any hearings were held. See *The Churchman*, July 20, 1901, Murphy Papers, UNC.

13. *Child Labor in Alabama*, 3–6; McKelway, "Child Labor in the South," McKelway Papers, L.C.

14. *The Boston Evening Transcript*, October 30, 1901.

15. *Child Labor in Alabama*, 11–20.

16. The reply initially appeared in *The Boston Evening Transcript* and was reprinted in *The Monthly Leader*, December, 1901.

17. *Child Labor in Alabama*, 21–27.

18. *Ibid.*, 27–28.

19. Murphy, *The South and Her Children, A Rejoinder in the Child Labor Discussion*, 3, hereinafter, *The South and Her Children*.

20. *The Case Against Child Labor: An Argument*, 3–5, 22–27.

21. *Ibid.*, 6–18.

22. *Ibid.*, 27–34.

23. *Ibid.*, 19, 34–36, 38, 41–45.

24. August 28, 1902, as reproduced in *The South and Her Children*, 4–11.

25. *Ibid.*, 4–9; McKelway, "Child Labor and Its Attendant Evils," *Sewanee Review*, XVI (April, 1908), 219.

26. *The South and Her Children*, 13, 15, 17–21.

27. Murphy, *A Child Labor Law*, 1–10.

28. *Child Labor and Business*, 1–5.

29. September 2, 1902.

30. Bulletin B never appeared.

31. October 29, 1902.

32. Davidson, *Child Labor Legislation*, 39.

33. *Child Labor Legislation, Review of Laws in the United States*, 10, 28.

34. *Pictures from Mill Life. Mill Children in Alabama*, 3–4, 7, 9.

35. *Ibid.*, 11.

36. Davidson, *Child Labor Legislation*, 36.

37. Murphy, "Southern Prosperity is not Shackled to Child Labor," *Charities*, X (May 2, 1903), 453.

38. Davidson, *Child Labor Legislation*, 34–37, citing Murphy to Gompers, October 11, 18, November 5, 10, December 10, 1902, January 9, 1903.

39. Murphy to Villard, November 22, 1902, Villard Papers, Harvard University.

40. *Idem, ibid.*; Davidson, *Child Labor Legislation*, 47.

41. *Montgomery Advertiser*, February 20, 1903; Murphy, "Child Labor in Alabama," *The Annals of the American Academy of Political and Social Science*, XXI (March, 1903), 331–332; Davidson, *Child Labor Legislation*, 49.

42. Murphy, *Annals, loc. cit.*

43. *Ibid.*; Davidson, *Child Labor Legislation*, 50.

44. Elizabeth H. Davidson, "The Child Labor Problem in North Carolina, 1883–1903," *North Carolina Historical Review*, XIII (April, 1936), 112, 116, 120–121; McKelway to the Editor of *The Wilmington Star*, November 6, 1909, McKelway Papers, L.C.

45. The address is reproduced in Murphy, *Problems of the Present South*, Chapter V, 129–149.

46. May 16, 1903.

47. Oral testimony of McKelway before Senator Walch's Committee, May 11, 1915, B.T.W. Papers, L.C.; McKelway's Memorial Oration, Gardner Murphy Papers, Topeka.

48. Davidson, *Child Labor Legislation*, 111, 118, 121.

49. *Ibid.*, 123; Maud Murphy, *E.G.M.*, 72–73.

50. Typescript, Murphy Papers, UNC.

51. *Ibid.*, 1–4.

52. *Ibid.*, 4–8.

53. *Ibid.*, 8–12.

54. Minute Book, National Child Labor Committee, First to Tenth Meetings, April, 1904–April, 1906, National Child Labor Committee Papers, Library of Congress, hereinafter cited as N.C.L.C. Book #1, L.C.

55. Leaflet, *National Child Labor Committee*, Murphy Papers, UNC.

56. "The National Child-labor Committee," *Charities*, XII (June 4, 1904), 574–576.

57. Folks, "Child Labor and the Law," *ibid.*, XIII (October 1, 1904), 20.

58. Adler's Memorial Oration, Gardner Murphy Papers, Topeka.

59. N.C.L.C. Book #1, May 4, 1904, L.C.

60. Folks to Murphy, September 2, 1904, Murphy Papers, UNC.

61. N.C.L.C. Book #1, October 3, November 10, 1904, February 6, 1905, L.C.

62. *Ibid.*, November 16, 1905; leaflet, *National Child Labor Committee*, Murphy Papers, UNC.

63. Programs, *ibid.*

64. McKelway, "Legislative Hints for Social Reformers," and "Ten Years of Child Labor Reform," McKelway Papers, L.C.

65. Murphy to McKelway, January 23, 1905, Murphy Papers, UNC.

66. McKelway, "Legislative Hints for Social Reformers," McKelway Papers, L.C.; Elizabeth H. Davidson, "Child Labor Reforms in North Carolina Since 1903," *North Carolina Historical Review*, XIV (April, 1937), 112, 114–118; Joseph L. Morrison, *Josephus Daniels Says . . . An Editor's Political Odyssey from Bryan to Wilson and F.D.R., 1894–1913*, 155–157, 211–212, citing *Charlotte Observer*, January 1, June 20, 1905; Herbert J. Doherty, Jr., "Alexander J. McKelway: Preacher to Progressives," *Journal of Southern History*, XXIV (May, 1958), 179–180, and "Voices of Protest from the New South," *Mississippi Valley Historical Review*, XLII (June, 1955), 61–62.

67. Davidson, *Child Labor Legislation,* 129–130; Minute Book, National Child Labor Committee, Eleventh to Nineteenth Meetings, October 24, 1906–April 29, 1908, National Child Labor Committee Papers, Library of Congress, hereinafter cited at N.C.L.C. Book #2, L.C.

68. N.C.L.C. Book #1, November 16, 1905, L.C.

69. Maud Murphy, E.G.M., 86.

70. Caffey to Murphy, November 30, 1906, Murphy Papers, UNC; de-Forest to Murphy, May 28, 1907, *ibid.*

71. Lindsay to Murphy, June 3, 1905, *ibid.*

72. N.C.L.C. Book #2, containing the letter of Murphy to Adler, December 18, 1906, January 29, 1907, L.C.

73. Lindsay to Murphy, January 10, 1907, Murphy Papers, UNC.

74. Lindsay to George Foster Peabody, January 25, 1907, *ibid.*; Davidson, *Child Labor Legislation,* 134–135; Owen R. Lovejoy to Peabody, January 31, 1908, Peabody Papers, L.C.; Oswald G. Villard to Lillian D. Wald, September 9, 1907, Villard Papers, Harvard University; Wald to Villard, September 27, 1907, *ibid.*

75. *Montgomery Advertiser,* January 13, 1907; Eliot to Murphy, January 18, 1907, Murphy Papers, UNC; Murphy to Roosevelt, February 4, 1907, *ibid.*

76. Murphy to Oswald G. Villard, February 24, 1907, Villard Papers, Harvard University.

77. Roosevelt to Murphy, January 17, 1907, Gardner Murphy Papers, Topeka.

78. Murphy to Villard, February 17, 24, 1907, Villard Papers, Harvard University.

79. *The Federal Regulation of Child Labor, A Criticism of the Policy Represented in the Beveridge-Parsons Bill,* 1–7.

80. *Ibid.,* 8–11.

81. *Ibid.,* 12–14.

82. *Ibid.,* 15–28.

83. *Ibid.,* 28–30.

84. *Ibid.,* 28–36.

85. Davidson, *Child Labor Legislation,* 133.

86. See 157 *infra.*

87. December 2, 1907.

88. Murphy was in Texas when the Alabama committee voted to adopt this policy, and he disclaimed all direct responsibility for it.

89. Murphy to Adler, May 27, 1907, Murphy Papers, UNC.

90. June 26, 1906.

91. Davidson, *Child Labor Legislation,* 216.

92. Murphy to Villard, March 10, 1907, Villard Papers, Harvard University.

93. Dated March 29, 1907, Murphy Papers, UNC.

94. This is the seventh and last stanza of the poem which is dated March 20, 1907. The poem is in the Southern Education Board Papers, A. P. Bourland Collection, University of North Carolina.

95. Murphy to Villard, March 10, 1907, Villard Papers, Harvard University.

96. As reprinted the work was entitled: *The Child Labor Question in Alabama—A Plea for Immediate Action*, National Child Labor Committee Pamphlet 59, hereinafter, *Plea for Immediate Action*; McKelway to Murphy, January 17, 1911, as cited in Davidson, *Child Labor Legislation*, 220.

97. *Plea for Immediate Action*, 1–6.

98. *Ibid.*, 6–8.

99. *Ibid.*, 8–12; accounts of this are also in the *Mobile Register*, July 13, 1907, and *The New York Evening Post*, July 18, 1907.

100. *Plea for Immediate Action*, 12n; Murphy, "Child Labor in Alabama," *New York Evening Post*, September 19, 1907.

101. *Ibid.*

102. Murphy to Villard, September 17, 1907, Villard Papers, Harvard University.

103. Roosevelt to Murphy, November 15, 1907, Murphy Papers, UNC.

104. deForest to Murphy, May 28, 1907, Murphy Papers, UNC; National Child Labor Committee, *Third Annual Report—for the Fiscal Year Ended September 30, 1907*, 12–13; Davidson, *Child Labor Legislation*, 135–137.

105. Murphy to Villard, January 2, 1908, Villard Papers, Harvard University.

106. Lovejoy to Murphy, January 6, 1908, Murphy Papers, UNC.

107. deForest to Murphy, January 8, 1908, *ibid.*

108. "Child Labor in 1913," *Child Labor Bulletin* (November, 1913), 9, Murphy Papers, UNC.

Chapter 4.

1. James W. Silver, "Mississippi: The Closed Society," *Journal of Southern History*, XXX (January, 1964), 4.

2. For example, see Murphy to Washington, August 4, 1902, B.T.W. Papers, L.C.

3. *Idem*, October 20, November 18, 1902, *ibid.*

4. Washington to Oswald G. Villard, October 10, 1904, Villard Papers, Harvard University.

5. Woodward, *Origins*, 424–425; Washington to Villard, April 20, 1908, Villard Papers, Harvard University.

6. Washington to Villard, September 7, 1908, *ibid.*

7. J. W. Dinsmore to George W. Cable, June 21, 1909, Cable Papers, Tulane University.

8. Francis Garrison to Villard, September 12, 1908, Villard Papers, Harvard University.

9. Samuel Proctor, *Napoleon Bonaparte Broward, Florida's Fighting Democrat*, 251–252; Edwin A. Alderman, *The Growing South*, 12–14, 18, 20.

10. Little to Washington, July 2, 1905, Villard Papers, Harvard University.

11. Oscar Handlin, "Desegregation in Perspective," *Current History*, XXXII (May, 1957), 257.

12. To the Editor of *The Atlanta Constitution*, August 31, 1905, Villard Papers, Harvard University.

13. Thomas F. Gossett, *Race: The History of An Idea in America*, 285.

14. *Ibid.*, 283.

15. See 191–193 *infra*.

16. Murphy, *The Task of the South. An Address before the Faculty and Students of Washington and Lee University, Lexington, Virginia, December 10th A.D., 1902*, 2nd ed., 8–12.

17. *Ibid.*, 12–24, 26–37; Broadus Mitchell, "Economics in the South," *Current History*, XXXII (May, 1957), 270.

18. *Montgomery Advertiser*, February 15, 1903; Maud Murphy, *E.G.M.*, 63–64.

19. Wm. Loeb, Jr. to Murphy, February 25, 1903, Gardner Murphy Papers, Topeka; Theodore Roosevelt to Washington, September 14, 1901, March 4, 1903, B.T.W. Papers, L.C.; Woodward, *Origins*, 464–468; Henry F. Pringle, *Theodore Roosevelt, A Biography*, 247–250; Seth M. Scheiner, "President Theodore Roosevelt and the Negro, 1901–1908," *Journal of Negro History*, XLVII (July, 1962), 170–176.

20. Shaw Papers, N.Y. Library.

21. February 7, 1903, *ibid.*

22. Vincent P. DeSantis, "The Republican Party and the Southern Negro, 1877–1897," *Journal of Negro History*, XLV (April, 1960), 87; Seth M. Scheiner, "President Theodore Roosevelt and the Negro, 1901–1908," *ibid.*, XLVII (July, 1962), 180–181; Edwin Mims, "President Theodore Roosevelt," *South Atlantic Quarterly*, IV (January, 1905), 58–61; Woodward, *Origins*, 465–466.

23. Emma Lou Thornbrough, "The Brownsville Episode and the Negro Vote," *Mississippi Valley Historical Review*, XLIV (December,

1957), 481; Roosevelt to Murphy, January 17, 1907, Gardner Murphy Papers, Topeka.

24. Villard to Washington, November 16, 1906, B.T.W. Papers, L.C.; James A. Tinsley, "Roosevelt, Foraker, and the Brownsville Affray," *Journal of Negro History*, XLII (January, 1956), 43–49, 54–55.

25. Washington introduction of J. H. Dillard, n.d., B.T.W. Papers, L.C.

26. Remarks in *Westminister Gazette* made at annual meeting of the Anti-Slavery and Aborigines Protection Society, April 12, 1916, Page Papers, Harvard University.

27. Clippings, Murphy Papers, UNC.

28. Maud Murphy, *E.G.M.*, 56.

29. Madison Square Garden Speech Typescript, Murphy Papers, UNC; Murphy to J. H. Kirkland, November 29, 1907, Ogden Papers, L.C.

30. Madison Square Garden Speech.

31. Murphy to Villard, May 22, 29, 1903, Villard Papers, Harvard University.

32. *Outlook*, LXXIV (June 13, 1903), 391.

33. Murphy, *The Peonage Cases in Alabama. Three Letters*, 3–6.

34. *Ibid.*, 6–8.

35. *Ibid.*, 8–12.

36. *Ibid.*, 12–18.

37. Murphy to Villard, July 23, 1903, Villard Papers, Harvard University.

38. *Idem*, July 25, 1903, *ibid*.

39. Murphy to Washington, July 28, 1903, B.T.W. Papers, L.C.

40. CLXXX (January, 1905), 109–133.

41. January 21, 1905, Murphy Papers, UNC.

42. January 13, 1905, *ibid*.

43. *The Present South*, preface, 208.

44. *Ibid.*, 22–23, 46, 129, 160, 238, 258.

45. *Ibid.*, 7, 11, 170, 190, 263–265, 282–283; Bruce L. Clayton, "An Intellectual on Politics: William Garrott Brown and the Ideal of a Two-Party South," *South Atlantic Quarterly*, LXIII (Winter, 1964), 352.

46. Guion G. Johnson, "The Ideology of White Supremacy," in Fletcher Green (ed.), *Essays in Southern History*, 145.

47. "Our Duty to the Negro," *South Atlantic Quarterly*, II (October, 1903), 373.

48. *The Present South*, 12–13, 16, 18, 20, 49, 93, 149, 183–184, 189, 194, 199, 241, 269.

49. *Ibid.*, 19–20, 68, 179, 189, 269.

50. *Ibid.*, 81–89, 271.

51. *Ibid.*, 153, 155, 165–168, 174–186, 260–273.

52. *Ibid.*, 32–33 60–62, 71, 77, 81, 86, 102–103, 162. Chapter VII, 205–250, deals with education and presents a strong plea for federal aid. Chapter IV, "The Industrial Revival and Child Labor," and Chapter V, "Child Labor and the Industrial South," 95–149, present Murphy's views on the child labor question.

53. *Southern Workman*, XXXIII (June, 1904), 324; other quotations are from an advertisement of *The Present South*, Gardner Murphy Papers, Topeka.

54. April 14, 1904, Murphy Papers, UNC.

55. Advertisement of *Problems of the Present South*, Gardner Murphy Papers, Topeka.

56. Schurz to Murphy, April 7, 1904, *ibid.*

57. Hay to Murphy, December 17, 1904, *ibid.*

58. Buttrick to Murphy, January 4, 1905, Murphy Papers, UNC.

59. Robert C. Ogden to Murphy, September 9, 1905, Ogden Papers, L.C.

60. Anson Phelps Stokes to Murphy, May 17, 1904, Gardner Murphy Papers, Topeka; Maud Murphy, *E.G.M.*, 79.

61. Murphy to Washington, August 20, 1904, B.T.W. Papers, L.C.

62. Ogden to Murphy, September 15, 1904, Letter Book, Ogden Papers, L.C.

63. Ogden to Roosevelt, December 5, 1914, SEB Papers, Dabney Ser., UNC.

64. Wm. Loeb Jr. to Ogden, December 6, 1904, *ibid.*

65. Washington to T. Thomas Fortune, November 22, 1904, B.T.W. Papers, L.C.

66. Ogden to Murphy, December 13, 1904, Letter Book, Ogden Papers, L.C.

67. Roosevelt to Murphy, January 17, 1907, Gardner Murphy Papers, Topeka.

68. Murphy to Villard, January 5, 8, 1905, Villard Papers, Harvard University.

69. Villard to Murphy, February 23, 1906, *ibid.*

70. See Raymond A. Cook, "The Man Behind The Birth of A Nation," *North Carolina Historical Review*, XXXIX (October, 1962), 519–523, 529–535.

71. Hart to Murphy, June 1, 1905, Murphy Papers, UNC; Murphy to Villard, February 16, 1906, Villard Papers, Harvard University; Villard to Murphy, February 23, 1906, *ibid.* Villard admitted to Robert C. Ogden that Hart "was becoming somewhat severe and extreme in his Northern view of things" and expressed the hope that Hart "might come in contact with some of the informing influences" of the Conference for Southern Education; see Ogden to Murphy, June 19, 1905, Ogden Papers, L.C.

72. Murphy to Villard, April 12, 1906, Villard Papers, Harvard University; Villard to Murphy, April 16, 1906, *ibid.* Villard could not believe anything was wrong at Tuskegee, having visited it only recently.

73. Washington to Murphy, November 9, 14, 1906, B.T.W. Papers, L.C.; Murphy to Washington, November 17, 1906, *ibid.*

74. Washington to Villard, October 10, 1908, Villard Papers, Harvard University.

75. XV (January, 1907), 1–30.

76. *Ibid.*, 1–10.

77. *Ibid.*, 11–30.

78. Washington to Murphy, January 5, 1907, B.T.W. Papers, L.C.; Murphy to Villard, January 14, 1907, Villard Papers, Harvard University. Washington also asked Murphy's suggestions for Tuskegee trustees. He recommended B. J. Baldwin and S. B. Marks, Jr. of Montgomery. See Murphy to Washington, June 3, 1907, B.T.W. Papers, L.C.

79. Murphy, "The Proposed Negro Episcopate—Part of a Letter to a Member of the House of Bishops," *Churchman* (September 21, 1907), 403–404.

80. Murphy to Ogden, September 14, 1907, Ogden Papers, L.C.

Chapter 5.

1. George F. Milton, "Compulsory Education and the Southern States," *Sewanee Review*, XVI (July, 1908), 299; Ambrose Caliver, "Certain Significant Developments in the Education of Negroes During the Past Generation," *Journal of Negro History*, XXXV (April, 1950), 113.

2. Murphy, *Task of the South*, 41–48, 51; Murphy, N.E.A., *Journal of the Proceedings and Addresses of the Forty-Second Annual Meeting Held At Boston, Massachusetts, July 6–10, 1903*, XL (1903), 133–136, hereinafter *N.E.A. Journal, 1903.*

3. "Some Phases of Southern Education," *South Atlantic Quarterly*, II (April, 1903), 138.

4. "The School as the Exponent of Democracy in the South," *Sewanee Review*, XVI (January, 1908), 24.

5. Edgar W. Knight, "The Peabody Fund and Its Early Operations in North Carolina," *South Atlantic Quarterly*, XIV (April, 1915), 168–171, 179–180; Henry L. Swint, "Rutherford B. Hayes, Educator," *Mississippi Valley Historical Review*, XXXIX (June, 1952), 45–50, 57–58; Harold W. Mann, *Atticus Greene Haygood, Methodist*

Bishop, Editor and Educator, 147–148, 182–195; Curtis W. Garrison (ed.), "Slater Fund Beginnings: Letters from General Agent Atticus G. Haygood to Rutherford B. Hayes," *Journal of Southern History*, V (May, 1939), 223–223; John Hope Franklin, "Jim Crow Goes to School: The Genesis of Legal Segregation in Southern Schools," *South Atlantic Quarterly*, LVII (Spring, 1959), 226, 232.

6. Allen J. Going, "The South and the Blair Education Bill," *Mississippi Valley Historical Review*, XLIV (September, 1957), 267–275, 281–283, 289–290.

7. *N.E.A. Journal, 1903*, 129–133.

8. George W. Cable, "Is the South Doing All It Can for Public Education," MS, Cable Papers, Tulane University.

9. Page to E. A. Alderman, August 21, 1896, Alderman Papers, University of Virginia; Burton J. Hendrick, *The Training of An American, The Earlier Life and Letters of Walter H. Page, 1855–1913*, 175–192.

10. Alderman, "Charles Brantley Aycock—An Appreciation," *North Carolina Historical Review*, I (July, 1924), 244, 248–249, 271; Josephus Daniels, "Charles Brantley Aycock—Historical Address," *ibid.*, 262–263; Robert B. House, "Aycock and Universal Education," *ibid.*, XXXVII (April, 1960), 212–214; Dumas Malone, *Edwin A. Alderman, A Biography*, 23–29, 35, 38–39, 51–53, 61, 67, 71, 76; Clement Eaton, "Edwin A. Alderman—Liberal of the New South," *North Carolina Historical Review*, XXIII (April, 1946), 206–209, 215–219; "Dr. Edwin A. Alderman—A Brief Appreciation," *University of Virginia Bulletins*, New Series, IV (October, 1904), 238–240; Edwin Mims, "A Semi-Centennial Survey of North Carolina's Intellectual Progress," *North Carolina Historical Review*, XXIV (April, 1947), 246; Daniels, *Editor in Politics*, 322–323; Rose Howell Holder, *McIver of North Carolina*, vii, 55–63, 70–80, 94, 113–117, 127, 161, 176–183.

11. Wycliffe Rose, "The Educational Movement in the South," Murphy Papers, UNC; Julian D. Dreher, "A Short Account of the First Conference for Christian Education in the South, Capon Springs, West Virginia, June 29 to July 2, 1898," SEB Papers, Dabney Ser., UNC.

12. Minutes of the Capon Springs Conference and Conference for Education in the South, Vol. XXXVI, SEB Papers, UNC, hereinafter cited as Conference Minutes; Southern Education Board, Scrapbook #2, *ibid.*; *New York Evening Post*, June 26, 1899.

13. Murphy to Frissell, March 24, June 4, 1900, Robert C. Ogden Papers, University of North Carolina, hereinafter cited as Ogden Papers, UNC; *idem*, June 16, 1900, Murphy Papers, UNC; "The Conference and Its Growth, 1898–1914," hereinafter cited as "The Conference, 1898–1914," Ogden Papers, UNC; Rose, *loc. cit.*

14. *Ibid.*; Dabney to Dickerman, April 10, 1909, SEB Papers, Dabney Ser., UNC.

15. *Proceedings of the Fourth Conference*, 21.

16. *Ibid.*, 12.

17. "Results of Informal Conference, Greensboro, N.C., September 13, 1901," SEB Papers, Dabney Ser., UNC; Southern Education Board Minutes, Vol. XXXVIII, SEB Papers, UNC, hereinafter cited as SEB Minutes.

18. The latter three were also to be the district directors.

19. SEB Minutes.

20. Ogden stated Curry's role was to be that of a "general adviser or consulting engineer," while the actual work was to be directed by others.

21. Ogden to Murphy, November 11, 1901, SEB Papers, Dabney Ser., UNC; Ogden to Booker T. Washington, November 11, 1901, B.T. W. Papers, L.C.

22. *Montgomery Advertiser*, November 28, December 19, 1901; clippings, Murphy Papers, UNC.

23. D. and G. Murphy, *Maud Murphy*, 18–19.

24. *Montgomery Advertiser*, December 15, 1901.

25. Albert Shaw to Murphy, December 4, 1901, SEB Papers, Dabney Ser., UNC; Murphy to Dabney, December 19, 1901, *ibid.*; Murphy to Shaw, December 28, 1901, Shaw Papers, New York Library.

26. Frissell to Ogden, December 31, 1901, SEB Papers, Miscellaneous Ser., UNC.

27. Murphy to Washington, January 1, 2, 23, 1902, B.T.W. Papers, L.C.; Murphy to Curry, February 4, 1902, Letter Book, Murphy Papers, UNC.

28. Alderman, "Robert Curtis Ogden, Volunteer Statesman," *University of Virginia Alumni Bulletin*, IX (January, 1916), 5–9; Page to Mrs. William Potter Wilson, May 20, 1913, Ogden Papers, L.C.

29. Ogden to Dr. Cuyler, March 30, 1904, Ogden Papers, L.C.; Philip Whitwell Wilson, *An Unofficial Statesman—Robert C. Ogden*, 206–214, hereinafter Wilson, *Ogden*; Ogden to Oswald G. Villard, March 10, 1905, Villard Papers, Harvard University; Ogden to Rev. Samuel H. Bishop, March 27, 1906, *ibid.*

   "In the relations between the races, I take the stand that guides me in in all the social affairs of my life," Ogden wrote Julius D. Dreher (March 20, 1906, Ogden Papers, L.C.). "I deal with the individual alone, and make my determination entirely upon my own preferences. It is my natural disposition to be quite particular in social matters, but I do include among friends, for whom I have profound respect, at least a half dozen colored men."

30. Wilson, *Ogden*, 206–207; Ogden to Rev. Rollin A. Sawyer, February 16, 1906, Ogden Papers, L.C.; Ogden to W. H. Baldwin, Jr., April 5, 1907, *ibid.*; Edwin M. Shepard to Peabody, June 6, 1905, Peabody Papers, L.C. Underlying factors also were the relative secrecy with which the board functioned and the demogogic opposition to all educational advancement.

31. Ogden to Villard, March 10, 1905, Villard Papers, Harvard University.

32. Murphy to Washington, January 8, 1902, B.T.W. Papers, L.C.; Dabney to Murphy, February 8, 1902, SEB Papers, Dabney Ser., UNC.

33. "Organization of the General Education Board," *ibid.*; *A Statement Concerning the Southern Education Board . . . Circular of the Southern Education Board*, Series I (June, 1902); Murphy, *Task of the South*, 1–6; Raymond B. Fosdick, *Adventure in Giving, The Story of the General Education Board, A Foundation Established by John D. Rockefeller*, vii, 3–25; Mrs. John D. Hammond, "The Work of the General Education Board in the South," *South Atlantic Quarterly*, XIV (October, 1915), 348–351; "The General Education Board and the American College," *ibid.*, XV (April, 1907), 244–247.

34. G. S. Dickerman to Washington, April 14, 1902, Letter Book, Murphy Papers, UNC; Maud Murphy, *E.G.M.*, 59.

35. *Proceedings of the Fifth Conference*, 1, 20–26, 36, 55–61.

36. SEB Minutes, Meeting of May 14, 1902; Maud Murphy, *E.G.M.*, 58.

37. Dabney to Murphy, March 5, April 10, 1902, SEB Papers, Dabney Ser., UNC; Murphy to Dabney, April 16, May 9, 1902, *ibid.*

38. Charles G. Lewis, *Philander Priestley Claxton, Crusader for Public Education*, 114–117.

39. Dabney to Murphy, April 10, February 14, May 23, 1902, SEB Papers, Dabney Ser., UNC; Murphy to Dabney, May 23, 1902, *ibid.*; Murphy to Peabody, June 23, 1902, Peabody Papers, L.C.

40. *Progress Within the Year, Circular of the Southern Education Board*, Series I (October, 1902).

41. Murphy to Peabody, June 23, 1902, Peabody Papers, L.C.; Maud Murphy, *E.G.M.*, 59.

42. The Board concurred with Murphy's views, and the following year the poem was incorporated in its minutes; see SEB Minutes, August 10, 1902, August 7, 1903. It read:

> Where two great poplars lift their slender height
> Between the freighted hills and waters clear—
> Twin beacons of his hospitality clear—
> He gave us kindly welcome. In our right
> He named anew the woody steeps of light,
> And, soft distilling from his royal mere,
> He brought the meaning of a love sincere,

And made "our" home a lodging for delight.
A place he made for converse and for rest;
He builded here a lodge for brotherhood.
We shall remember; and the solemn good
Of these true, human hours shall long attest
The grace that wrought a welcome for his guest
From out those noble waters and the silent wood.

43. Murphy to Curry, September 24, 1902, J.L.M. Curry Papers, L.C.

44. Murphy to Dabney, November 5, 1902, SEB Papers, Dabney Ser., UNC; Dabney to Murphy, November 13, 1902, *ibid.*

45. *Task of the South*, 24–27.

46. *Ibid.*, 39–41.

47. *Ibid.*, 41–48, 51; *N.E.A. Journal*, 1903, 129–133.

48. Cited in Maud Murphy, *E.G.M.*, 66.

49. Murphy to Washington, January 8, 1902, B.T.W. Papers, L.C.; SEB Minutes, session beginning January 7, 1903.

50. Ogden to Murphy, January 21, 23, February 3, 1900, Ogden Papers, L.C.; Ogden to Alderman, February 3, 1903, Letter Book, *ibid.*

51. Murphy to Joseph B. Graham, March 11, 16, 1903, Letter Book, Murphy Papers, UNC.

52. Murphy to Clay, March 30, 1903, *ibid.*; Ogden to Murphy, February 7, 17, March 6, 7, 9, 1903, Letter Book, Ogden Papers, L.C.

53. Murphy to Mrs. B. B. Valentine, March 12, 28, 1903, Letter Book, Murphy Papers, UNC; Murphy to N. Rufus Rhodes, March 30, 1903, *ibid.*; Murphy to Hill, April 3, 1903, *ibid.*

54. "The Conference, 1898–1914," 3–8; *Proceedings of the Sixth Conference*, 10–11, 39–45.

55. *Ibid.*, 10.

56. Dickerman to Murphy, March 30, 1903, SEB Papers, Dickerman Letter Book, UNC; Maud Murphy, *E.G.M.*, 70–71. Here, as in several other instances, Mrs. Murphy's dates are incorrect. See also, Ogden to Rev. Theodore L. Cuyler, April 2, 1904, Ogden Papers, L.C.

57. Maud Murphy, *E. G. M.*, 67; *Montgomery Advertiser*, May 29, 1903. "Culture and Democracy" is Chapter VIII of *The Present South*, 251–288.

58. Murphy to Dabney, June 25, 1903, SEB Papers, Dabney Ser., UNC; Ogden to Dabney, July 2, 1903, *ibid.*; statement on 1903 Summer School, *ibid.*

59. *N.E.A. Journal, 1903*, 129–137.

60. *Ibid.*

61. *Ibid.*, 133–136.

62. SEB Minutes, meeting beginning August 7, 1903; Dabney to Murphy, August 1, 1903, SEB Papers, Dabney Ser., UNC; Ogden to Murphy,

September 28, October 1, 1903, Letter Book, Ogden Papers, L.C.; Murphy to Mrs. B. B. Valentine, December 8, 1903, Letter Book, Murphy Papers, UNC.

63. *Alabama's First Question*, 1–6.

64. *Ibid.*, 7.

65. Murphy to Ogden, March 5, 8, 1904, Ogden Papers, L.C.

66. *Idem*, March 8, 1904, *ibid.*

67. Murphy to Dabney, February 6, 1904, SEB Papers, Dabney Ser., UNC; Ogden to Murphy, March 12, April 7, 9, 1904, Letter Book, Ogden Papers, L.C.; Murphy to Ogden, April 6, 8, 1904, *ibid.* After the Conference, Ogden wrote, "The Negro press is charging us with surrendering to the South and the Southern press charges us with being simply friends of the Negroes in disguise. It is amusing to read the two sorts of criticism in the light of each other." (Ogden to Dabney, May 21, 1904, SEB Papers, Dabney Ser., UNC.)

68. *Proceedings of the Seventh Conference*, 18, 112, 131–135.

69. Ogden to Murphy, July 15, 1904, Letter Book, Ogden Papers, L.C.; SEB Minutes, Summer 1904, *ibid.*

70. Dickerman to John Graham Brooks, July 19, 1904, Dickerman Scrapbook, SEB Papers, UNC; Dickerman to Murphy, August 1, 1904, *ibid.*; *Proceedings of the Eighteenth Annual Convention of the Association of Colleges and Preparatory Schools of the Middle States and Maryland*, XVIII–XXII (1904–1908), 64–74.

71. *Ibid.*, 70–74.

72. Murphy to Peabody, January 12, 1905, Peabody Papers, L.C.; Murphy to Ogden, January 17, 1905, Ogden Papers, L.C.; Ogden to Murphy, January 18, 1905, Letter Book, *ibid.*; SEB Minutes, March 8, 9, 1905.

73. Murphy to Ogden, March 14, 17, 22, April 4, 5, 10, 1905, Ogden Papers, L.C.; *idem*, April 4, 5, 1905, Education Series, Letters I, *ibid.*; *idem*, March 23, 1905, B.T.W. Papers, L.C.

74. Notice of legal action taken following the wreck, Ogden Papers, L.C.; *Chicago News*, April 29, 1905; Ogden to Dabney, May 9, 1905, Ogden Papers, L.C.

75. C. S. Dickerman, "The Conference for Education in the South and the Southern Education Board," Chapter XI, *Proceedings of the Tenth Conference*, 313; *Proceedings of the Eight Conference*, 70, 148–152.

76. *Ibid.*, 8–10.

77. Maud Murphy, *E.G.M.*, 84; Ogden to Murphy, September 9, 1905, Letter Book, Ogden Papers, L.C.

78. Murphy to Peabody, December 12, 1905, Peabody Papers, L.C.

79. *Idem*, January 24, 1906, *ibid.*; SEB Minutes, January 25, 1906; Ogden to Murphy, January 27, February 14, 1906, Letter Book, Ogden Papers, L.C.

80. Ogden to Murphy, March 9, 1906, Ogden Papers, L.C.; Ogden to Mc-Iver, March 16, 1906, SEB Papers, Dabney Ser., UNC; Ogden to Dabney, April 16, 1906, *ibid*.; "Informal Conference—Called by Ogden, Union League Club, April 25, 1906," SEB Papers, Bourland Ser., UNC.

81. "The Conference, 1898–1914," 11–12; *Proceedings of the Ninth Conference*, 13–16; Dickerman to Murphy, May 25, 1906, Dickerman Scrapbook, SEB Papers, UNC; Joseph Cannon Bailey, *Seaman A. Knapp, Schoolmaster of American Agriculture*, 3, 20–21, 31, 37, 42–50, 91, 98, 101, 109–110, 132–141, 152, 169–178, 185, 196, 202, 216–228, 245–249, 226–267; Page to Buttrick, February 10, 17, 1907, Page Papers, Harvard University; Raymond B. Fosdick, *Adventures in Giving, The Story of the General Education Board, A Foundation Established by John D. Rockefeller*, 39–43.

82. Ogden to Murphy, June 6, 1906, Letter Book, Ogden Papers, L.C. Ogden wrote that matters at Tuskegee "are causing me constant anxiety; in fact there is anxiety everywhere—so much so that there is little left in life to enjoy. And yet I must make no complaint, especially when I think of your long struggle." June 27 (*idem, ibid*.), he declared, "The responsibilities for Hampton and Tuskegee are just now pressing very hard. The latter needs a great deal of executive work for its improvement."

83. SEB Minutes, August 6–8, 1906; "Summer Meeting, Southern Education Board, August 6–8, 1906," Ogden Papers, L.C.

84. Maud Murphy, *E.G.M.*, 84; SEB Minutes, December 3–5, 1906; Dickerman to Ogden, December 12, 1906, Dickerman Scrapbook, SEB Papers, UNC.

85. Murphy to Ogden, December 31, 1906, SEB Papers, Dabney Ser., UNC; Murphy to Alderman, January 4, 1907, *ibid*.

86. Ogden to Murphy, January 4, March 3, 1907, Ogden Papers, L.C.; Murphy to Dickerman, January 1, 1907, Dickerman Scrapbook, SEB Papers, UNC; Dickerman to Frissell, March 10, 1907, *ibid*.; Murphy to Alderman, March 13, 1907, Ogden Papers, UNC; Murphy to Ogden, March 3, 1907, Educational Series, Ogden Papers, L.C.

87. *Proceedings of the Tenth Conference*, 18–23, 37–38.

88. Washington to Villard, April 21, 1903, Villard Papers, Harvard University. The Treasurer's statement for the year ending December 31, 1905 (SEB Papers, UNC) reported a budget of $24,908.05 for the Southern board; of this the General Board gave $4,000, Peabody and Ogden $1,500 each, Frank R. Chambers $5,000, and Andrew Carnegie $10,000; in addition, Ogden and Peabody each made $2,500 contributions.

89. *Proceedings of the Tenth Conference*, 40–45. A detailed account of Southern school progress under Board leadership is in G. S. Dick-

erman (with the assistance of Wickliffe Rose), *Educational Progress in the South, A Review of Five Years, Field Reports of the Southern Education Board*, 263–300.

90. "The Conference, 1898–1914," 12.

91. Dickerman to Ogden, July 6, 1907, Dickerman Scrapbook, SEB Papers, UNC; Murphy to Washington, May 4, June 1, 1907, B.T.W. Papers, L.C.; Tribute to Ogden, July 1, 1907, *ibid.*; Murphy to Peabody, July 28, 1907, Peabody Papers, L.C.

92. "Summer Meeting, 1907," Ogden Papers, L.C.; SEB Minutes, August 5, 1907, SEB Papers, Miscellaneous Ser., UNC; Louis Harlan, "The Southern Education Board and the Race Issue in Public Education," *Journal of Southern History*, XXIII (May, 1957), 193–194.

93. Louis R. Harlan, *Separate and Unequal, Public School Campaigns and Racism in the Southern Seaboard States, 1901–1915* carefully chronicles the board's compromise with Southern racism. He writes (p. 95), while fighting demagogues, the Northern philanthropists joined the upper class Southern conservatives "who quietly administered discrimination."

94. Murphy to Dickerman, November 14, 1907, SEB Papers, Dabney Ser., UNC; Murphy to Buttrick, November 14, 1907, *ibid.*

95. "Progress in Southern Education," *Tradesman*, (January 1, 1908), 385–386.

96. Murphy to Ogden, November 26, 29, 1907, SEB Papers, Dabney Ser., UNC.

97. Calendar of Events, *ibid.*

98. SEB Minutes, December 10–11, 1907.

99. Mitchell to Murphy, February 19, 1908, Murphy Papers, UNC.

100. Dickerman to Ogden, December 15, 1907, Dickerman Scrapbook, SEB Papers, UNC; Dickerman to Dr. J. S. Mitchell, January 1, 4, 1908, *ibid.*

101. Murphy Papers, UNC.

102. *Proceedings of the Eleventh Conference*, 9, 29, 101; Murphy to J. Y. Joyner, February 4, 1908, SEB Papers, Joyner Ser., UNC; Dickerman to A. J. Steele, March 28, 1908, Dickerman Scrapbook, SEB Papers, UNC; Murphy to Ogden, April 28, 1908, Gardner Murphy Papers, Topeka.

103. Included in a letter to Dickerman, May 18, 1908, Ogden Papers, UNC.

104. "Summer Meeting, August 4–5, 1908," Ogden Papers, L.C.; Murphy to Ogden, January 9, 1909, *ibid.*

105. *Idem*, October 20, 1908, New Series, Letters I, *ibid.*

106. November 10, 1908, *ibid.*

107. SEB Minutes, January 12–13, 1909.

108. January 9, 1909, Ogden Papers, L.C.

109. SEB Minutes, April 17, 1909, February 2, 1910.

110. Mitchell to Murphy, February 19, 1908, Murphy Papers, UNC; *Montgomery Advertiser*, February 20, 1908.

111. Wiggins to Murphy, February 20, 1908, Peabody Papers, L.C.

112. Dillard to Murphy, February 18, 1908, *ibid*.

113. Murphy to Washington, March 29, 1908, B.T.W. Papers, L.C.; Murphy to Peabody, May 30, 1908, Peabody Papers, L.C.; Murphy to Ogden, October 20, 1908, Educational Series, Letters I, Ogden Papers, L.C.

114. Murphy to Washington, January 30, 1908, B.T.W. Papers, L.C.

115. Burton J. Hendrick, *The Life of Andrew Carnegie*, II, 262.

116. Washington to Murphy, April 20, 1908, B.T.W. Papers, L.C.; Murphy to Peabody, May 30, 1908, Peabody Papers, L.C.; Pritchett to Murphy, March 30, December 14, 1908, Murphy Papers, UNC; *idem*, October 30, 1908, SEB Papers, Joyner Ser., UNC.

117. Dickerman to Ogden, November 13, 1908, Dickerman Copybook, SEB Papers, UNC; Joyner to Murphy, November 20, 1908, SEB Papers, Joyner Ser., UNC.

118. Francis G. Peabody to Murphy, February 20, 1908, George Foster Peabody Papers, L.C.

Chapter 6.

1. Murphy, "Backward or Forward," *South Atlantic Quarterly*, VIII (January, 1909), 19–38.

2. Washington to Francis J. Garrison, October 12, 1905, September 6, 1906, Villard Papers, Harvard University; Washington to Wallace Buttrick, September 30, 1906, B.T.W. Papers, L.C.; Washington to Page, November 6, 1906, October 13, 1911, Page Papers, Harvard University.

3. Murphy, "Backward or Forward," *loc. cit.*, 19–22.

4. Arthur Krock (ed.), *The Editorials of Henry Watterson*, 313.

5. W. W. Ball, "Improvement in Race Relations in South Carolina: The Cause," *South Atlantic Quarterly*, XXXIX (October, 1940), 385–389, 393.

6. Murphy, "Backward or Forward," *loc. cit.*, 23–38.

7. January 29, 1909, B.T.W. Papers, L.C.

8. Washington to Murphy, February 9, 1909, *ibid.*; Murphy to Washington, February 15, 1909, *ibid.*

9. Maud Murphy, *E.G.M.*, 101.

10. The table of contents was: I. The Children of the Mills (the Open Letter to the Legislature of Alabama), prepared; II. Child Labor and the Reaction (Reworked version of the address before the Ethical Culture Society of New York), partially ready; III. The Millions Out of School, unprepared; IV. The Deportation of A Perplexity, prepared; V. A Word for Tuskegee (the Madison Square Garden address), prepared; VI. Are There Lessons in Jamaica?, unprepared; VII. The Courts, the Schools and the Labor Question (Immigration as effected by security and opportunity), unprepared; VIII. How to Make the Negro Work (education as the stimulus of wants), unprepared; IX. The Economic Defect of "Economics" (reply to A. H. Stone), unprepared; X. The Public Function of the Public School" (Princeton address, rewritten), prepared; XI. "Shall the Fourteenth Amendment be Enforced?" (article from *The North American Review*), prepared; XII. "Backward or Forward?" (article from *The South Atlantic Quarterly*), prepared; XIII. Child Labor and the New Federalism, prepared; XIV. The Old Leadership and the New South ("The Task of the Leader" from *The Sewanee Review*), prepared.

11. Murphy Papers, UNC.

12. Though not always agreeing with Murphy, Francis J. Garrison noted this. See Garrison to Villard, October 26, 1905, Villard Papers, Harvard University. (Garrison indirectly quoted Murphy on this.)

13. Murphy to Washington, March 8, July 16, 1909, B.T.W. Papers, L.C. Longmans, Green and Co. also became the subsequent publisher of *The Present South*, which, like *The Basis of Ascendancy*, retailed for $1.50.

14. *The Basis of Ascendancy*, xiv, 138, 143, 176–177, 190, 195, 215–217, 223, 226.

15. Cable Diary, December 21, 1888, Cable Papers, Tulane University.

16. Thomas F. Gossett, *Race: The History of An Idea in America*, 275; Richard B. Nixon, *Henry W. Grady, Spokesman of the New South*, 214.

17. "The Silent South," *South Atlantic Quarterly*, VI (April 1907), 209.

18. George B. Tindall, "The Significance of Howard W. Odum to Southern History: A Preliminary Estimate." *Journal of Southern History*, XXIV (August, 1958), 286–287.

19. *The Basis of Ascendancy*, 5, 46, 62, 133, 136, 138, 192, 198, 200, 221–222, 230–237.

20. Cable Diary, December 20, 1888, Cable Papers, Tulane University.

21. *The Basis of Ascendancy*, 8, 10, 17–20, 74, 123, 127–128, 139, 157–168.

22. Bassett to Villard, November 17, 1905, Villard Papers, Harvard University.

23. *The Basis of Ascendancy*, viii, xv–xviii, 3, 78, 82–89, 93–94, 102, 197.

24. *Ibid.*, 27–34, 40–42, 51, 56–57, 108, 111, 145–148.

25. *Ibid.*, 97, 99, 112, 123, 150–154, 210–212 218, 240–248.

26. June 4, 1909, B.T.W. Papers, L.C. For two months before its publication in June, 1909, Murphy had been quite ill and "unspeakably wretched." "That it was ever finished was due to Mrs. Murphy's devoted interest and care," he wrote.

27. June 22, 1909, Villard Papers, Harvard University.

28. June 24, 1909.

29. R. R. Moton to Murphy, September 22, 1909, Murphy Papers, UNC; Wickliffe Rose to Ogden, July 10, 1909, Ogden Papers, L.C.

30. To Murphy, n.d., B.T.W. Papers, L.C., and "The Negro and the 'Solid' South," *Independent*, (1909), clipping, Murphy Papers, UNC.

31. Mitchell to Murphy, July 19, 1909, *ibid.*

32. Peabody to Murphy, November 16, 1909, *ibid.*; Dillard to Murphy, January 18, 1910, *ibid.*

33. *New York Daily Tribune*, October 30, 1909.

34. Unknown critic to Mrs. Berry, November 19, 1909, Ogden Papers, L.C.

35. March 7, 1906, Villard Papers, Harvard University.

36. March 12, 1909, *ibid.*

37. Murphy to the Editor of *The Evening Post*, March 12, 1909, Murphy Papers, UNC.

38. Published by Doubleday, Page and Co. in 1908.

39. Washington to Carroll D. Wright, March 26, 1907, Villard Papers, Harvard University. After the work appeared, Washington hoped its pessimism would result in its doing little harm. "It is hard to get up enthusiasm in connection with a funeral procession," he wrote. Murphy urged *The Outlook* to have David F. Houston, then President of the University of Texas, review the book. See Murphy to Washington, August 26, 1908, B.T.W. Papers, L.C.; Washington to Murphy, August 29, 1908, *ibid.*; Murphy to the Editor of *The Outlook*, August 26, 1908, *ibid.*

40. Murphy to Villard, July 17, 19, 1909, Villard Papers, Harvard University.

41. Washington to Villard, August 28, 1909, *ibid.*

42. Murphy to Villard, September 7, 1909, *ibid.*; Murphy to Washington, July 27, 1909, B.T.W. Papers, L.C.

43. Villard to Murphy, September 7, 1909, Villard Papers, Harvard University; Murphy to Villard, September 8, 1909, *ibid.*

44. John H. Franklin, *From Slavery to Freedom, A History of American Negroes*, 2nd edition, 437–438.

45. Elliott M. Rudwick, *W.E.B. DuBois, A Study of Minority Group Leadership*, 88, hereinafter, Rudwick, *DuBois*.

46. Villard to Washington, December 13, 1910, Villard Papers, Harvard University; Villard to Mrs. W. H. Baldwin, Jr., December 20, 1910, *ibid.*; Villard to Charles Dyer Norton, September 20, 1910, *ibid.*

47. Washington to Villard, March 21, April 8, 1913, *ibid.* Interesting material relating to the DuBois-Washington feud and the origins of the N.A.A.C.P. include Rudwick, *DuBois*; Emma Lou Thornbrough, "The National Afro-American League, 1887–1908," *Journal of Southern History*, XXVII (November, 1961), 494–512; Elliott M. Rudwick, "The Niagra Movement," *Journal of Negro History*, XLII (July, 1957), 177–200, and "W. E. B. DuBois in the Role of Crisis Editor," *ibid.*, XLIII (July, 1958), 214–240; Warren D. St. James, *The National Association For the Advancement of Colored People: A Case Study in Pressure Groups*. Charles Flint Kellogg's *NAACP, A History of the National Association for the Advancement of Colored People*, I, 1909–1920, is invaluable.

48. Murphy to Washington, June 4, 1909, B.T.W. Papers, L.C.; Murphy to Villard, September 8, 1909, Villard Papers, Harvard University.

49. February 8, 1909, Gardner Murphy Papers, Topeka. The printed version omits Hoke Smith's and Charley Murphy's names.

50. Murphy to Villard, July 17, 1909, Villard Papers, Harvard University.

51. April 3, 1909, Peabody Papers, L.C.

52. Gailor to Murphy, April 25, 1908, Gardner Murphy Papers, Topeka.

53. Murphy to Gailor, April 30, 1908, *ibid.*

54. Murphy to DuBose Murphy, February 12, 1908, DuBose Murphy Papers, Abilene; Murphy to Gardner, March 20, 1908, Gardner Murphy Papers, Topeka.

55. Undated, *ibid.*

56. Pamphlet, Murphy Papers, UNC.

57. Murphy to Gardner, November 26, 1912, Gardner Murphy Papers, Topeka; Maud Murphy, *E.G.M.*, 107–108.

58. *Ibid.*, 105–106; D. and G. Murphy, *Maud King Murphy*, 21. Murphy greatly admired the British astronomer, Lord Kelvin, and added the "Mc" since he had never seen McKready spelled with a "K."

59. Advertisement of *A Beginner's Star Book*, Gardner Murphy Papers, Topeka.

60. D. and G. Murphy, *Maud King Murphy*, 21; clipping from *Popular Astronomy* (June–July, 1931), Murphy Papers, UNC.

61. Frissell to Murphy, January 12, 1912, *ibid.*; Cary to Murphy, April 23, 1912, *ibid.*; Abbott to Murphy, April 18, 1912, *ibid.*

62. Murphy to Gardner, Easter Day, 1912, Gardner Murphy Papers, Topeka.

63. *Idem*, April 30, 1910, *ibid.*; Ogden to Peabody, March 30, 1910, Peabody Papers, L.C.; Maud Murphy, *E.G.M.*, 106.

64. Murphy to Gardner, February 12, 1911, Easter Day, 1912, Gardner Murphy Papers, Topeka; Washington to Murphy, December 10, 1910, B.T.W. Papers, L.C.; Maud Murphy, *E.G.M.*, 109–110.

65. Washington to Murphy, August 5, 1911, B.T.W. Papers, L.C.; Murphy to Ogden, April 9, 1911, Gardner Murphy Papers, Topeka; Murphy to Gardner, October 28, 1912, *ibid.*

66. D. and G. Murphy, *Maud King Murphy*, 23–28; *American Men of Science, A Biographical Directory, The Social and Behavorial Sciences*, 10th ed., 776; *Who's Who in America*, 1964–65, XXXIII, 1453. Maud Murphy lived in New York City until her death in 1957 at the age of ninety-two. Though blind the last few years of her life, her mental acuteness and interest in life continued until her death. (This information was also obtained through interviews with Gardner Murphy and Alice Gardner Murphy, DuBose Murphy's daughter.)

67. Wm. B. Hill to Murphy, June 16, 1911, Murphy Papers, UNC.

68. Murphy to Ogden, August 13, 1912, Ogden Papers, L.C.

69. Murphy to Gardner, November 15, 1912, Gardner Murphy Papers, Topeka; Maud Murphy, *E.G.M.*, 109–110.

70. January 15, 1913, Gardner Murphy Papers, Topeka.

71. Murphy to Helen Ogden Purvis, March 13, 1910, Ogden Papers, L.C.

72. Maud Murphy to Wickliffe Rose, June 23, 1913, SEB Papers, Misc. Ser., UNC; Maud Murphy, *E.G.M.*, 111. Murphy's grave is near that of Daniel Chester French on Chestnut Path, a ridge facing Author's Ridge, on which Louisa May Alcott, Nathaniel Hawthorne, Ralph Waldo Emerson, Henry David Thoreau, and others are buried. The inscription on his tomb reads: "Christ's Faithful Servant Until Life's End."

73. Program Card, Gardner Murphy Papers, Topeka.

74. Owen R. Lovejoy to Friends of Edgar Gardner Murphy, November 28, 1913, Murphy Papers, UNC.

75. "Edgar Gardner Murphy Memorial Meeting, New York City, December 7, 1913," Typescript, Gardner Murphy Papers, Topeka.

76. Minutes, October 25, 1913, Ogden Papers, UNC.

77. "Edgar Gardner Murphy: An Appreciation," *Sewanee Review*, XXII (October, 1914), 495–496.

78. "Edgar Gardner Murphy," CIV (July 5, 1913), 496–497.

Bibliography

Manuscripts

Edwin A. Alderman Papers, Edwin A. Alderman Library, University of Virginia.

George W. Cable Papers, Howard-Tilton Library, Tulane University.

W. Burke Cochran Papers, New York Public Library.

J. L. M. Curry Papers, Library of Congress.

Alexander McKelway Papers, Library of Congress.

DuBose Murphy Papers, in possession of Leonard B. Murphy, Abilene, Texas.

Edgar Gardner Murphy Papers, University of North Carolina.

Gardner Murphy Papers, in possession of Gardner Murphy, Topeka, Kansas.

National Child Labor Committee Papers, Library of Congress.

Robert C. Ogden Papers, Library of Congress and University of North Carolina.

Walter Hines Page Papers, Houghton Library, Harvard University.

George Foster Peabody Papers, Library of Congress.

Albert Shaw Papers, New York Public Library.

Southern Education Board Papers, including Bourland Series, Dabney Series, Joyner Series, and Miscellaneous Series, University of North Carolina.

Oswald G. Villard Papers, Houghton Library, Harvard University.

Booker T. Washington Papers, Library of Congress.

Newspapers and Periodicals

The Alabama Journal, April, 1901.
Bishop's Junior Church News (San Antonio), February, 1893.
Chillicothe Gazette, 1894–1897.
Chillicothe Leader-Gazette, January, 1894.
Chillicothe News, 1894–1897.
The Church Record (Tuscaloosa), November–December, 1900.
The Montgomery Advertiser, 1898–1903, 1907.
The New York Evening Post, 1900–1909.
The Outlook, LXXIV (May–August, 1903), CIV (May–August, 1913).
Providence Journal, January, 1899.
San Antonio Express, August, 1893.
The Southern Workman, XXXI–XXXIII (1902–1904).

Edgar Gardner Murphy Publications

Alabama's First Question. Montgomery: 1904.
"Backward or Forward?" *South Atlantic Quarterly*, VIII (January, 1909), 19–38.
The Basis of Ascendancy, A Discussion of Certain Principles of Public Policy Involved in the Development of the Southern States. New York: 1909.
A Beginner's Star-Book. New York: 1912.
"Brotherhood and Brotherhoods," *St. Andrew's Cross* (September, 1893).
The Case Against Child Labor: An Argument. Montgomery: 1902.
"Child Labor in Alabama," *Annals of the American Academy of Political and Social Science*, XXI (March, 1903), 331–332.
"Child Labor in Alabama," *New York Evening Post*, September 19, 1907.
Child Labor in Alabama, An Appeal to the People and Press of New England, With a Resulting Correspondence. Montgomery: 1901.
Child Labor in Alabama, The Nichols-Sears-Murphy Correspondence. Montgomery: 1902.
Child Labor and Business. Montgomery: 1902.
Child Labor and "Politics." Montgomery: 1902.
Child Labor and the Public. Montgomery: 1902.
A Child Labor Law. Montgomery: 1902.
Child Labor Legislation, Review of Laws in the United States. Montgomery: 1902.

The Child Labor Question in Alabama—A Plea for Immediate Action. Pamphlet No. 59, National Child Labor Committee. New York: 1907.

An Episcopal Church for the Negroes of Montgomery, Alabama. Leaflet in Murphy Biographical Folder, Library, Alabama Department of Archives and History, Montgomery.

The Federal Regulation of Child Labor, A Criticism of the Policy Represented in the Beveridge-Parsons Bill. New York: 1907.

"First Principles," *Homiletic Review* (January, 1893).

"The Georgia Atrocity and Southern Opinion," *Outlook*, LXII (May 20, 1899), 179–180.

The Larger Life, Sermons and An Essay. New York: 1897.

Letter to the Editor, *Outlook*, LVIII (February 5, 1898), 394.

"Matthew Arnold and the English Church," *Churchman* (March 5, 1898).

"The Ministry of Absolution," *Outlook*, LIX (August 6, 1898), 816–817.

"The National Child-Labor Committee," *Charities*, XII (June 4, 1904), 574–576.

"The New American Saint," *Outlook*, LV (February 13, 1897), 487–488.

An Open Letter On Suffrage Restriction, and Against Certain Proposals of the Platform of the State Convention, 4th ed. Montgomery: 1901.

The Peonage Cases in Alabama, Three Letters. New York: 1903.

Pictures from Life. Mill Children in Alabama. Montgomery: 1903.

"Progress in Southern Education," *Tradesman* (January 1, 1908), 385–386.

"Progress in the South," *Outlook*, LXVIII (June 29, 1901), 475–476.

Progress Within the Year, Circular of the Southern Education Board. Series I (October, 1902), No. 4.

"The Proposed Negro Episcopate—Part of a Letter to a Member of the House of Bishops," *Churchman* (September 21, 1907), 403–404.

"The Public Function of the Public School," *Proceedings of the Eighteenth Annual Convention of the Association of Colleges and Preparatory Schools of the Middle States and Maryland, 1904, XVIII–XXII* (1904–1908), 64–74.

"The Pulpit and the War," *North American Review*, CLXVI (June, 1898), 751–752.

Review of *Clerical Life and Work, St. Andrew's Cross* (May, 1895).

"The Schools of the People," *Journal of the Proceedings and Addresses of the Forty-Second Annual Meeting* [National Education Association] *Held at Boston, Massachusetts*, July 6–10, 1903, XL (1903).

"Self-Fulfillment," *Homiletic Review* (October, 1893).

"Shall the Fourteenth Amendment be Enforced?" *North American Review*, CLXXX (January, 1905), 109–133.

The South and Her Children, A Rejoinder in the Child Labor Discussion. Montgomery: 1902.

"Southern Prosperity is not Shackled to Child Labor," *Charities,* X (May 2, 1903), 453–456.

A Statement Concerning the Southern Education Board, Circular of the Southern Education Board. Series I (June, 1902), No. 3.

Sternbuch für Anfänger, Eine Anleitung zum Auffinden der Sterne und zum astronomischer Gebrauch des Opernglases, des Feldstechers und des Teleskops. (Kelvin McKready, pen name, translated by Dr. Max Ikle.) Leipzig: 1913.

"The Task of the Leader," *Sewanee Review,* XV (January, 1907), 1–30.

The Task of the South. An Address before the Faculty and Students of Washington and Lee University, Lexington, Virginia, December 10th A.D., 1902, 2nd ed., New York: 1903.

"Teachings of Jesus and the Development of Doctrine," *Papers, Addresses and Discussions at the Eighteenth Church Congress in the United States, Held in the City of Pittsfield, Mass., June 7, 8, 9 and 10, 1898.* New York: 1898.

"Two Aspects of Confirmation," *The Living Church* (April 24, 1897).

The White Man and the Negro at the South. An Address delivered under invitation of the American Academy of Political and Social Science, the American Society for the Extension of University Teaching, and the Civic Club of Philadelphia, in the Church of the Holy Trinity, Philadelphia, on the Evening of March 8th, A.D. 1900. N.p., n.d.

Words for the Church. New York: 1897.

Articles

Alderman, Edwin A. "Charles Brantley Aycock—An Appreciation," *North Carolina Historical Review,* I (July, 1924), 243–250.

Alderman, Edwin A. "Robert Curtis Ogden, Volunteer Statesman," *University of Virginia Alumni Bulletin,* IX (January, 1916), 5–9.

Bailey, Kenneth K. "Southern White Protestantism at the Turn of the Century," *American Historical Review,* LXVIII (April, 1963), 618–635.

Ball, W. W. "Improvement in Race Relations in South Carolina: The Cause," *South Atlantic Quarterly,* XXXIX (October, 1940), 385–393.

Brewer, James H. "Editorials From the Damned," *Journal of Southern History,* XXVIII (May, 1962), 225–233.

Calista, Donald J. "Booker T. Washington: Another Look," *Journal of Negro History*, XLIX (October, 1964), 240–255.

Calvier, Ambrose. "Certain Significant Developments in the Education of Negroes During the Past Generation," *Journal of Negro History*, XXXV (April, 1950), 111–134.

"Child Labor in 1913," *Child Labor Bulletin* (November, 1913), 8–9.

Clayton, Bruce L. "An Intellectual on Politics: William Garrott Brown and the Ideal of a Two-Party South," *North Carolina Historical Review*, XLII (Summer, 1965), 319–334.

Cook, Raymond A. "The Man Behind The Birth of A Nation," *North Carolina Historical Review*, XXXIX (October, 1962), 519–540.

Daniels, Josephus. "Charles Brantley Aycock—Historical Address," *North Carolina Historical Review*, I (July, 1924), 251–276.

Davidson, Elizabeth H. "The Child-Labor Problem in North Carolina, 1883–1903," *North Carolina Historical Review*, XIII (April, 1936), 105–121.

Davidson, Elizabeth H. "Child-Labor Reforms in North Carolina Since 1903," *North Carolina Historical Review*, XIV (April, 1937), 109–134.

Davidson, Elizabeth H. "Early Development of Public Opinion Against Southern Child Labor," *North Carolina Historical Review*, XIV (July, 1937), 230–250.

DeSantis, Vincent P. "The Republican Party and the Southern Negro, 1877–1897," *Journal of Negro History*, XLV (April, 1960), 71–87.

Doherty, Herbert J., Jr. "Alexander J. McKelway: Preacher to Progressives," *Journal of Southern History*, XXIV (May, 1958), 177–190.

Doherty, Herbert J., Jr. "Voices of Protest from the New South, 1875–1910," *Mississippi Valley Historical Review*, XLII (June, 1955), 45–66.

Dowd, Jerome. "Child Labor," *South Atlantic Quarterly*, I (January, 1902), 41–43.

"Dr. Edwin A. Alderman—A Brief Appreciation," *University of Virginia Bulletin*, New Series, IV (October, 1904), 238–240.

DuBose, William P. "Edgar Gardner Murphy: An Appreciation," *Sewanee Review*, XXII (October, 1914), 495–496.

Few, William P. "The Constructive Philanthropy of a Southern Cotton Mill," *South Atlantic Quarterly*, VIII (January, 1909), 82–90.

Folks, Homer. "Child Labor and the Law," *Charities*, XII (October 1, 1904), 19–25.

Franklin, John H. "Jim Crow Goes to School: The Genesis of Legal Segregation in Southern Schools," *South Atlantic Quarterly*, LVIII (Spring, 1959), 225–235.

Garner, James W. "Lynchings and the Criminal Law," *South Atlantic Quarterly*, V (October, 1906), 333–341.

Garner, James W. "Recent Agitation of the Negro Question in the South," *South Atlantic Quarterly*, VII (January, 1908), 11–22.

"The General Education Board and the American College," *Sewanee Review*, XV (April, 1907), 244–247.

Glasson, William H. "The Statistics of Lynchings," *South Atlantic Quarterly*, V (October, 1906), 342–348.

Going, Allen J. "The South and the Blair Education Bill," *Mississippi Valley Historical Review*, XLIV (September, 1957), 267–290.

Guerry, Moultrie. "Makers of Sewanee: William Porcher DuBose," *Sewanee Review*, XLI (October, 1933), 483–494.

Hammond, Mrs., John D. "The Work of the General Education Board in the South," *South Atlantic Quarterly*, XIV (October, 1915), 348–357.

Handlin, Oscar. "Desegregation in Perspective," *Current History*, XXXII (May, 1957), 257–260.

Harlan, Louis R. "Booker T. Washington and the White Man's Burden," *American Historical Review*, LXXI (January, 1966), 441–467.

Harlan, Louis R. "The Southern Education Board and the Race Issue in Public Education," *Journal of Southern History*, XXIII (May, 1957), 189–202.

House, Robert B. "Aycock and Universal Education," *North Carolina Historical Review*, XXXVII (April, 1960), 211–216.

Kilgo, John C. "Our Duty to the Negro," *South Atlantic Quarterly*, II (October, 1903), 369–385.

Kilgo, John C. "The Silent South," *South Atlantic Quarterly*, VI (April, 1907), 200–211.

Kilgo, John C. "Some Phases of Southern Education," *South Atlantic Quarterly*, II (April, 1903), 137–151.

Knight, Edgar W. "The Peabody Fund and its Early Operation in North Carolina," *South Atlantic Quarterly*, XIV (April, 1915), 168–180.

Link, Arthur S. "The Progressive Movement in the South, 1870–1914," *North Carolina Historical Review*, XXIII (April, 1946), 172–195.

McKelway, Alexander J. "Child Labor and its Attendant Evils," *Sewanee Review*, XVI (April, 1908), 214–227.

Mabry, William A. "Ben Tillman Disfranchised the Negro," *South Atlantic Quarterly*, XXXVII (April, 1938), 170–183.

Mabry, William A. "Louisiana Politics and the 'Grandfather Clause'," *North Carolina Historical Review* (October, 1936), 290–310.

Mabry, William A. "Negro Suffrage and Fusion Rule in North Carolina," *North Carolina Historical Review*, XII (April, 1935), 79–102.

Marshall, Dr. John S. "From Aristotle to Christ, or The Philosophy of William Porcher DuBose," *Sewanee Review*, LI (January–March, 1943), 148–159.

Milton, George F. "Compulsory Education and the Southern States," *Sewanee Review*, XVI (January, 1908), 18–61.

Mims, Edwin. "President Theodore Roosevelt," *South Atlantic Quarterly*, IV (January, 1905), 48–62.

Mims, Edwin. "A Semi-Centennial Survey of North Carolina's Intellectual Progress," *North Carolina Historical Review*, XXIV (April, 1947), 235–257.

Mitchell, Broadus. "Economics in the South," *Current History*, XXXII (May, 1957), 267–272.

Mitchell, Broadus. "Two Industrial Revolutions," *South Atlantic Quarterly*, XX (October, 1921), 287–304.

Mitchell, S. C. "The School as an Exponent of Democracy in the South," *Sewanee Review*, XVI (January, 1908), 18–25.

Moton, Robert R. "The South and the Lynching Evil," *South Atlantic Quarterly*, XVIII (July, 1919), 191–196.

Nash, Henry S. "Dr. DuBose's 'Gospel in the Gospels'," *Sewanee Review*, XV (January, 1907), 111–120.

Ovington, Mary W. "The National Association for the Advancement of Colored People," *Journal of Negro History*, IX (April, 1924), 107–116.

Patton, James W. "The Southern Reaction to the Ogden Movement," in *Education in the South, Institute of Southern Culture Lectures at Longwood College, 1959*, Farmville, Virginia, 1959.

Rudwick, Elliott M. "The Niagara Movement," *Journal of Negro History*, XLII (July, 1957), 177–200.

Rudwick, Elliott M. "W.E.B. DuBois in the Role of *Crisis* Editor," *Journal of Negro History*, XLII (July, 1958), 214–240.

Scheiner, Seth M. "President Theodore Roosevelt and the Negro, 1901–1908," *Journal of Negro History*, XLVII (July, 1962), 169–182.

Smith, Robert G. "Mill on the Dan: Riverside Cotton Mills, 1882–1901," *Journal of Southern History*, XXI (February, 1955), 38–66.

"Stirring Up the Fires of Race Antipathy," *South Atlantic Quarterly*, II (October, 1903), 298–305.

Swint, Henry L. "Rutherford B. Hayes, Educator," *Mississippi Valley Historical Review*, XXXIX (June, 1952), 45–60.

Thornbrough, Emma L. "The Brownsville Episode and the Negro Vote," *Mississippi Valley Historical Review*, XLIV (December, 1957), 469–493.

Thornbrough, Emma L. "More Light on Booker T. Washington," *Journal of Negro History*, XLII (January, 1958), 34–49.

Thornbrough, Emma L. "The National Afro-American League, 1887–1908," *Journal of Southern History*, XXVII (November, 1961), 494–512.

Tindall, George B. "The Question of Race in the South Carolina Constitutional Convention of 1895," *Journal of Negro History*, XXXVII (July, 1952), 277–303.

Tindall, George B. "The Significance of Howard W. Odom to Southern History: A Preliminary Estimate," *Journal of Southern History*, XXIV (August, 1958), 285–307.

Tinsley, James A. "Roosevelt, Foraker, and the Brownsville Affray," *Journal of Negro History*, XLI (January, 1956), 43–65.

Wallace, D. D. "The South Carolina Convention of 1895," *Sewanee Review*, IV (May, 1896), 348–360.

Washington, Booker T. "My View of Segregation Laws," *New Republic*, V (December 4, 1915), 113–114.

Washington, Booker T. "The Montgomery Race Conference," *Century Magazine*, XL (August, 1900), 630–632.

White, John E. "The Need of a Southern Program on the Negro Problem," *South Atlantic Quarterly*, VI (April, 1907), 177–188.

Winston, Robert Watson. "An Unconsidered Aspect of the Negro Question," *South Atlantic Quarterly*, I (January, 1902), 265–268.

Books

Alderman, Edwin A. *The Growing South*. New York: 1908.

American Men of Science, A Biographical Directory. 4 vols. 10th ed., New York: 1962.

Bailey, Joseph C. *Seaman A. Knapp, Schoolmaster of American Agriculture*. New York: 1945.

Bardolph, Richard. *The Negro Vanguard*. New York: 1959.

Broderick, Francis L. *W.E.B. DuBois, Negro Leader in Time of Crisis*. Stanford: 1959.

Brooks, John G. *An American Citizen, The Life of William Henry Baldwin, Jr.* Boston: 1910.

Clark, Thomas D. *Three Paths to the Modern South, Education, Agriculture, and Conservation*. Eugenia Dorothy Blount Lamar Memorial Lectures No. 8. Athens: 1965.

Cubberley, Ellwood P. *Public Education in the United States, A Study and Interpretation of American Educational History*. New York: 1947.

Curti, Merle E. *The Social Ideas of American Education*. New York: 1935.

Dabney, Charles W. *Universal Education in the South*. 2 vols., Chapel Hill: 1936.

Dabney, Virginius. *Liberalism in the South*. Chapel Hill: 1932.

Daniels, Josephus. *Editor in Politics*. Chapel Hill: 1941.

Davidson, Elizabeth H. *Child Labor Legislation in the Southern Textile States*. Chapel Hill: 1939.

Dickerman, G. S., with the assistance of Wickliffe Rose (ed.). *Educational Progress in the South, A Review of Five Years, Field Reports of the Southern Education Board*. New York: 1907.

DuBois, W.E.B. *The Souls of Black Folks, Essays and Sketches*. New York: 1953.

Fosdick, Raymond B. *Adventure in Giving: The Story of the General Education Board, A Foundation Established by John D. Rockefeller*. New York: 1962.

Franklin, John H. *From Slavery to Freedom, A History of American Negroes*. 2nd ed., New York: 1956.

Ginger, Ray. *The Age of Excess, The United States from 1877 to 1914*. New York: 1965.

Good, H. C. *A History of American Education*. New York: 1956.

Gossett, Thomas F. *Race, The History of An Idea in America*. Dallas: 1963.

Grantham, Dewey W., Jr. *The Democratic South*. Eugenia Dorothy Blount Lamar Memorial Lectures No. 6. Athens: 1963.

Grantham, Dewey W., Jr. *Hoke Smith and the Politics of the New South*. Baton Rouge: 1958.

Green, Fletcher (ed.). *Essays in Southern History*. Chapel Hill: 1949.

Handlin, Oscar. *The Newcomers, Negroes and Puerto Ricans in A Changing Metropolis*. Cambridge: 1959.

Harlan, Louis R. *Separate and Unequal, Public School Campaigns and Racism in the Southern Seaboard States, 1901–1915*. Chapel Hill: 1958.

Harris, Julia C. *The Life and Letters of Joel Chandler Harris*. New York: 1918.

Hendrick, Burton J. *The Life of Andrew Carnegie*. 2 vols., Garden City: 1932.

Hendrick, Burton J. *The Training of An American, The Earlier Life and Letters of Walter H. Page, 1855–1913*. Boston: 1928.

Hesseltine, William B., and David L. Smiley. *The South in American History*. 2nd ed., Englewood Cliffs: 1960.

Hocutt, Olivia B. "The Conference for Education in the South; Its Work and Influence." Unpublished Master's thesis, University of North Carolina, 1932.

Hoffstadter, Richard. *Social Darwinism in American Thought*. Rev. ed., New York: 1959.

Holder, Rose H. *McIver of North Carolina*. Chapel Hill: 1957.

Holt, Rackham. *George Washington Carver, An American Biography*. Garden City: 1943.

Johnson, Allen, *et. al.* (ed.). *The Dictionary of American Biography*. 22 vols., New York: 1928–1958.

Kendrick, Benjamin B., and Alex M. Arnett. *The South Looks at Its Past*. Chapel Hill: 1935.

Kerwin, Albert D. *Revolt of the Red Necks, Mississippi Politics, 1876–1925*. Lexington: 1951.

Knight, Edgar W. *Education in the United States*. Boston: 1929.

Knight, Edgar W. *Public Education in the South*. Boston: 1922.

Krock, Arthur (ed.). *The Editorials of Henry Watterson*. New York: 1923.

Levinson, Paul. *Race, Class, and Party, A History Of Negro Suffrage and White Politics in the South*. New York: 1963.

Larsen, William, *Montague of Virginia, The Making of A Southern Progressive*. Baton Rouge: 1965.

Lewis, Charles V. *Philander Priestley Claxton, Crusader for Public Education*. Knoxville: 1948.

McMillan, Malcolm C. *Constitutional Development in Alabama, 1798–1901: A Study in Politics, the Negro, and Sectionalism*. Chapel Hill: 1955.

Malone, Dumas. *Edwin A. Alderman, A Biography*. New York: 1940.

Mann, Harold W. *Atticus Greene Haygood: Methodist Bishop, Editor, and Educator*. Athens: 1965.

Mandel, Bernard. *Samuel Gompers, A Biography*. Antioch: 1963.

Marcossin, Isaac F. *"Marse Henry," A Biography of Henry Watterson*. New York: 1951.

Mathews, Basil J. *Booker T. Washington, Educator and Inter-Racial Interpreter*. Cambridge: 1948.

Meier, August. *Negro Thought in America, 1880 to 1915, Racial Ideologies in the Age of Booker T. Washington*. Ann Arbor: 1963.

Mims, Edwin. *The Advancing South, Stories of Progress and Reaction*. Garden City: 1926.

Mims, Edwin. *Chancellor Kirkland of Vanderbilt*. Nashville: 1940.

Morrison, Joseph L. *Josephus Daniels Says . . . An Editor's Political Odyssey from Bryan to Wilson and F.D.R., 1894–1913*. Chapel Hill: 1962.

Murphy, DuBose and Gardner. *Maud King Murphy, 1865–1957*. N.p., n.d.

Murphy, Maud K. *Edgar Gardner Murphy, From Records and Memories*. New York: 1943.

National Child Labor Committee. *Third Annual Report—For the Fiscal Year Ended September 30, 1907.* New York: 1907.

Newby, I. A. *Jim Crow's Defense, Anti-Negro Thought in America, 1900–1930.* Baton Rouge: 1965.

Nixon, Richard B. *Henry W. Grady, Spokesman of the New South.* New York: 1943.

Owen, Thomas M. *History of Alabama and Dictionary of Alabama Biography.* 4 vols., Chicago: 1921.

Page, Walter H. *The School that Built A Town: with an Introductory Chapter by Roy E. Larsen.* New York: 1952.

Pittinger, W. Norman (ed.). *William Porcher DuBose, Unity in the Faith.* Greenwich: 1957.

Proceedings of the Fourth to Thirteenth Conferences for Education in the South. Raleigh, etc.: 1901–1910.

Pringle, Henry F. *Theodore Roosevelt, A Biography.* New York: 1931.

Proctor, Samuel. *Napoleon Bonaparte Broward, Florida's Fighting Democrat.* Gainesville: 1950.

Race Problems of the South—Report of the Proceedings of the First Annual Conference Held Under the Auspices of the Southern Society for the Promotion of the Study of Race Conditions and Problems in the South . . . at . . . Montgomery, Alabama, May 8, 9, 10, A.D. 1900. Richmond: 1900.

Rudwick, Elliott M. *W.E.B. DuBois, A Study of Minority Group Leadership.* Philadelphia: 1960.

Ryan, W. Carson, J. Minor Gwynn, and Arnold K. King (eds.). *Secondary Education in the South.* Chapel Hill: 1946.

Simpkins, Francis B. *Pitchfork Ben Tillman, South Carolinian.* Baton Rouge: 1944.

Southern Commission on the Study of Lynching. *Lynchings and What They Mean.* Atlanta: 1931.

Spenser, Samuel R., Jr. *Booker T. Washington and the Negro's Place in American Life.* Boston: 1955.

Ware, Louise. *George Foster Peabody, Banker, Philanthropist, Publicist.* Athens: 1951.

Warren, D. St. James. *The National Association for the Advancement of Colored People: A Case Study in Pressure Groups.* New York: 1958.

Washington, Booker T. *My Larger Education.* New York: 1911.

Washington, Booker T. *Up From Slavery.* New York: 1901.

Who's Who in America, 1964–1965. New York: 1965.

Wilson, Philip W. *An Unofficial Statesman—Robert C. Ogden.* Garden City: 1924.

Winston, George T. *A Builder of the New South, Being the Story of the Life Work of Daniel Augustus Tompkins.* Garden City: 1920.

Woodson, Carter G. *The Negro in Our History.* 8th ed., Washington: 1945.

Woodward, C. Vann. *Origins of the New South, 1877–1913.* Baton Rouge: 1951.

Woodward, C. Vann. *The Strange Career of Jim Crow.* 2nd ed., New York: 1966.

Woodward, C. Vann. *Tom Watson, Agrarian Rebel.* New York: 1938.

Index

North Carolina, University of, 57, 111, 142

Oates, Gov. William C., 121
Odum, Howard W., 192
Ogden, Robert C., 38, 40, 43, 44, 50, 87, 92, 117, 148, 155, 159, 161, 162, 164–165, 168, 171, 172, 174, 175, 179, 180, 181, 182, 184, 185, 197, 211; as President of Conference for Education in the South, 144; attacks upon, 150–151; attitude towards the Negro, 35; chooses Murphy as Executive Secretary of Southern Education Board, 147; compromises racial views, 150; consults with Murphy, 42–43; dominates educational movement, 149; earlier career, 35; elected Vice-President of Conference for Christian Education, 143; influences Theodore Roosevelt, 130–131; opposes modification of Fifteenth Amendment, 44; organizes Southern Education Board, 146–147; relationship with General Education Board, 151, 152; special train's wreck, 167; supports Hampton and Tuskegee Institutes, 34–35
Ohio, 10, 11, 12, 13, 16, 17, 91
Oklahoma, 56
Old Point Comfort, Va., 179
"Old South," 125, 135
Old South Church, Boston, 119
Orr, Mrs. Lillian Milner, 80, 85
Outlook, The, 18, 38, 54, 123, 128, 215–216
Oxford Movement, 17, 20

Page, Thomas Nelson, 55, 167
Page, Walter Hines, 3, 40, 50, 119, 145, 146, 151, 154, 170, 176, 179; as education reformer, 141, 142; opposes modification of Fifteenth Amendment, 41, 44; op-

poses racial journal, 51; view of the race problem, 26, 40
Parable of the Good Samaritan, 26
Parable of the Prodigal Son, 14
Peabody, Prof. Francis G., 115, 185
Peabody Fund, 33, 46, 53, 139, 146
Peabody, George F., 96, 129, 139, 143, 146, 151, 153, 155, 158, 166, 167, 168, 170–171, 197, 202, 205, 206, 214; background, 53; becomes Episcopalian, 53; contributes to Montgomery Y.M.C.A., 53
Peace Corps, 194
Pennsylvania, 34–35, 36, 38, 42, 43, 51, 90, 91, 92, 100, 158
Pennsylvania, University of, 90
peonage, 121–124
Percy, William Alexander, 4
Perry Picture Co., 25
Personality, A Bio-Social Approach to Origins and Structure, 212
Phi Beta Kappa, 5
Philadelphia, Penn., 34–35, 36, 38, 42, 43, 92, 158
philanthropists, 33, 42, 143, 147, 148, 176–177
philanthropy, 40, 149, 154, 156, 157–158
Phillips Andover Academy, 34
Phillips, Dr. J. H., 71, 164, 167
Pictures from Life . . . , 82–83
Piedmont Hotel, Atlanta, 181
Pinehurst, N.C., 172–174
Pittinger, W. Norman, 4
Pittsfield, Mass., 19–20
"Plea for Immediate Action, A," 104–106
poll tax, 61, 62
poor whites, 42
Popular Astronomy, 210
Populist Party, 82, 193
Populist revolt, 27
Presbyterian Church, 30
Presbyterian Standard, 86
Present South, The, 125–130, 132, 189, 190, 191